Penn Quarter
Pages 88–105

Capitol Hill
Pages 44–55

PENN
QUARTER

THE
MALL

CAPITOL
HILL

Washington Channel

Anacostia River

0 meters 750
0 yards 750

The Mall
Pages 56–87

P9-BYB-640

EYEWITNESS TRAVEL

WASHINGTON, DC

EYEWITNESS TRAVEL

WASHINGTON, DC

Main contributors:
Susan Burke and Alice L. Powers

Project Editor Claire Folkard
Art Editors Tim Mann, Simon J.M. Oon
Senior Editor Helen Townsend
Editors Emily Anderson, Felicity Crowe
US Editor Mary Sutherland
Designers Gillian Andrews, Eli Estaugh,
Elly King, Rebecca Milner
DTP Designers Sam Borland, Maite Lantaron
Picture Researchers Brigitte Arora, Katherine Mesquita
Production Mel Allsop

Contributors
Susan Burke, Alice L. Powers, Jennifer Quasha, Kem Sawyer

Photographers
Philippe Dewet, Kim Sayer, Giles Stokoe, Scott Suchman

Illustrators
Stephen Conlin, Gary Cross, Richard Draper, Chris Orr & Associates, Mel Pickering,
Robbie Polley, John Woodcock

Printed in China

First American Edition, 2000
16 17 18 19 10 9 8 7 6 5 4 3 2 1

Published in the United States by
DK Publishing, 345 Hudson Street,
New York, New York 10014

**Reprinted with revisions 2002, 2003, 2004, 2005, 2006, 2008,
2009, 2010, 2011, 2012, 2013, 2014, 2015, 2016**

Copyright © 2000, 2016 Dorling Kindersley Limited, London
A Penguin Random House Company

ISSN 1542-1554
ISBN 978-1-4654-3969-7

Floors are referred to throughout in accordance with
American usage; ie the "first floor" is at ground level.

MIX
Paper from
responsible sources
FSC
www.fsc.org   FSC™ C018179

Front cover main image: Early morning at Jefferson Memorial and Tidal Basin

 Iwo Jima Statue, with the Washington Monument and the United States Capitol in the background

Contents

How to Use this Guide **6**

Fountain in Dumbarton Oaks

Introducing Washington, DC

Great Days in
Washington, DC **10**

Putting Washington, DC
on the Map **14**

The History of
Washington, DC **18**

Washington, DC
at a Glance **32**

Washington, DC
Through the Year **38**

View toward the Lincoln Memorial from
Arlington National Cemetery

Columns from the US Capitol building, now in the National Arboretum

Map seller outside the National Gallery of Art on the Mall

The George, a boutique hotel

Quirky decor at Acadiana restaurant

Monticello, home of Thomas Jefferson in Charlottesville, Virginia

HOW TO USE THIS GUIDE

This guide helps you to get the most from your stay in Washington, DC. It provides detailed practical information and expert recommendations. *Introducing Washington, DC* maps the city and the region, sets it in its historical and cultural context, and gives an overview of the main attractions. *Washington, DC Area by Area* is the main sightseeing section, giving detailed information on all the major sights, with photographs, illustrations and maps. *Farther Afield* looks at sights outside the city center, and *Beyond Washington, DC* explores other places within easy reach of the city. Carefully researched suggestions for restaurants, hotels, entertainment, and shopping are found in the *Travelers' Needs* section, while the *Survival Guide* contains useful advice on everything from changing money to traveling on Washington's Metrorail system.

Washinton, DC Area by Area

The center of Washington has been divided into five sightseeing areas. Each section opens with a portrait of the area, summing up its character and history and listing all of the sights to be covered. Sights are numbered and clearly located on an *Area Map*. After this comes a large-scale *Street-by-Street Map* focusing on the most interesting part of the area.

Finding your way about the area section is made easy by a numbering system. This refers to the order in which the sights are described on the pages that complete the section.

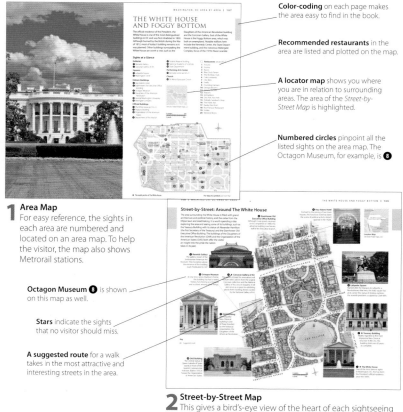

Color-coding on each page makes the area easy to find in the book.

Recommended restaurants in the area are listed and plotted on the map.

A locator map shows you where you are in relation to surrounding areas. The area of the *Street-by-Street Map* is highlighted.

Numbered circles pinpoint all the listed sights on the area map. The Octagon Museum, for example, is ❽

1 Area Map
For easy reference, the sights in each area are numbered and located on an area map. To help the visitor, the map also shows Metrorail stations.

Octagon Museum ❽ is shown on this map as well.

Stars indicate the sights that no visitor should miss.

A suggested route for a walk takes in the most attractive and interesting streets in the area.

2 Street-by-Street Map
This gives a bird's-eye view of the heart of each sightseeing area. The numbering of the sights ties in with the area map and the fuller descriptions on the pages that follow.

Washington, DC at a Glance

Each map in this section concentrates on a specific theme: *Museums and Galleries in Washington, DC* and *Monuments and Memorials in Washington, DC*. The top sights are shown on the map.

Each sightseeing area is color-coded.

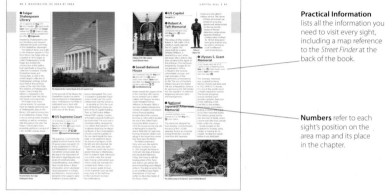

Practical Information lists all the information you need to visit every sight, including a map reference to the *Street Finder* at the back of the book.

Numbers refer to each sight's position on the area map and its place in the chapter.

3 Detailed Information on each Sight

All important sights in each area are described in depth in this section. They are listed in order, following the numbering on the *Area Map*. Practical information on opening hours, telephone numbers, websites, admission charges, and facilities available is given for each sight. The key to the symbols used can be found on the back flap.

The Visitors' Checklist provides the practical information you will need to plan your visit.

Stars indicate the most interesting architectural details of the building, and the most important works of art or exhibits on view inside.

The façade of each major sight is shown to help you spot it quickly.

Numbered circles point out major features of the sight listed in a key.

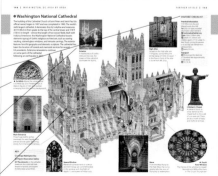

4 Washington, DC's Major Sights

These are given two or more full pages in the sightseeing area in which they are found. Historic buildings are dissected to reveal their interiors; and museums and galleries have color-coded floor plans to help you find important exhibits.

INTRODUCING WASHINGTON, DC

GREAT DAYS IN WASHINGTON, DC

Washington boasts not only world-renowned works of art and majestic monuments, but picturesque neighborhoods and beautiful gardens. Here are itineraries for some of the best of the attractions and unexpected treasures, arranged first under themes and then by length of stay. All the sights can be reached on foot or by public transportation. Feel free to dip into the itineraries as you wish. Price guides on pages 10–11 show the daily cost for two adults or for a family of two adults and two children including lunch.

The White House, the Presidential residence

Monumental City

Two adults allow at least $40

- **Lincoln Memorial**
- **World War II Memorial**
- **Corcoran Gallery of Art**
- **The White House**

Morning

Start your day at the **Lincoln Memorial** *(see p87)*, six blocks south of the Foggy Bottom Metro stop. Inside, on the north and south walls, you will find inscriptions of President Lincoln's **Gettysburg Address** *(see p165)*. In front of the memorial, to the left of the Reflecting Pool, is the moving **Vietnam Veterans Memorial** *(see p85)*. Engraved on black granite are the names of Americans who died in the war. Then make your way through the shady Constitution Gardens back to the Reflecting Pool. To the right is the **Korean War Veterans Memorial** *(see p85)* and nearby is the **World War II Memorial** *(see p84)*. Here you can see the Freedom Wall, its inscriptions, and the bas-reliefs showing the US at war. After this memorial, move on to 17th Street where there are several historic buildings including the **Organization of American States** and the **Daughters of the American Revolution** *(see p116)*. Pass the **Corcoran Gallery of Art**, one of the country's first art galleries *(see p115)*. Have lunch at one of the cafés near Pennsylvania Avenue.

Afternoon

Stroll down Pennsylvania Avenue, passing the Renwick Gallery, Blair House (where presidential guests stay), and **The White House** *(see pp110–11)*. Walk around the White House to the Visitor Center at 1450 Pennsylvania Avenue. Afterwards, visit the **US National Archives** *(see p92)* to see historic documents including the *Declaration of Independence* and the *Bill of Rights*. End your day with a tour of **Ford's Theater** *(see p98)* where Lincoln was shot, followed by a meal in **Chinatown** *(see pp98–9)* or **Penn Quarter** *(see pp88–105)*.

Black History

Two adults allow at least $20

- **Frederick Douglass House**
- **Mary McLeod Bethune Site**
- **U Street landmarks**
- **African American Civil War Museum and Memorial**

Morning

If traveling by car, spend the morning at the **Frederick Douglass House**, an estate in Anacostia *(see p147)*. Douglass was a fugitive slave who became a famous abolitionist. Almost all of the furnishings here are original (look out for the walking stick collection). Cross the river to **The Shaw Neighborhood** *(see p143)* with its lovely Victorian houses, where prominent African-Americans lived in the 1940s. Visit the **Mary McLeod Bethune Council House** *(see p142)*, home of the civil rights leader and founder of the National Council of Negro Women.

Lunch at **Ben's Chili Bowl** *(see p189)* on U Street, a place that was once the Minnehaha silent movie theater.

Lincoln Theatre, the venue for many of Duke Ellington's performances

◀ An 1801 aquatint view of Washington

Georgetown's pretty gardens and houses, a delightful neighborhood to stroll through

Afternoon

Stroll along U Street, once known as Black Broadway. Audiences went wild when Duke Ellington performed at the **Lincoln Theatre** *(see p142)*. He lived nearby at numbers 1805 and 1816 13th Street. Visit the **African American Civil War Museum and Memorial**, honoring black soldiers *(see p135)*. End the day in style in Georgetown with dinner and jazz at **Blues Alley** *(see pp198–9)*.

Art and Shopping

Two Adults allow at least $35

- **National Gallery of Art**
- **Lunch on the Mall**
- **Georgetown Shopping**
- **Washington Harbor**

Morning

To experience the full scope of art covered at the **National Gallery of Art** *(see pp60–63)*, visit both the West Building (13th–19th century European and American art) and the East Building (galleries closed for renovation). Take time to reflect on the exhibits and rest your legs by having a coffee break at the Espresso Bar on the Concourse level. Outside, in the Garden Court (north side of East Building), find the Andy Goldsworthy installation entitled *Roof*, a study of

domes. Wander through the enchanting Sculpture Garden to the Pavilion Café, a charming spot for lunch.

Afternoon

Now head to cobblestoned **Georgetown** *(see pp122–9)*. You could take the 90-minute walk *(see pp150–51)*, but if shopping is your ultimate goal, go to M Street or Wisconsin Avenue for numerous galleries and shops and a range of stylish goods – lamps, Italian ceramics, prints, and cutting-edge fashion. To finish, have tea in the Garden Terrace at the **Four Seasons Hotel** *(see p178)*, or have a drink at **Washington Harbor** while watching the boats *(see p124)*, then stroll through the Georgetown waterfront park next to the harbor.

A Family Day

Family of Four allow at least $55

- **Visit the National Zoo**
- **National Air and Space Museum**
- **Washington Monument**

Morning

Start early at the **National Zoo** *(see pp140–41)*, checking at its Visitor Center for feeding times, talks, and training sessions (entry is free). See clouded

leopards and giant pandas on the Asia Trail and the Sumatran tigers in Great Cats. At the Great Ape House orangutans scale a 400-ft (130-m) "O Line." Have lunch at the Mane Restaurant or at one of the snack bars.

Afternoon

Go by metro to the **National Air and Space Museum** *(see pp64–7)*. Discover facts such as the cruising speed of the *Spirit of St. Louis*, or the reason Skylab was covered with a coating of gold. Catch a film at the IMAX theatre, where you can experience flying without leaving the ground. Then head for the **Washington Monument** *(see p80)* and take the elevator to the top for the spectacular view (advance booking required). Finish off at the **Kennedy Center** *(see pp120–21)* in Foggy Bottom, for free entertainment on the Millennium Stage at 6pm.

Washington Monument, for a fabulous view of the city

The Martin Luther King, Jr. memorial, surrounded by cherry blossom

2 days in Washington, DC

- Marvel at the White House
- Watch first-class entertainment at the Kennedy Center
- Discover great paintings at the National Gallery of Art

Day 1
Morning Start the day with a roam around the nation's legislative heart, the **US Capitol** *(pp52–3)*, admiring its Neo-Classical architecture. Then stroll the grand mile-long **National Mall** *(pp56–87)*, lined on either side with museums. Stop at the **National Museum of American History** *(pp76–9)* to see the First Ladies exhibition, the flag that inspired the national anthem, and Abraham Lincoln's top hat. Afterward, take the elevator (tickets can be booked online) to the top of the city's tallest landmark, the **Washington Monument** *(p80)*.

Afternoon Marvel at one of the world's most recognizable homes, the **White House** *(pp110–13)*, residence of the US president, then take a virtual tour at the **White House Visitor Center** *(p113)*. End the day with a show at the **Kennedy Center** *(pp120–21)*, renowned for its music, theater, and ballet productions.

Day 2
Morning While away a few hours exploring the trove of great painting at the **National Gallery of Art** *(pp60–63)*. Then head to

the **National Air & Space Museum** *(pp64–7)*, which showcases exhibits ranging from the Wright brothers' first airplane to the latest space rockets.

Afternoon Walk along **Tidal Basin** *(p81)*, which is particularly pretty when the cherry trees are in blossom. Take in the striking monuments honoring past presidents, including the **Jefferson Memorial** *(p81)* and **Franklin D. Roosevelt Memorial** *(pp86–7)*. A short distance from here is the awe-inspiring **Lincoln Memorial** *(p87)*, which looms large over the Reflecting Pool. Make your way to the **Smithsonian Museum of American Art & National Portrait Gallery** *(pp100–103)*, which houses portraits of all the American presidents.

3 days in Washington, DC

- Learn about the nation's history at the many memorials
- Shop along Wisconsin Avenue in Georgetown
- Enjoy the view from the Washington Monument

Day 1
Morning Stroll the scenic **Tidal Basin** *(p81)*, passing the **Jefferson Memorial** *(p81)*, **Franklin D. Roosevelt Memorial** *(pp86–7)*, and the statue of civil rights leader **Martin Luther King, Jr.** *(p85)*. Visit the imposing **Lincoln Memorial** *(p87)*, and then spend time exploring the poignant

Vietnam Veterans Memorial *(p85)* and **World War II Memorial** *(p84)*. Next, ascend the **Washington Monument** *(p80)*, for far-reaching views.

Afternoon Stand in awe of the **White House** *(pp110–13)* and explore the **White House Visitor Center** *(p113)* to see the rooms where history is made. Nearby, the **Smithsonian Museum of American Art & National Portrait Gallery** *(pp100– 103)* tells the nation's story through paintings and photographs. End the day with an evening show at the infamous **Ford's Theatre** *(p98)*, the scene of Abraham Lincoln's assassination.

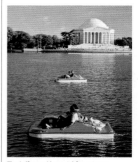

The Jefferson Memorial from across Tidal Basin

Day 2
Morning After a tour of the soaring Rotunda and statuary hall of the **US Capitol** *(pp52–3)*, witness history in action at the **US Supreme Court** *(p50)*. Then stop at the impressive **Library of Congress** *(pp48–9)* to admire the stunning Great Hall and Main Reading Room. For something different, head to the **National Gallery of Art** *(pp60–63)*, which houses a remarkable collection of painting and sculpture.

Afternoon Explore the riveting **Newseum** *(p95)*, documenting events from the past and present in both print and digital formats. Then pop into the enormous **National Museum of Natural History** *(pp72–3)*. The Hall of Mammals and Ocean Hall are a must. Wind down with a performance at the **Kennedy Center** *(pp120–21)*.

Day 3

Morning Head to the **National Mall** *(pp58–9)* for a variety of world-class museums. Highlights include the **National Air & Space Museum** *(pp64–7)*, the **National Museum of American History** *(pp76–9)*, and the **Hirschhorn Museum** *(p68)* for modern art.

Afternoon Visit the city's most historic quarter, **Georgetown** *(pp122–9)*, to meander its pretty streets lined with Federal town houses and browse the shops on **Wisconsin Avenue** *(pp124–5)*. Follow with a tour of the splendid **Dumbarton Oaks** estate *(p129)*, and then dine at one of the riverside restaurants at **Washington Harbor** *(p124)*.

A pretty, tree-lined street in Washington's historic quarter, Georgetown

5 days in Washington, DC

- Visit George Washington's estate at Mount Vernon
- Pay your respects at Arlington Cemetery
- Explore the portraits at the Smithsonian Museum

Day 1

Morning See American history in the making at the **US Capitol** *(pp52–3)*, and then take in some culture at the **National Gallery of Art** *(pp60–63)*. Ride the elevator to the top of the **Washington Monument** *(p80)* for magnificent views of the city and the **World War II Memorial** *(p84)*.

Afternoon A walk along **Tidal Basin** *(p81)* will lead you to the **Jefferson Memorial** *(p81)*, **Franklin D. Roosevelt Memorial** *(pp86–7)*, and **Lincoln Memorial** *(p87)*. Look out for the statue of **Martin Luther King, Jr.** *(p85)* en route. Nearby is the **Vietnam Veterans Memorial** *(p85)*. After, head to the **Smithsonian Museum of American Art & National Portrait Gallery** *(pp100–103)*, which displays portraits of all the US presidents.

Day 2

Morning Admire the rooms of the **White House** *(pp110–13)* at the **White House Visitor Center** *(p113)*, then see it for real. Nearby, the **Corcoran Gallery** *(p115)*, closed for renovation, will feature works from the National Gallery of Art and the original Corcoran collection, once it reopens.

Afternoon Discover **Dumbarton Oaks** estate *(p129)* for a leisurely walk in the circular garden. Then continue to **Georgetown** *(pp122–9)*, to look around its shops on **Wisconsin Avenue** *(pp124–5)*. Afterward, take a stroll along the **Chesapeake and Ohio Canal** *(pp124–5)* towpath. Round off the day with a show at the **Kennedy Center** *(pp120–21)*.

Day 3

Morning Visit the stately quarters of the nation's tribunal, the **US Supreme Court** *(p50)*, and marvel at the colossal reading rooms in the **Library of Congress** *(pp48–9)*. The historic treasures of the **National Archives** *(pp92–3)*, including the original Declaration of Independence and the US Constitution, and Bill of Rights, are worth a closer look.

Afternoon Watch history come to life in the newsreels of the **Newseum** *(p95)*. Next, pick between the **National Museum of American History** *(pp76–9)*, the **National Air & Space Museum** *(pp64–7)*, or the **Hirschhorn Museum** *(p68)*, which line the **National Mall** *(pp58–9)*. Later, visit **Ford's Theatre** *(p98)* and explore the trendy restaurants in the **Penn Quarter** *(pp90–91)*.

Day 4

Morning Immerse yourself at the heart-rending **United States Holocaust Memorial Museum** *(pp82–3)*. Then, for something relaxing, visit the Ocean Hall at the **National Museum of Natural History** *(pp72–3)*.

Afternoon Head out for a tour of the magnificent **Washington National Cathedral** *(pp144–5)*. At night, choose one of the variety of restaurants in **Adams-Morgan** *(p139)* or dine in one of the restaurants at lively **Washington Harbor** *(p124)*.

Day 5

Morning Spend the morning at **Mount Vernon** *(pp162–3)*, George Washington's beautiful riverside estate, and tour the mansion, grounds, and gardens.

Afternoon Take a moving trip to **Arlington National Cemetery** *(pp132–3)* for the tombs of John F. Kennedy and the nation's war heroes. Follow this with a visit to **Old Town Alexandria** *(pp160–61)*, whose streets are lined with boutiques, restaurants, and historic sights aplenty.

The impressive Neo-Classical architecture of the US Capitol

Putting Washington, DC on the Map

Washington, DC is situated near the East Coast of North America, surrounded by the state of Maryland and separated from Virginia by the Potomac River. It covers an area of 108 sq km (67 sq miles) and has a population of 600,000. As the capital of the United States, and seat of federal government, the city is a major focus of American life. It is a very popular tourist destination, attracting millions of visitors each year. The beautiful countryside of Maryland and Virginia is also easily reached from the capital city.

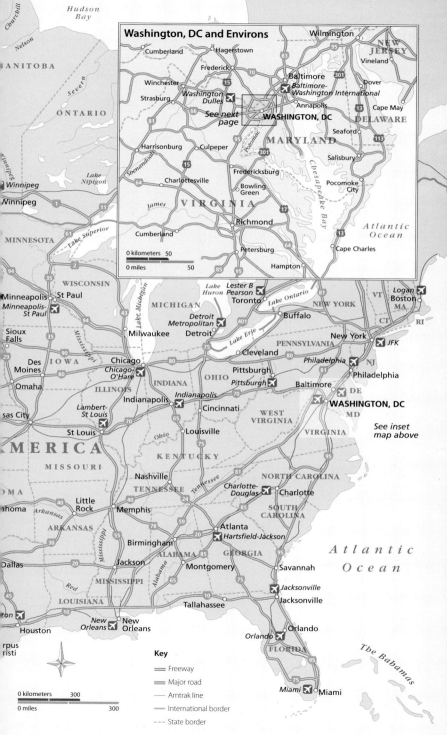

Greater Washington, DC

The city of Washington was created not only as a new capital for the United States but also as the seat of government, independent from the other states. It was laid out in a diamond-shaped area with a grid system of roads. One side of the square was lost after land was ceded back to Virginia in 1846. Although the city has sprawled beyond its original limits, officially the District of Columbia remains within the boundaries indicated. Washington is an easy city to get around, with an efficient modern metro system.

MARYLAND

VIRGINIA

Gaithersburg

BETHESDA

Dulles International Airport

VIENNA

FALLS CHURCH

ARLINGTON

FAIRFAX

ALEXANDRIA

HUNTING

ARLING CEMET

ROCKVILLE PIKE
VEIRS MILL RO
OLD GEORGETOWN ROAD
EAST W
RIVER ROAD
CLARA BARTON PARKWAY
GEORGE WASHINGTON MEMORIAL PARKWAY
CANAL ROAD
GEORGETOWN PIKE
LEESBURG PIKE
GLEBE ROAD
DOLLEY MADISON BOULEVARD
MAPLE AVENUE
CHAIN BRIDGE ROAD
LEE HIGHWAY
LEE HIGHWAY
ARLINGTON BOULEVARD
LEESBURG PIKE
CAPITAL BELTWAY
COLUMBIA PIKE
RIVER TURNPIKE
BRADDOCK ROAD
SHIRLEY MEMORIAL HIGHWAY
FRANCONIA ROAD
RICHMOND HIGHWAY
KING
OLD KEENE MILL ROAD
PARKWAY
FAIRFAX COUNTY

Richmond

Key

- Central Washington
- Built-up area
- Freeway
- Major road
- Train line
- Metro line/station
- State border

0 kilometers   2.5
0 miles   2.5

For additional map symbols *see back flap*

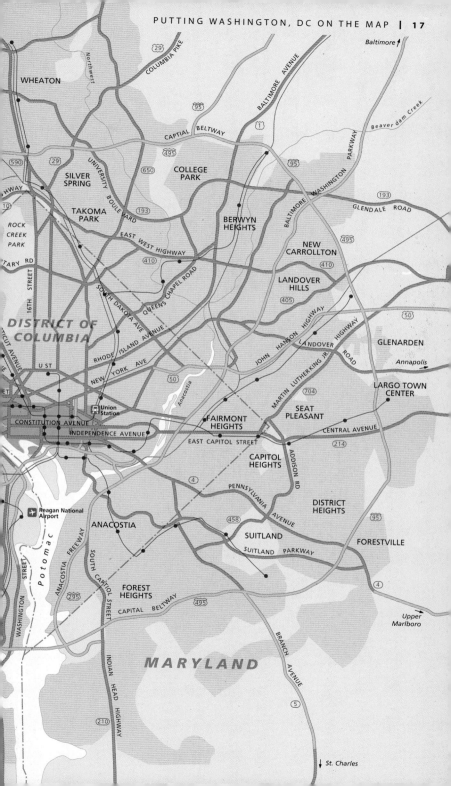

THE HISTORY OF WASHINGTON, DC

Native Americans settled in what is now the District of Columbia as long as 6,000 years ago. Archeologists have discovered traces of three villages in the area; the largest was called Nacotchtanke. Its people, the Anacostines, settled along the Potomac River and a smaller tributary now named the Anacostia River.

English Settlement

In December 1606 Captain John Smith of the Virginia Company, under the charge of King James I of England, set sail from England for the New World. Five months later he arrived in the Chesapeake Bay and founded the Jamestown colony. A skilled cartographer, Smith was soon sailing up the Potomac River. In 1608 he came to the area that would later become Washington.

The English settlers who followed supported themselves through the fur trade, and later cultivated tobacco and corn (maize). The marriage in 1614 between John Rolfe, one of the settlers, and Pocahontas, daughter of the Indian chief Powhatan, kept the peace between the English and the Indians for eight years. Struggles over land ownership between the English and the Powhatan Indians, whose ancestors had lived there for centuries, led to massacres in 1622. The English finally defeated the Indians in 1644, and a formal peace agreement was made in 1646.

The first Africans arrived in the region on board a Dutch ship in 1619 and worked as indentured servants on plantations. They were given food and lodging as payment for serving for a fixed number of years. However, within the next 40 years the practice changed so that black people were purchased for life, and their children became the property of their master. As the number of plantations grew, so did the number of slaves.

In the late 1600s another group of settlers, this time Irish-Scottish, led by Captain Robert Troop, established themselves here. Along the Potomac River two ports, George Town (later known as Georgetown) and Alexandria, soon became profitable centers of commerce. Here planters had their crops inspected, stored, and shipped. In both towns streets were laid out in rectangular patterns. With rich soil, plentiful land, abundant labor, and good transportation, the region rapidly grew in prosperity.

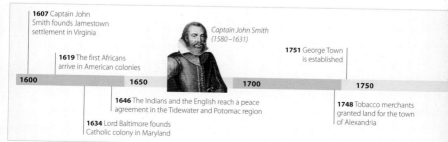

1607 Captain John Smith founds Jamestown settlement in Virginia

1619 The first Africans arrive in American colonies

Captain John Smith (1580–1631)

1751 George Town is established

1600 **1650** **1700** **1750**

1646 The Indians and the English reach a peace agreement in the Tidewater and Potomac region

1634 Lord Baltimore founds Catholic colony in Maryland

1748 Tobacco merchants granted land for the town of Alexandria

◀ George Washington by Rembrandt Peale, painted 1824–5

Revolutionary Years

Some 100 years after the first settlers arrived, frustration over British rule began to grow, both in the Potomac region and elsewhere in the 13 American colonies. In 1775, the colonies began their struggle for independence. On April 19, shots were fired at Lexington, Massachusetts by American colonists who wanted "no taxation without representation," thus beginning the War of Independence.

On July 4, 1776, the Declaration of Independence was issued as colonists attempted to sever ties with Britain. Revolt led to revolution, and the newly formed United States won an important victory at Saratoga, New York in 1777. The French came to the aid of the Americans and finally, on October 19, 1781, the British, led by Lord Cornwallis, surrendered at Yorktown, Virginia. This ended the war and assured the independence of the United States. The peace treaty was signed in Paris on September 3, 1783. Britain agreed to boundaries giving the US all territory to the south of what is now Canada, north of Florida, and west to the Mississippi River.

The Continental Congress, a legislative body of representatives from the newly formed states, appointed a committee to draft the country's first constitution. The result was the Articles of Confederation, which established a union of the newly created states but provided the central government with little power. This later gave way to a stronger form of government, created by the delegates of the Federal Constitutional Convention in Philadelphia in May, 1787. George Washington was unanimously chosen to be president. He took office on April 30, 1789.

Meeting in New York of the first delegates of Congress to discuss the location for a new capital city

A New City

The Constitution of the United States, ratified in 1788, allowed for the creation of a seat of government, not to exceed 10 square miles, which would be ruled by the United States Congress. This area was to be independent and not part of any state. At the first meeting of Congress in New York City in 1789, a dispute arose between northern and southern delegates over where the capital should be located. Secretary of the Treasury Alexander Hamilton and Secretary of State Thomas Jefferson worked out an agreement whereby the debts incurred by northern states during the Revolution would be taken over by the government, and in return the capital would be located in

1781 The British surrender at Yorktown

1783 The US and Britain sign the Treaty of Paris

1787 The Federal Constitutional Convention meets in Philadelphia

1793 President Washington lays the Capitol's cornerstone

1775   **1780**   **1785**   **1790**

1775 The first battles of the American Revolution are fought at Lexington and Concord

Articles of Confederation

1789 Delegates gather in New York City to discuss a location for the capital

1791 President Washington obtains land for the capital city

1792 Construction begins on the President's House (later the White House)

the south. George Washington chose an area that incorporated land from both Maryland and Virginia, and included the towns of Alexandria and Georgetown. It was to be known as the city of Washington. At Suter's Tavern in Georgetown, Washington convinced local residents to sell their land for £25 an acre. He chose a surveyor, Andrew Ellicott, and his assistant Benjamin Banneker, a free African-American, to lay out the streets and lots.

Ellicott's engraved map of 1792, based on L'Enfant's plan

Washington also invited Major Pierre Charles L'Enfant to create a grand design for the new capital city (see p69).

In 1800 the government was moved to Washington. President John Adams and his wife Abigail took up residence in the new President's House, designed by James Hoban, which was later renamed the White House by Theodore Roosevelt. The city remained empty of residents for many years while the building works took place.

War of 1812

Tension with Britain over restrictions on trade and freedom of the seas began to escalate during James Madison's administration. On June 18, 1812, the US declared war on Britain. In August 1814, British troops reached Washington and officers at the Capitol fled, taking the Declaration of Independence and the Constitution with them. First Lady Dolley Madison escaped from the White House with Gilbert Stuart's portrait of George Washington. On August 24, the British defeated the Americans at Bladensburg, a suburb of Washington. They set fire to the War Department, the Treasury, the Capitol, and the White House. Only a night of heavy rain prevented the city's destruction. The Treaty of Ghent, which finally ended the war, was signed on February 17, 1815 in the Octagon.

The British attack on Washington, DC in August 1814

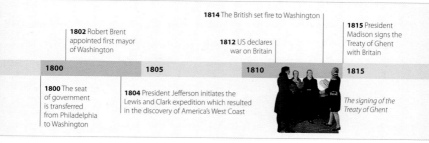

1814 The British set fire to Washington

1802 Robert Brent appointed first mayor of Washington

1812 US declares war on Britain

1815 President Madison signs the Treaty of Ghent with Britain

| 1800 | 1805 | 1810 | 1815 |

1800 The seat of government is transferred from Philadelphia to Washington

1804 President Jefferson initiates the Lewis and Clark expedition which resulted in the discovery of America's West Coast

The signing of the Treaty of Ghent

The Baltimore and Ohio Railroad's "Tom Thumb" locomotive racing a horse-drawn car

Rebirth

With the end of the War of 1812 came a period of renewed optimism and economic prosperity in Washington. Washingtonians wanted to make their city a bustling commercial capital. They planned to build the Chesapeake and Ohio Canal to connect Washington to the Ohio River Valley and thus open trade with the west. Construction on the Baltimore and Ohio Railroad line also got under way. As the population grew, new hotels and boarding-houses, home to many of the nation's congressmen, opened up. Newspapers, such as the *National Intelligencer,* flourished.

In 1829, James Smithson, an Englishman, bequeathed a collection of minerals, books, and $500,000 in gold to the United States, and the Smithsonian Institution was born.

Construction began on three important government buildings, each designed by Robert Mills (1781–1855): the Treasury Building, the Patent Office, and the General Post Office building. Also at this time, the Washington National Monument Society, led by George Watterston, chose a 600-ft (183-m) obelisk to become the Washington Monument, again designed by the architect Robert Mills.

Slavery Divides the City

Racial tension was beginning to increase around this time, and in 1835 it erupted into what was later known as the Snow Riot. After the attempted murder of the widow of architect William Thornton, a botany teacher from the North was arrested for inciting black people because plant speci-mens had been found wrapped in the pages of an abolitionist newspaper. A riot ensued, and in the course of the fighting a school for black children and the interior of a restaurant owned by Beverly Snow, a free black man, were destroyed. As a result, and to the anger of many people, black and white, laws were passed denying free black people licenses to run saloons or eating places.

Nothing has been more divisive in Washington's history than the issue of slavery. Many Washingtonians were slaveholders; others became ardent abolitionists. The homes of several abolitionists and free black people, as well as black churches, were used as hiding places for fugitive slaves. On an April night in 1848, 77 slaves attempted to escape the city, and boarded a small schooner on the Potomac River. But the following night they were captured and brought back to Washington, where they

1828 President John Quincy Adams breaks ground for the Chesapeake and Ohio Canal

James Smithson (1765–1829)

1844 The invention of the telegraph speeds the distribution of news from Washington

| 1825 | 1830 | 1835 | 1840 | 18 |

1829 James Smithson leaves a fortune worth more than $500,000 to the United States

1827 The Washington Abolition Society is organized

1835 Baltimore and Ohio Railroad links Washington and Baltimore. Racial tension leads to the Snow Riot

1846 Construction on the Smithsonian Castle begins. Alexandria is retroceded to Virginia

were sold at auction. The incident served only to heighten the tension between pro-slavery and anti-slavery groups. Slavery was abolished in Washington in 1862.

The Civil War

In 1860, following the election of President Abraham Lincoln, several southern states seceded from the Union in objection to Lincoln's stand against slavery. Shots were fired on Fort Sumter in Charleston, South Carolina on April 12, 1861, and the Civil War began. By the summer, 50,000 volunteers arrived in Washington to join the Army of the Potomac under General George B. McClellan. Washington suddenly found itself in the business of housing, feeding, and clothing the troops, as well as caring for the wounded. Buildings and churches became makeshift hospitals. Many people came to nurse the wounded, including author Louisa May Alcott and poet Walt Whitman.

Thousands of northerners came to help the war effort. They were joined by hordes of black people heading north to escape

Black residents of Washington celebrating the abolition of slavery in the District of Columbia

slavery, so that by 1864 the population of Washington had doubled that of 1860, reaching 140,000.

After skirmishes on July 12, 1864, witnessed by Lincoln himself at Fort Stevens, the Confederates retreated. By March 1865 the end of the war appeared to be close at hand. Parades, speeches, and band concerts followed Confederate General Robert E. Lee's surrender on April 9, 1865. Yet the celebratory mood was short-lived. Disturbed by the Union Army's victory, John Wilkes Booth assassinated President Lincoln at Ford's Theatre during the third act of *Our American Cousin* on April 14, 1865. Lincoln was taken to the house of tailor William Petersen, across the street from the theater, where he died the next morning (see p98).

Victory parade through Washington, DC to celebrate the end of the Civil War in April 1865

1851 Major expansion of the Capitol begins

1859 Senate wing of the Capitol is completed

1857 House of Representatives wing of the Capitol is completed

1861 Civil War begins when shots are fired on Fort Sumter, South Carolina

1862 Slavery is abolished in the District of Columbia

1850   **1855**   **1860**   **1865**

1848 77 slaves attempt to escape from Washington by schooner. Ground is broken for the Washington Monument

1863 The Emancipation Proclamation is issued

1865 General Robert E. Lee surrenders to the Union. President Lincoln is assassinated

President Lincoln

1860 President Abraham Lincoln elected

Post Civil War

The Freedmen's Bureau was created to help provide African Americans with housing, food, education, and employment. In 1867 General Oliver Otis Howard, commissioner of the bureau, used $500,000 of the bureau's funds to purchase land to establish a university for African Americans. He was president of this institution, later named Howard University, from 1869 to 1873.

On February 21, 1871, a new "territorial government" was formed to unite Georgetown, the city of Washington, and the County of Washington into the District of Columbia. A governor and a board of public works were appointed by President Ulysses S. Grant. Alexander "Boss" Shepherd, a member of the board of public works, paved streets, installed streetlights, laid sidewalks, planned parks, and designed an advanced sewerage system. But the District's debts rose uncontrollably. As a result, Congress quickly tightened its reins and established home rule. It took over some of the District's debts, and appointed three commissioners to work within a set budget.

Washington became a city of contrasts, attracting both rich and poor. One of the most distinguished literati in the city was Henry Adams, best known for his autobiographical work, *The Education of Henry Adams*. He lived on Lafayette Square next door to John Hay, Secretary of State and also a man of letters. One of Washington's most prominent African Americans, Frederick Douglass, lived at Cedar Hill, across the river in Anacostia. Born a slave in Maryland, he escaped north to freedom where he started an abolitionist newspaper. During the Civil War he became an adviser to President Lincoln.

Many lived well, including the growing middle class, which moved to the new suburbs of Mount Pleasant and LeDroit Park, yet a large number of the poor made their home in Washington's hidden alleys.

The Library of Congress under construction

A New Century

In 1901 Senator James McMillan of Michigan spearheaded a plan to improve the design of Washington by partaking in the "city beautiful" movement, in vogue at the time. L'Enfant's plan was finally completed, and the Mall between the Washington Monument and the US Capitol was laid out. Architects Daniel Burnham, Charles F. McKim, and others planned the building of a memorial to honor President Abraham Lincoln.

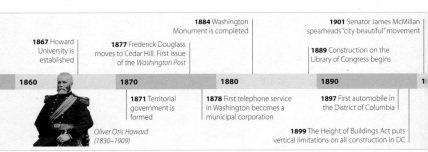

1867 Howard University is established

1877 Frederick Douglass moves to Cedar Hill. First issue of the *Washington Post*

1884 Washington Monument is completed

1901 Senator James McMillan spearheads "city beautiful" movement

1889 Construction on the Library of Congress begins

| 1860 | 1870 | 1880 | 1890 | 1 |

1871 Territorial government is formed

1878 First telephone service in Washington becomes a municipal corporation

1897 First automobile in the District of Columbia

1899 The Height of Buildings Act puts vertical limitations on all construction in DC

Oliver Otis Howard (1830–1909)

Suffragettes demanding a hearing for imprisoned leader Alice Paul

restaurants. It became home to many successful musicians and writers; Duke Ellington and the opera star Madame Evanti lived here, as did poets Langston Hughes and Paul Dunbar. Alain Locke, a professor of philosophy at Howard, and Jean Toomer, author of *Cane*, were also residents.

When the US entered World War I in 1917, growing numbers of women came to Washington to fill the posts vacated by men. Suffragists took to the streets to campaign for the right to vote. The National Women's Party, led by Alice Paul, picketed the White House to urge President Wilson to endorse a constitutional amendment to give women the vote.

African Americans in Washington were not only banned from voting but also faced discrimination in housing and education. After a local black battalion was excluded from a World War I victory parade, tension mounted. On July 20, 1919, riots erupted on the streets and did not stop for four days. Although discrimination continued, the 1920s were a period of commercial, artistic, and literary success for the black community. The area around U Street and Howard University attracted small businesses, theaters, nightclubs, and

Roosevelt Ushers in a New Deal

Following the stock market crash of 1929, federal workers received salary cuts, and many other Washingtonians lost their jobs. As a result, President Roosevelt created the "New Deal," an ambitious public works program to reduce unemployment. People were paid to do a range of tasks, from planting trees on the Mall to completing some of the city's edifices, such as the Supreme Court, the government office buildings of the Federal Triangle, and the National Gallery of Art.

Roosevelt's wife, Eleanor, was a champion of the poor and a tireless reformer. In 1939, when Marian Anderson, the African American singer, was denied permission by the Daughters of the American Revolution to perform at Constitution Hall, Eleanor Roosevelt arranged for her to sing at the Lincoln Memorial instead, to a crowd of 75,000.

President Franklin D. Roosevelt with First Lady Eleanor

1906 Teddy Roosevelt's daughter, Alice, is married in the White House

1908 Opening of Union Station, designed by Daniel Burnham

1918 Washington celebrates Armistice Day

1919 Race riots continue for four days

Marian Anderson (1897–1993)

1910

1920

1930

1940

1917 US enters World War I

1920 The 19th amendment, granting suffrage to women, is ratified

1929 The Great Depression begins

1933 New Negro Alliance is formed to improve the status of black people

1939 Marian Anderson performs at the Lincoln Memorial

After the US entered World War II in December 1941, Washington's population soared. Women from all across the country arrived in the capital, eager to take on government jobs while the men were overseas. They faced housing shortages, and long lines as they waited to use rationing coupons for food and services. The city also offered a respite for soldiers on leave. Actress Helen Hayes, a native Washingtonian, opened the Stage Door Canteen where celebrities provided food and entertainment.

Soldiers on patrol after the death of Martin Luther King, Jr.

The Civil Rights Movement

In 1953 the Supreme Court's ruling in the Thompson Restaurant case made it illegal for public places to discriminate against black people. With the passage of other anti-discrimination laws, life in Washington began to change. In 1954, the recreation department ended its public segregation. In the same year, on May 17, the Supreme Court ruled that "separate educational facilities are inherently unequal."

On August 28, 1963, more than 200,000 people arrived in the capital for the "March on Washington" to support civil rights. From the steps of the Lincoln Memorial, Marian

John F. Kennedy, Jr. salutes his father's casket at Arlington Cemetery in 1963

Anderson sang again and Reverend Martin Luther King, Jr. shared his dream in words that would echo for generations (see p99).

In November 1963, the nation was stunned by the assassination of President John F. Kennedy in Dallas, Texas. An eternal flame was lit at his funeral in Arlington Cemetery by his widow, Jacqueline. Five years later, on April 4, 1968, Martin Luther King was shot. Killed at the age of 39, he is revered as a hero and a martyr.

The opening of the Kennedy Center for Performing Arts in 1971 indicated the growing international character of the city. Several art museums with impressive collections (the East Wing of the National Gallery of Art, the Hirshhorn, the National Museum of American Art, and the National Portrait Gallery) also opened to enrich the city's cultural life. The construction of the Metro helped alleviate traffic problems. The embassies, the foreign banking community (the World Bank, the International Monetary Fund, and the Inter-American Development Bank), and the increasing number of immigrants, provided a cosmopolitan flavor.

1940 First plane lands at National Airport

1945 The first atomic bomb is dropped on Hiroshima, ending World War II

1973 Washingtonians gain the right to elect a mayor

1963 Martin Luther King gives "I Have a Dream" speech

1969 250,000 anti-Vietnam War protesters march

1976 Metro opens. National Air and Space Museum opens

| 1940 | 1950 | 1960 | 1970 | 1 |

1941 The National Gallery of Art opens. After Japan attacks Pearl Harbor, the US enters World War II

Dr. Martin Luther King, Jr. (1929–68)

1964 Washington residents vote in a presidential election for the first time

1974 President Richard Nixon resigns following criminal investigation

1978 Marion Barry elected mayor for the first of four terms

1982 Dedication of the Vietnam Veterans Memorial, designed by Maya Ying Lin

Home Rule

Residents of the District of Columbia have never been given full representation in American politics, as they have no congressman. (Until the 23rd Amendment of 1961 they could not even vote for president – the 1964 election was the first in which they took part.) In 1967, with people clamoring for a greater say in local government, President Lyndon Johnson replaced the system of three commissioners, set up by Congress in 1871, with an appointed mayor and a city council with greater responsibility in policy and budget issues. The result was the city's first elected mayor in over 100 years, Walter E. Washington. Residents were permitted to elect a non-voting delegate to Congress in 1971, and the Home Rule Act of 1973 allowed the people to elect both mayor and city council.

In 1978 Marion Barry succeeded as mayor. Born in Mississippi and raised in Tennessee, he came to Washington in 1965 to work for civil rights. He was the city's mayor for 16 of the next 20 years, but toward the end of his tenure, a large deficit and dissatisfaction with city politics developed. Middle-class families, both white and black, continued to flee the increasingly crime-ridden city for the safety of the suburbs. In 1995 Congress stripped the mayor

Mayor Bowser opening the 10th Anniversary Festival, 2015

of much of his power and appointed a five-person "financial control board" to oversee the city's affairs. The election in 1998 was won by Anthony Williams, an outsider, who offered a fresh outlook and financial stability. Congress returned to the mayor much of the authority it had taken away. Within months of taking his new office it appeared that Mayor Williams was turning the city around. The budget was operating with a surplus, the population had stabilized, and unemployment was down.

A new administration under Adrian Fenty, elected in 2006, transformed the city's image. No longer dubbed the crime capital of the US, Washington, DC has again become a mecca for tourists and a safer place for its residents. In 2010, Fenty was defeated by moderate democrat Vincent Gray; in 2015, Gray was defeated by Muriel Bowser.

In 2009 Barack Obama became the first African-American president in US history – a momentous occasion.

Fireworks lighting the Washington Monument during the 2000 celebrations

1993 Opening of the US Holocaust Memorial Museum

President Bill Clinton (b.1946)

2005 George W. Bush inaugurated for a second term as US president

2011 Rare 5.8 magnitude earthquake hits DC

2012 Barack Obama re-elected for a second term as president

2015 Muriel Bowser elected mayor

1990　2000　2010　2020

2001 September 11 Terrorist attack on the Pentagon

2010 Vincent Gray elected mayor

2014 Mayor Vincent Gray defeated in the Democratic primary

2009 Barack Obama becomes the first African-American president

The American Presidents

The presidents of the United States have come from all walks of life; at least two were born in a log cabin – Abraham Lincoln and Andrew Jackson. Others, such as Franklin D. Roosevelt and John F. Kennedy, came from privileged backgrounds. Millard Fillmore attended a one-room schoolroom and Jimmy Carter grew peanuts. Many, including Ulysses S. Grant and Dwight D. Eisenhower, were military men, who won public popularity for their great achievements in battle.

Benjamin Harrison (1889–93)

Chester A. Arthur (1881–5)

Millard Fillmore (1850–53)

Franklin Pierce (1853–7)

Zachary Taylor (1849–50)

James K. Polk (1845–9)

Rutherford B. Hayes (1877–81)

W.H. Harrison (1841)

George Washington (1789–97) was a Revolutionary War general. He was unanimously chosen to be the first president of the United States.

James Madison (1809–17), known as the Father of the Constitution, was co-author of the Federalist Papers.

Andrew Johnson (1865–9)

| 1775 | 1800 | 1825 | 1850 | 1875 |

| 1775 | 1800 | 1825 | 1850 | 1875 |

John Adams (1797–1801), a lawyer and historian, was the first president to live in the White House.

James Monroe (1817–25)

John Quincy Adams (1825–9)

John Tyler (1841–5)

Martin Van Buren (1837-41)

James A. Garfield (1881)

Ulysses S. Grant (1869–77)

Grover Cleveland (1885–9)

Thomas Jefferson (1801–9), architect, inventor, landscape designer, diplomat, and historian, was the quintessential Renaissance man.

James Buchanan (1857–61)

Andrew Jackson (1829–37) defeated the British at the Battle of New Orleans in the War of 1812.

Abraham Lincoln (1861–5) won the epithet, the Great Emancipator, for his role in the abolition of slavery. He led the Union through the Civil War.

Grover Cleveland (1893–7)

William McKir (1897–19

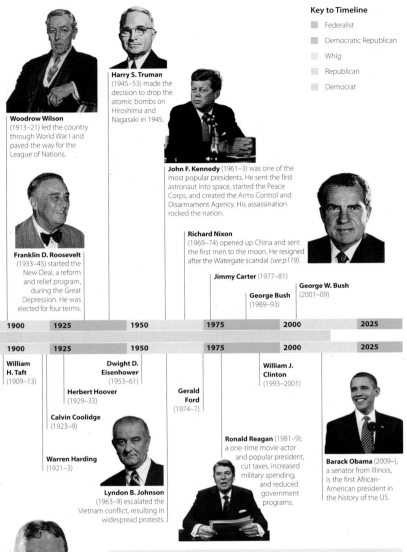

Key to Timeline

- Federalist
- Democratic Republican
- Whig
- Republican
- Democrat

Woodrow Wilson (1913–21) led the country through World War I and paved the way for the League of Nations.

Harry S. Truman (1945–53) made the decision to drop the atomic bombs on Hiroshima and Nagasaki in 1945.

John F. Kennedy (1961–3) was one of the most popular presidents. He sent the first astronaut into space, started the Peace Corps, and created the Arms Control and Disarmament Agency. His assassination rocked the nation.

Richard Nixon (1969–74) opened up China and sent the first men to the moon. He resigned after the Watergate scandal (see p119).

Franklin D. Roosevelt (1933–45) started the New Deal, a reform and relief program, during the Great Depression. He was elected for four terms.

Jimmy Carter (1977–81)

George Bush (1989–93)

George W. Bush (2001–09)

| 1900 | 1925 | 1950 | 1975 | 2000 | 2025 |

| 1900 | 1925 | 1950 | 1975 | 2000 | 2025 |

William H. Taft (1909–13)

Dwight D. Eisenhower (1953–61)

Herbert Hoover (1929–33)

Calvin Coolidge (1923–9)

Warren Harding (1921–3)

Gerald Ford (1974–7)

William J. Clinton (1993–2001)

Lyndon B. Johnson (1963–9) escalated the Vietnam conflict, resulting in widespread protests.

Ronald Reagan (1981–9), a one-time movie actor and popular president, cut taxes, increased military spending, and reduced government programs.

Barack Obama (2009–), a senator from Illinois, is the first African-American president in the history of the US.

Theodore Roosevelt (1901–9) created many national parks and oversaw the construction of the Panama Canal.

The Role of the First Lady

In the 19th century, the First Lady acted primarily as hostess and "behind-the-scenes" adviser. Later, when Eleanor Roosevelt held her own press conferences, the role of First Lady changed greatly. Jackie Kennedy gave support to the arts, Rosalynn Carter attended Cabinet meetings, Barbara Bush promoted literacy, and Hillary Clinton ran her own political campaign. Michelle Obama follows in this vein, campaigning for charitable causes, including the prevention of childhood obesity and support for military families.

Eleanor Roosevelt at a press conference in the 1930s

How the Federal Government Works

In September 1787, the Constitution of the United States of America was signed *(see p93)*. It was created as "the supreme Law of the Land," to ensure that it would take precedence over state laws. The powers of the federal government were separated into three distinct areas: the legislative branch to enact the laws, the executive branch to enforce them, and the judicial branch to interpret them. No one branch, however, was to exert too much authority, and the system of checks and balances was instituted. Provisions were made for amending the Constitution, and by December 1791 the first ten amendments, called the Bill of Rights, were ratified.

Checks and Balances

The system of checks and balances means that no one branch of government can abuse its power.

The Executive Branch: The President can recommend and veto legislation and call a special session of Congress. The President appoints judges to the courts and can grant pardons for federal offenses.

The Judicial Branch: The Supreme Court interprets laws and treaties and can declare an act unconstitutional. The Chief Justice presides at an impeachment trial of the President.

The Legislative Branch: Congress can override a presidential veto of a bill with a two-thirds majority. Presidential appointments and treaties must be approved by the Senate. Congress also oversees the jurisdiction of the courts and can impeach and try the President and federal judges.

The Senate, sitting in session in the US Capitol.

The Executive Branch

The President, together with the Vice President, is elected for a four-year term. The President suggests, approves, and vetoes legislation. The Executive also develops foreign policy and directs relations with other countries, serves as Commander-in-Chief of the armed forces, and appoints ambassadors. Secretaries to the Cabinet, composed of various heads of departments, meet regularly to advise the President on policy issues. Several agencies and councils, such as the National Security Council and the Office of Management and Budget, help determine the executive agenda.

Seal of the President

Ulysses S. Grant served as the US President from 1869 to 1877.

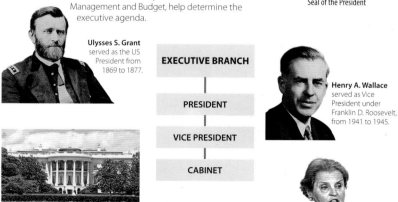

EXECUTIVE BRANCH

PRESIDENT

VICE PRESIDENT

CABINET

Henry A. Wallace served as Vice President under Franklin D. Roosevelt, from 1941 to 1945.

The White House is the official residence of the US President.

Madeleine Albright, the first woman to serve as Secretary of State, was appointed in 1997.

The Judicial Branch

The Supreme Court and other federal courts determine the constitutionality of federal, state, and local laws. They hear cases relating to controversies between states and those affecting ambassadors or citizens of different states. They also try cases on appeal. The Supreme Court consists of nine justices appointed for life by the President.

The Supreme Court is the highest court in the United States and is the last stop in issues of constitutionality.

Thurgood Marshall was the first African American to be a Supreme Court Justice. He held the position from 1967 to 1991.

JUDICIAL BRANCH

9 SUPREME COURT JUSTICES

OF WHOM ONE IS CHIEF SUPREME COURT JUSTICE

Oliver Wendell Holmes, Supreme Court Justice from 1902 to 1932, was a strong advocate of free speech.

Earl Warren was Supreme Court Justice from 1953 to 1969. He wrote the unanimous opinion in *Brown v. Board of Education* (1954). *(See p50).*

The Legislative Branch

The Congress of the United States consists of two bodies, the House of Representatives and the Senate. Representatives to the House are elected by the voters in each state for a two-year term. The number of Representatives for each state is determined by the state's population. The Senate is composed of two Senators from each state, elected for six-year terms. Congress regulates commerce and is empowered to levy taxes and declare war. This branch also makes the laws: bills discussed, written, and revised in legislative committees must be passed first by the House and by the Senate before being approved by the President.

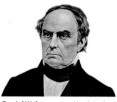

Daniel Webster served both in the House of Representatives (1813–17) and in the Senate (1822–41).

LEGISLATIVE BRANCH

HOUSE OF REPRESENTATIVES

SENATE

Sam Rayburn was a popular and distinguished Speaker of the House.

Edward Kennedy, leader of the United States' most famous political family, served in the Senate from 1962 until his death in 2009.

The US Capitol is home to both the House of Representatives and the Senate.

WASHINGTON, DC AT A GLANCE

Washington is more than just the political capital of the United States. It is also the home of the Smithsonian Institution, and as such is the cultural focus of America. Its many superb museums and galleries have something to offer everyone. Always one of the most popular sights, the president's official residence, the White House, attracts millions of visitors each year. Equally popular is the National Air and Space Museum, which draws vast numbers of visitors to its awe-inspiring displays of air- and spacecraft. Also of particular interest are Washington's many monuments and memorials. The huge Washington Monument, honoring the first US president, dominates the city skyline. In contrast, the war memorials, dedicated to the thousands of soldiers who died in battle, are quietly poignant.

Washington's Top Ten Attractions

The White House *See pp110–13*

Vietnam Veterans Memorial
See p85

National Air and Space Museum
See pp64–7

National Gallery of Art
See pp60–63

Kennedy Center
See pp120–21

Washington National Cathedral *See pp144–5*

Arlington National Cemetery
See pp132–3

Washington Monument
See p80

Lincoln Memorial
See p87

US Capitol
See pp52–3

◄ Statue of General Grant in front of the United States Capitol

Museums and Galleries in Washington, DC

Few cities can claim to have as many museums and galleries in such a concentrated area as Washington. The Mall forms the main focus because it is lined with museums. Most of these are part of the Smithsonian Institution *(see p74)*, which is funded by the government. They cover a wide range of exhibits, from great works of art to space shuttles, to mementos of major events in American history. Admission to most of the museums and galleries is free.

National Museum of American History
This statue of a toga-clad George Washington is one of millions of artifacts in this museum of American history *(see pp76–9)*.

Georgetown

The White House and Foggy Bottom

Corcoran Gallery of Art
This Beaux Arts building is in the midst of a major renovation. Once it reopens, the National Gallery of Art will manage its collection and exhibitions *(see p115)*.

Potomac River

Tidal Basin

US Holocaust Memorial Museum
Photographs, videos, and re-created concentration camp barracks bring to life the brutality of the Holocaust and illustrate the terrible fate of Jews and others in World War II Nazi Germany *(see pp82–3)*.

Smithsonian American Art Museum and the National Portrait Gallery
This museum houses the world's largest collection of American paintings, sculpture, photographs, and crafts *(see pp100–3)*.

National Museum of Natural History
A huge African elephant is the focal point of the building's main foyer. The museum's fascinating exhibits trace the evolution of animals and explain the creation of gems and minerals *(see pp72–3)*.

Penn Quarter

National Gallery of Art
The futuristic East Building houses the 20th-century art in this collection, while the 1930s West Building is home to older works *(see pp56–63)*.

The Mall

Capitol Hill

0 meters 500
0 yards 500

National Air and Space Museum
Washington's most popular museum has exhibits from aviation and space history, including the Wright Brothers' first airborne plane and the Apollo 14 space module *(see pp64–7)*.

Monuments and Memorials in Washington, DC

As the political center of the United States, and home of its president, Washington has a great number of monuments and memorials honoring America's key figures and historic events. The most well-known among these are the Washington Monument and the Lincoln Memorial – sights of great interest to all who visit the city. For those who wish to remember the countless men and women who lost their lives fighting for their nation, there are poignant monuments, set in tranquil parks, where visitors can reflect in peace.

Korean War Veterans Memorial Created in 1995, the 19 stainless steel, larger than life-size statues of this memorial recall the thousands who died in the Korean War *(see p85)*.

Georgetown

Lincoln Memorial This emotive and inspirational marble figure has often been the focus of civil rights protests *(see p87)*.

The White House and Foggy Bottom

Iwo Jima Statue (US Marine Corps Memorial) This iconic memorial depicts US Marines capturing the Japanese island of Iwo Jima at the end of World War II *(see p136)*.

| 0 meters | 500 |
| 0 yards | 500 |

Potomac River

Vietnam Veterans Memorial Visitors to this dramatic memorial are confronted by a sobering list of names on the V-shaped granite walls *(see p85)*.

Martin Luther King, Jr. Memorial
Surrounded by cherry blossom trees and including an inscription on the wall, this is the first memorial on the Mall to an African-American *(see p85)*.

Washington Monument
One of the most enduring images of Washington, this 555 ft (170 m) marble obelisk can be seen from all over the city. Built in two stages, the monument was finally completed in 1884 *(see p80)*.

Penn Quarter

Capitol Hill

The Mall

Jefferson Memorial
This Neo-Classical building houses a bronze statue of President Jefferson, a key player in America's struggle for independence *(see p81)*.

Franklin D. Roosevelt Memorial
This vast memorial, in the form of a 7 acre (3 hectares) park, includes statuary, waterfalls, and ornamental gardens *(see pp86–7)*.

WASHINGTON, DC THROUGH THE YEAR

A wide variety of events takes place in Washington, DC all through the year. In late March or early April, when the famous cherry blossoms bloom, the city really comes to life. Parades and outdoor festivals begin, and continue through the summer as more and more people come to explore the DC area in June, July, and August.

The White House is a focus for many visitors, and it plays host to annual events such as the Easter Egg Roll in the spring and the Garden Tours in the spring and fall. Some of the more popular events are listed below; for further details on these and other events in the city, contact the Destination DC tourist office *(see p207)*.

Spring

The air is clear in springtime in Washington, DC, with crisp mornings and warm, balmy days. The cherry tree blossoms surrounding the Tidal Basin are world famous and should not be missed, although the area does get very busy. Memorial Day is a big event in DC; it marks the official beginning of summer, and is celebrated in many ways.

March
Washington Home and Garden Show, Walter E. Washington DC Convention Center, 801 Mount Vernon Place, NW (7th St and New York Ave, NW). **Tel** (202) 249-4039. A vast array of garden items and things for the home.
St. Patrick's Day *(Sun before Mar 17)*, Constitution Ave, NW. Parade celebrating Irish culture. There are also celebrations in Old Town Alexandria.
Cherry Blossom Kite Festival *(last Sat)*, Washington

Monument. **Tel** (202) 633-1000. Kite designers fly their best models and compete for prizes.

April
National Cherry Blossom Festival *(late Mar–early Apr)*, Constitution Ave, NW. **Tel** 1-877-442-5666. Parade and concerts to celebrate the blooming of Washington's famous cherry trees.
White House Egg Roll *(Easter Mon)*, White House Lawn. www.whitehouse.gov/easteregg roll. Children's races with eggs.
White House Spring Garden Tours *(second weekend)*, White House gardens. **Tel** (202) 456-7041. Tour of the Jacqueline Kennedy Garden and more.
Thomas Jefferson's Birthday *(Apr 13)*, Jefferson Memorial. **Tel** (202) 426-6821. Military drills, speeches, and wreath-laying.
Shakespeare's Birthday Celebration *(end of Apr)*, Folger Shakespeare Library, 201 E Capitol St, SE. **Tel** (202) 544-4600. A day of music, plays, food, and children's events.

Mother-and-daughter team in the Easter Egg Roll at the White House

May
Flower Mart *(first Fri & Sat)*, Washington National Cathedral. **Tel** (202) 537-6200. Flower booths, music, and crafts.
Memorial Day Weekend Concert *(last Sun)*, West Lawn of Capitol. **Tel** (202) 619-7222. National Symphony Orchestra performs.
Memorial Day *(last Mon)*, Arlington National Cemetery. **Tel** (703) 607-8000. US Navy Memorial. **Tel** (202) 737-2300. Vietnam Veterans Memorial. **Tel** (202) 619-7222. Wreath-laying, speeches, and music to honor war veterans.
Memorial Day Jazz Festival *(last Mon)*, Old Town Alexandria. **Tel** (703) 746-5592. Live, big-band jazz music.
Twilight Tattoo Military Pageant *(7pm every Wed, May & Jun)*, Fort McNair. **Tel** (202) 685-2888. Military parade presenting the history of the US Army.

Cherry tree blossoms surrounding Jefferson Memorial at the Tidal Basin

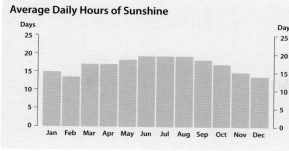

Average Daily Hours of Sunshine

Sunshine Chart

The amount of sunshine in Washington does not vary greatly – even in winter half the days will enjoy blue skies. In summer the sunshine is at its most persistent, although it is best to be prepared for the occasional rainstorm. The chart gives the number of days per month with little or no cloud.

Summer

In June, July, and August, visitors come to Washington, DC from far and wide. The streets and parks are packed with people enjoying the sunshine. Many attractions become overcrowded, so it is important to call ahead and make reservations at this time of year.

The summer months can also be extremely hot and humid; even so, parades and outdoor fairs are usually very popular. Independence Day on July 4 is particularly exciting, with a parade during the day and fireworks at night.

June

Smithsonian Festival of American Folklife *(late Jun–early Jul)*, The Mall. **Tel** (202) 633-6440. A huge celebration of folk culture, including music, dance, games, and food.

Capitol Pride *(mid-Jun)*, Pennsylvania Ave, NW. Street festival and parade celebrating the gay communities of DC.

DC Caribbean Carnival *(last Sat in Jun)*, Georgia Ave, NW. A colorful parade of more than 3,000 masqueraders, plus food, dance, and music.

DC Jazz Festival *(end Jun)*, venues all over the city. www. dcjazzfest.org. A five-day jazz festival attracting the best musicians in the country.

July

Independence Day *(Jul 4)*, Constitution Ave & US Capitol, other areas. Concert on west front of the Capitol. A parade along Constitution Avenue,

Fireworks over Washington, DC on the Fourth of July

with fireworks from the base of the Washington Monument. Other areas such as Old Town Alexandria and Mount Vernon have parades and fireworks.

Bastille Day *(Jul 14)*. A celebration involving food, music, and dance. Events are held in the French Embassy and selected cafés and restaurants.

Mary McLeod Bethune Celebration *(Jul 10)*, Bethune Statue, Lincoln Park, E Capitol St, SE, between 11th St & 13th St. **Tel** (202) 673-2402. Memorial wreath-laying, gospel music, and speeches.

Capital Fringe Festival *(Jul)*, venues all over the city. Modeled on Edinburgh's Fringe festival, the focus is on theater, dance, puppetry, and the spoken word. Film and visual arts also feature.

Screen on the Green *(Beginning at dusk: Mon evening Jul–Aug)*, The Mall. **Tel** 1-877-262-5866. A Washington summer tradition. Classic movies are shown on giant screens.

August

Shakespeare Free for All *(mid-Aug)*, Sidney Harmon Hall, 610 F St, NW. www. shakespearetheatre.org. Nightly performances by the Shakespeare Theater Company, free of charge.

Arlington County Fair *(mid-Aug)*, Thomas Jefferson Center, Arlington, VA. **Tel** (703) 829-7471. www.arlingtoncountyfair.us. Food, crafts, music, and fairground rides.

National Frisbee Festival *(late Aug)*, Washington Monument. **Tel** (202) 619-7222. A weekend celebrating the game of Frisbee, including a free Frisbee contest for champions and amateurs alike.

Performers at the Capital Fringe Festival

Average Monthly Rainfall

Rainfall Chart
It is impossible to escape the rain completely in Washington. The heaviest rainfall occurs during May through August, when it can come as a welcome break from the humidity. Rainfall tails off in September and October and reaches its lowest ebb in late winter. It rarely lingers for long in the city.

A school band performing in front of the Lincoln Memorial

Fall

With the air turning cooler, Labor Day (the first Monday in September) bids goodbye to the summer. The fall (autumn) season covers September, October, and November. A popular event at this time of year is Halloween, when children dress up as their favorite creatures or characters to go trick-or-treating.

Halloween
Jack-O'-Lantern

September
Labor Day Weekend Concert *(Sun before Labor Day)*, West Lawn of the US Capitol. **Tel** (202) 619-7222. National Symphony Orchestra performs a concert.
Fiesta DC *(Sep)*, Columbia Heights neighborhood. www. fiestadc.org. A celebration of Latino culture.
International Children's Festival, Wolf Trap Park, Vienna, VA. **Tel** (703) 255-1900. Musical and dance performances are held from around the world.

National Book Fair *(Sep)*, Washington Convention Center. **Tel** (202) 707-5000. More than 80 award-winning authors, illustrators, and poets talk about their work and sign books.
Taste of Georgetown *(Sep)*, Wisconsin Ave, NW. **Tel** (202) 298-9222. Washington's finest restaurants showcase their talents.
Adams-Morgan Day Festival *(second Sun)*. Giant street party with music, food, and crafts.
Colonial Market and Fair, Mount Vernon, VA. **Tel** (703) 780-2000. Craft demonstrations and 18th-century entertainment.

October
Columbus Day *(second Mon)*, Columbus Memorial, Union Station. **Tel** (202) 289-1908. Speeches and wreath-laying in honour of the man who discovered America.
White House Fall Garden Tours *(mid-Oct)*. **Tel** (202) 456-7041. A chance to walk the grounds of the President's home.

Boo at the Zoo *(end Oct)*, Washington National Zoo. **Tel** (202) 397-7328 (book tickets in advance). Halloween celebration for children.
Halloween *(Oct 31)*. Young people trick-or-treating, dressed as ghosts, clowns, and witches. Dupont Circle and Georgetown are popular areas.

November
Veterans Day Ceremonies *(Nov 11)*, Arlington National Cemetery. **Tel** (703) 607-8000. Services, parades, and wreath-layings take place at various memorials around the city, commemorating United States military personnel who died in war. Veterans Day ceremonies are held at the Vietnam Veterans Memorial. **Tel** (202) 426-6841, and at the US Navy Memorial **Tel** (202) 737-2300).
Kennedy Center Holiday Festival *(late Nov–New Year's Eve)*. **Tel** (202) 467-4600. Musicals, ballet, and classical concerts for the holiday season.

Military guard on Veterans Day in Arlington National Cemetery

Average Monthly Temperature

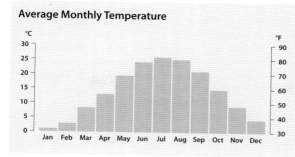

Temperature Chart
Washington's climate varies greatly. In winter the air is bitterly cold, with temperatures rising little above freezing. In July and August, however, it becomes very hot and extremely humid. The best time to visit the city is in the spring or fall, when the weather is pleasantly mild and the air is clear.

Winter

Temperatures can plummet below freezing during the winter months of December, January, and February. Hence the city is generally quieter at this time of year, making it a good time to see the most popular sights. Over the Christmas period, Washington becomes busy again with festive events to get people into the holiday spirit. Decorations are visible across the city, and many places offer Christmas tours.

Toward the end of winter, a number of famous birthdays are celebrated, including those of Martin Luther King, Jr. and Presidents Abraham Lincoln and George Washington.

December

National Christmas Tree Lighting *(mid-Dec)*, Ellipse south of the White House. www.thenationaltree.org. The President turns on the lights on the National Christmas tree (advance tickets only).

Washington National Cathedral Christmas Services *(throughout Dec)*. Tel (202) 537-6200. Holiday celebrations with festive music.
Christmas at Mount Vernon *(weekends late Nov–mid-Dec)*, Mount Vernon, VA. Tel (703) 780-2000. Experience an 18th-century Christmas.

January

Robert E. Lee's Birthday *(mid-Jan)*. Tours of the Lee-Fendall house in Alexandria. Tel (703) 548-1789.
Martin Luther King, Jr.'s Birthday *(third Mon)*. Commemorative events.
Restaurant week *(mid-Jan)*. Many of Washington's top restaurants offer prix fixe lunch or dinner specials.

Febuary

Chinese New Year *(first two weeks)*, N St, Chinatown. Tel *(202) 789-7000*. Parades, dancing, and live music.
African American History Month *(throughout Feb)*. Various events are held across the city:

contact the Smithsonian (Tel (202) 633-1000) and the National Park Service (Tel (202) 619-7222).
George Washington's Birthday Parade *(around Feb 15)*, Old Town Alexandria, VA. Tel (703) 838-4200.
Abraham Lincoln's Birthday, *(Feb 12)*, Lincoln Memorial. Tel (202) 619-7222. Wreath-laying ceremony followed by a reading of the Gettysburg Address.

Girl Scouts watching George Washington's Birthday Parade

Federal Holidays

New Year's Day (Jan 1)
Martin Luther King, Jr.'s Birthday (3rd Mon in Jan)
Presidents' Day (3rd Mon in Feb)
Easter Monday (Mar or Apr)
Memorial Day (last Mon in May)
Independence Day (Jul 4)
Labor Day (1st Mon in Sep)
Columbus Day (2nd Mon in Oct)
Veterans Day (Nov 11)
Thanksgiving (4th Thu in Nov)
Christmas Day (Dec 25)

The National Christmas tree outside a snow-covered White House

United States Capitol at sunrise ▶

WASHINGTON, DC AREA BY AREA

CAPITOL HILL

Soon after the Constitution was ratified in 1788, America's seat of government began to take root on Capitol Hill. The site was chosen in 1791 from 10 acres that were ceded by the state of Maryland. Pierre L'Enfant *(see p21)* chose a hill on the east side of the area as the foundation for the Capitol building and the center of the new city.

In more than 200 years, Capitol Hill has developed into a bustling microcosm of modern America. Symbols of the country's cultural development are everywhere, from its federal buildings to its centers of commerce, shops, and restaurants, as well as its multicultural residential areas.

The Capitol Hill area is frequented by the most powerful people in the United States. While access to official government buildings is strictly controlled for reasons of security, ordinary citizens may still find members of Congress greeting tour groups in the halls of the Capitol or dining at local restaurants.

Sights at a Glance

Historic Buildings
1 Library of Congress pp48–9
2 Folger Shakespeare Library
3 US Supreme Court
4 Sewall-Belmont House
5 United States Capitol pp52–3
13 Union Station

Museums and Galleries
14 National Postal Museum

Market
12 Eastern Market

Monuments and Memorials
6 Robert A. Taft Memorial
7 National Japanese American Memorial
8 Ulysses S. Grant Memorial

Parks and Gardens
9 US Botanic Garden
10 Bartholdi Park and Fountain

Church
11 Ebenezer United Methodist Church

Restaurants *see p183*
1 Acqua Al 2
2 Banana Café
3 Belga Café
4 Bistro Bis
5 Bullfeathers
6 Cava Mezze
7 Dubliner
8 Ethiopic
9 Five Guys
10 Good Stuff Eatery
11 Market Lunch
12 The Monocle
13 Montmartre
14 Sonoma
15 Tortilla Coast
16 Toscana Café
17 Tunnicliff's
18 We, the Pizza

See also Street Finder map 4

◀ United States Capitol with cherry blossom in foreground

For keys to symbols *see back flap*

Street-by-Street: Capitol Hill

The cityscape extending from the Capitol is an impressive combination of grand classical architecture and stretches of grassy open spaces. There are no skyscrapers here, only the immense marble halls and columns that distinguish many of the government buildings. The bustle and excitement around the US Capitol and US Supreme Court contrast with the calm that can be found by the reflecting pool or in a quiet residential street. Many of the small touches that make the city special can be found in this area, such as the antique lighting fixtures on Second Street, the brilliant bursts of flowers along the sidewalks, or the brightly painted façades of houses on Third Street near the Folger Shakespeare Library.

5 ★ US Capitol
The famous dome of the nation's seat of government is one of the largest in the world.

6 Robert A. Taft Memorial
A statue of Taft (1889–1953) stands in front of the bell tower that was erected to honor his principles and achievements.

8 Ulysses S. Grant Memorial
General Grant (1822–85), the Union leader in the American Civil War, is the central figure in a remarkable group of bronze equestrian statuary.

9 US Botanic Garden
Established in 1820, the Botanic Garden contains thousands of exotic and domestic plants.

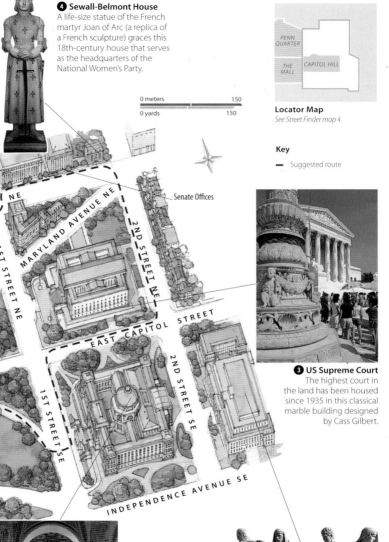

4 Sewall-Belmont House
A life-size statue of the French martyr Joan of Arc (a replica of a French sculpture) graces this 18th-century house that serves as the headquarters of the National Women's Party.

| 0 meters | 150 |
| 0 yards | 150 |

Locator Map
See Street Finder map 4

Key

— Suggested route

Senate Offices

3 US Supreme Court
The highest court in the land has been housed since 1935 in this classical marble building designed by Cass Gilbert.

1 ★ Library of Congress
Thomas Jefferson sold his personal book collection to the Library of Congress after the British had burned the Capitol, which housed the Library, using the books as kindling.

2 Folger Shakespeare Library
A tribute to the Bard's works and times, the library also doubles as a museum displaying Elizabethan treasures.

❶ Library of Congress

Congress first established a reference library in the US Capitol in 1800. When the Capitol was burned in 1814, Thomas Jefferson offered his own collection as a replacement. The government bought his library, and his belief in a universality of knowledge became the foundation for the Library's acquisition policy. In 1897 the Library of Congress moved to an Italian Renaissance-style building designed by John L. Smithmeyer and Paul J. Pelz. The main building, the Thomas Jefferson Building, is a marvel of art and architecture, with its paintings, mosaics, and exhibitions, such as "Creating the United States" and "Thomas Jefferson's Library". The Library of Congress has the world's largest collection of books, with over 650 miles (1,050 km) of bookshelves housing 35 million volumes.

Front façade of the Jefferson Building

★ **Main Reading Room**
Eight huge marble columns and 10 ft (3 m) high female figures personifying aspects of human endeavor dwarf the reading desks in this room. The domed ceiling soars 160 ft (49 m) above the reading room floor.

African & Middle Eastern Reading Room
This is one of 10 reading rooms in the Jefferson Building where visitors can use books from the Library's collections.

KEY

① Exhibition Area

② Asian Reading Room

Mosaic of Minerva
This beautiful marble mosaic figure of Minerva of Peace, created by Elihu Vedder, dominates the staircase landing near the Visitors' Gallery, overlooking the Main Reading Room.

★ **Gutenberg Bible**
The 15th-century Gutenberg Bible was the first book printed using movable metal type. This is one of only three perfect vellum copies.

②

Main Entrance

Neptune Fountain
The bronze statue of Neptune, the Roman god of the sea, forms a striking feature at the front of the Jefferson Building.

★ **Great Hall**
Splendid marble arches and columns, grand staircases, imposing bronze statues, stained-glass skylights, mosaics, and murals all combine to create a magnificent entrance hall.

❷ Folger Shakespeare Library

201 E Capitol St, SE. **Map** 4 F4.
Tel (202) 544-4600. Ⓜ Capitol South.
Open 10am–5pm Mon–Sat. **Closed**
Federal hols. 📷 ♿ Tickets for plays,
concerts, and readings available from
box office. Ⓦ **folger.edu**

Inspired by Shakespeare's own era, this library and museum celebrate the works and times of the Elizabethan playwright.

The research library was a gift to the American people in 1932 from Henry Clay Folger who, as a student in 1874, began to collect Shakespeare's works. Folger also funded the construction of this edifice, built specifically to house his collection. It contains 310,000 Elizabethan books and manuscripts, as well as the world's largest collection of Shakespeare's writings, including a third of the surviving copies of the 1623 First Folio (first editions of Shakespeare's works). One of these first editions is displayed in the oak-paneled Great Hall, along with books and engravings.

The Folger hosts many cultural events. For example, there are regular performances of Shakespeare's plays in the library's 250-seat reconstruction of an Elizabethan theater. There is also an annual series of poetry readings, as well as numerous talks throughout the year. The Folger Consort early music ensemble, performs concerts of 12th- to 20th-century music.

The Great Hall in the Folger Shakespeare Library

The impressive Neo-Classical façade of the US Supreme Court

In the grounds of the library, the Elizabethan Garden has plants that are featured in Shakespeare's plays. Shakespeare's birthday is celebrated every April with jugglers, music, theater shows, and a tour of the library.

❸ US Supreme Court

1st St between E Capitol St and
Maryland Ave, NE. **Map** 4 E4.
Tel (202) 479-3000. Ⓜ Capitol South.
Open 9am–4:30pm Mon–Fri.
Closed Federal hols. 📷 💻 ♿
Lectures. Ⓦ **supremecourtus.gov**

The Supreme Court forms the judicial and third branch of the US government *(see pp30–31)*. It was established in 1787 at the Philadelphia Constitutional Convention and provides the last stop in the disposition of the nation's legal disputes and issues of constitutionality. Groundbreaking cases settled here include *Brown v. Board of Education*, which abolished racial segregation in schools, and *Miranda v. Arizona*, which declared crime suspects were entitled to a lawyer before being interrogated. The Court is charged to guarantee "Equal Justice Under Law," the motto emblazoned over the entrance.

As recently as 1929, the court was still meeting in various sections of the US Capitol building. Then, at Chief Justice William Howard Taft's urging, Congress authorized a separate building to be constructed. The result was a Corinthian edifice, designed by Cass Gilbert, that opened in 1935. Sculptures depicting the allegorical figures of the Contemplation of Justice and the Guardian of the Law stand beside the steps while on the pediment above the entrance are figures of Taft (far left) and John Marshall, the fourth Chief Justice (far right).

Visitors can watch the court in session Monday to Wednesday from October to April. Admission is on a first-come, first-served basis. During controversial cases visitors camp out overnight for coveted spots. When court is not in session, public lectures on the Supreme Court are held every hour on the half-hour in the Courtroom (contact for confirmation).

Hallway of the 18th-century
Sewall-Belmont House

❹ Sewall-Belmont House

144 Constitution Ave, NE. **Map** 4 E4.
Tel (202) 546-1210. Ⓜ Capitol
South, Union Station. **Open** noon–
5pm Wed–Sun. **Closed** Federal hols.
Donations welcome. 🗓 📷
🆆 sewallbelmont.org

Robert Sewall, the original owner
of this charming 18th-century
house, rented it out to Albert
Gallatin, the Treasury Secretary
under President Thomas
Jefferson, in the early 1800s. It
was here Gallatin entertained a
number of wealthy contributors
whose financial backing
brought about the Louisiana
Purchase in 1803, which doubled
the size of the United States.
During the British invasion in
1814, the house was the only site
in Washington to resist the
attack. While the US Capitol was
burning, American soldiers took
refuge in the house from where
they fired upon the British.

The National Women's
Party, who won the right for
American women to vote
in 1920, bought the house in
1929 with the help of feminist
Alva Vanderbilt Belmont.
Today, the house is still the
headquarters of the Party,
and visitors can admire the
period furnishings and suffragist
artifacts. The desk on which the,
as yet unratified, Equal Rights
Amendment of 1923 was
written by Alice Paul, leader of
the Party, is here.

❺ US Capitol

See pp52–3.

❻ Robert A. Taft Memorial

Constitution Ave and 1st St,
NW. **Map** 4 E4. Ⓜ Union
Station. ♿

This statue of Ohio senator
Robert A. Taft (1889–1953)
stands in a park opposite
the US Capitol. The
statue itself, by sculptor
Wheeler Williams, is
dwarfed by a vast, white
bell tower (the Carillon), that
rises up behind the figure of
the politician. The memorial,
designed by Douglas W. Orr,
was erected in 1959 as
a "tribute to the honesty,
indomitable courage, and
high principles of free
government symbolized by
his life." The son of President
William Howard Taft, Robert
Taft was a Republican, famous
for sponsoring the Taft-Hartley
Act, the regulator of collective
bargaining between labor
and management.

❼ National Japanese American Memorial

Louisiana and New Jersey
Avenues at D St, NW. **Map** 4 E3.
Ⓜ Union Station.

This memorial, designed by
Davis Buckley, commemorates
the story of the 120,000
Japanese Americans interned
during World War II and the
more than 800 Japanese

Statue of
Robert Taft

Americans who died in
military service. The names
of these servicemen are
carved on a curving
granite wall, while etched
on the top are the
names of the ten
detention camps where
Japanese American
civilians were confined.
An 18-foot long alumi-
num gong may be rung
by visitors, serving as
a call to reflection
and remembrance.

❽ Ulysses S. Grant Memorial

Union Square, west side of US
Capitol in front of Reflecting Pool.
Map 4 D4. Ⓜ Capitol South, Union
Station. **Open** Visitor center:
9am–5pm daily. ♿

This dramatic memorial
was sculpted by Henry
Merwin Shrady and dedicated
in 1922. With its 13 horses,
it is one of the world's most
complex equestrian statues.
The bronze groupings
around General Grant
provide a graphic depiction
of the suffering of the
Civil War. In the artillery
group, horses and soldiers
pulling a cannon are urged
on by their mounted leader.
The infantry group storms
into the heat of battle, where
a horse and rider have already
fallen under the charge.

Shrady worked on the
sculpture for 20 years, using
soldiers in training for his
models. He died two weeks
before it was dedicated.

The artillery group in the Ulysses S. Grant Civil War Memorial

❾ United States Capitol

The US Capitol is one of the world's best-known symbols of democracy. The center of America's legislative process for 200 years, its Neo-Classical architecture reflects the democratic principles of ancient Greece and Rome. The cornerstone was laid by George Washington in 1793, and by 1800 the Capitol was occupied. The British burned it down in the War of 1812, but restoration began in 1815. Many architectural and artistic features, such as the Statue of Freedom and Brumidi's murals, were added later. An impressive Capitol Visitor Center, located below the East Plaza, offers visitor access and facilities.

★ **The Rotunda**
Completed in 1865, the 180-ft (55-m) high Rotunda is capped by *The Apotheosis of Washington*, a fresco by Constantino Brumidi.

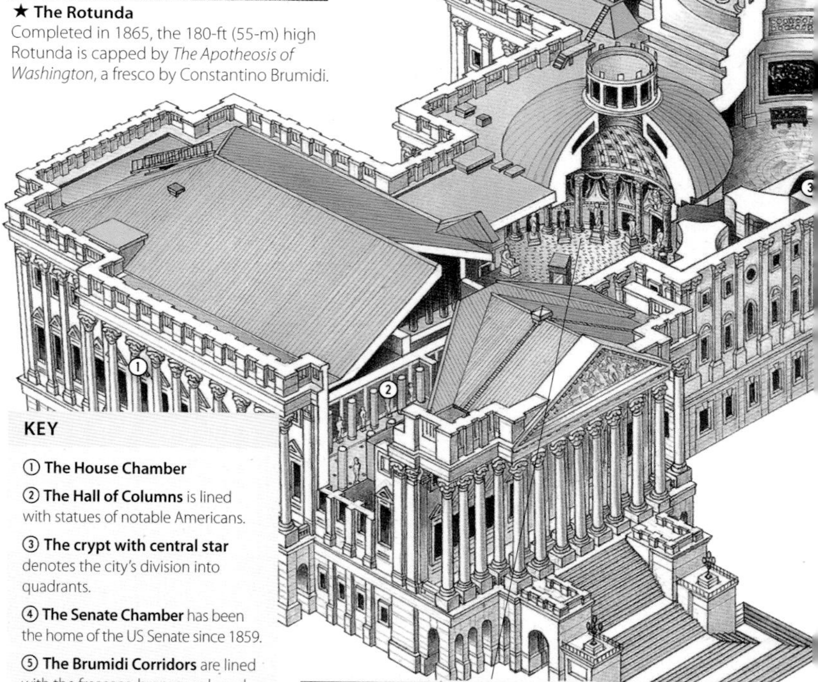

KEY

① **The House Chamber**

② **The Hall of Columns** is lined with statues of notable Americans.

③ **The crypt with central star** denotes the city's division into quadrants.

④ **The Senate Chamber** has been the home of the US Senate since 1859.

⑤ **The Brumidi Corridors** are lined with the frescoes, bronzework, and paintings of Italian artist Constantino Brumidi (1805–80).

⑥ **The Columbus Doors**, created by Randolph Rogers, are solid bronze and depict Christopher Columbus's life and his discovery of America, a theme echoed throughout the works of art in the Capitol.

★ **National Statuary Hall**
In 1864 Congress invited each state to contribute two statues of prominent citizens to stand in this hall.

The Dome
Designed by Thomas U. Walter, the cast-iron dome is undergoing major renovation until January 2017.

VISITORS' CHECKLIST

Practical Information
Main entrance: beneath East Front Plaza at First St and East Capitol St. **Map** 4 E4.
Tel (202) 224-3121. Visitor Center: (202) 226-8000; recorded information: (202) 225-6827.
🅦 **visitthecapitol.gov**
Open 8:30am–4:30pm Mon–Sat. Call for further information.
Closed Federal hols. 🎟 Passes required for free tours; book ahead on the website. ♿ 🅿 📷

Transport
Ⓜ Capitol South, Union Station, Federal Center. 🚌 32, 34, 36, 96.

Old Senate Chamber
Occupied by the Senate until 1859, this chamber was subsequently home to the Supreme Court for 75 years.

★ **Main Entrance/ Capitol Visitor Center**
Carved on the pediment are Classical female representations of America, flanked by figures of Justice and Hope. Guided tours start from the Capitol Visitor Center, located below the East Plaza.

US Capitol
Not only representative of the legislative heart of Washington, the Capitol marks the precise center of the city. The city's four quadrants radiate out from the middle of the building.

❾ US Botanic Garden

1st St and Independence Ave, SW.
Entrance: 100 Maryland Ave, SW.
Map 4 D4. **Tel** (202) 225-8333.
Ⓜ Federal Center SW. **Open** 10am–
5pm daily. ♿ ⓦ **usbg.gov**

The 80 ft (24 m) tall Palm
House is the centerpiece of the
Botanic Garden Conservatory.
The appearance of the 1933
building has been preserved
but modernized, creating
a spacious venue for the
collection of tropical and
subtropical plants, and the
comprehensive fern and
orchid collections. Other
specialties are plants native
to deserts in the Old and New
Worlds, plants of economic and
healing value, and endangered
plants rescued through an
international trade program.
    The Botanic Garden was
originally established to cultivate
plants that could be beneficial
to the American people. The
garden was revitalized in 1842,
when the Wilkes Expedition to
the South Seas brought back
an assortment of plants from
around the world, some of
which are still on display.
    A National Garden of plants
native to the mid-Atlantic region
was created on 3 acres (1 ha) of
land west of the Conservatory. It
includes a Water Garden, a Rose
Garden, and a terraced lawn.
Visitors can dial (202) 730-9303
from their cell phones for an
audio tour as they walk through.

❿ Bartholdi Park and Fountain

Independence Ave and 1st St, SW.
Map 4 D4. Ⓜ Federal Center SW. ♿
ⓦ **usbg.gov/bartholdi-park**

The graceful fountain that
dominates this jewel of a park
was created by Frédéric August
Bartholdi (sculptor of the Statue
of Liberty) for the 1876 Centennial.
Originally lit by gas, it was converted to electric lighting in
1881 and became a nighttime
attraction. Made of cast iron, the
symmetrical fountain is decorated with figures of nymphs and
tritons. Surrounding the fountain
are tiny model gardens, planted

The elegant Bartholdi Fountain,
surrounded by miniature gardens

to inspire the urban gardener.
They are themed, and include
Therapeutic, Romantic, and
Heritage plants, such as Virginia
sneezeweed, sweet William,
and wild oats.

⓫ Ebenezer United Methodist Church

4th St and D St, SE. **Tel** (202) 544-1636.
Map 4 F5. Ⓜ Eastern Market.
Open 10am–2pm Tue–Fri.
Closed Federal hols.

Ebenezer Church, established
in 1819, was the first black
church to serve Methodists in
Washington. Attendance grew
rapidly, and a new church, Little
Ebenezer, was built to take the
overflow. After the Emancipation

Proclamation in 1863 *(see p23)*,
Congress decreed that black
children should receive public
educa-tion. In 1864, Little
Ebenezer became the District of
Columbia's first school for black
children. The number of members
steadily increased and another
church was built in 1868, but
this was badly damaged by a
storm in 1896. The replacement
church, which was constructed
in 1897 and is still here today, is
Ebenezer United Methodist
Church. A model of Little
Ebenezer stands next to it.

⓬ Eastern Market

7th St and C St, SE. **Map** 4 F4.
Ⓜ Eastern Market. **Open** 7am–7pm
Tue–Fri, 7am–6pm Sat, 9am–5pm
Sun. **Closed** Jan 1, Jul 4, Thanksgiving,
Dec 25 & 26. ♿ at West end.
ⓦ **easternmarket-dc.org**

This block-long market hall has
been a fixture in Capitol Hill since
1871, and the provisions sold
today still have an Old World
flavor. Big beefsteaks and fresh
pigs' feet are plentiful, along with
gourmet sausages and cheeses
from all over the world. The
aroma of fresh bread, roasted
chicken, and flowers pervades
the hall. On Friday afternoons,
Saturdays, and Sundays the
covered stalls outside are filled
with crafts and farmers' produce;

The redbrick, late-19th-century Ebenezer United Methodist Church

Flowers for sale on the sidewalk outside the Eastern Market

on Sundays these popular stalls also host a flea market.

Eastern Market was designed by local architect Adolph Cluss. It was destroyed in a fire in 2007, but has been rebuilt with modern interiors that retain their old charm. It is one of the few public markets left in Washington, and the only one that is still used for its original purpose.

⑬ Union Station

50 Massachusetts Ave, NE. **Map** 4 E3. **Tel** (202) 289-1908. Ⓜ Union Station. **Open** daily. 🅿️ 🍴 👕 ♿ Ⓦ unionstationdc.com

When Union Station opened in 1908, its fine Beaux Arts design (by Daniel H. Burnham) set a standard that influenced architecture in Washington for 40 years. The elegantly proportioned white granite structure, its three main archways modeled on the Arch of Constantine in Rome, was the largest train station in the world. For half a century, Union Station was a major transportation hub, but as air travel became increasingly popular, passenger trains went into decline.

By the late 1950s, the size of the station outweighed the number of passsengers it served. For two decades, the railroad authorities and Congress debated its fate. Finally, in 1981, a joint public and private venture set out to restore the building. Union Station reopened in 1988, and today is the second-most-visited tourist attraction

in Washington. Its 96 ft (29 m) barrel-vaulted ceiling has been covered with 22-carat gold leaf. There are around 100 specialty shops and a food court to visit, and the Main Hall hosts cultural and civic events through-out the year. In 2011 an earthquake caused substantial damage to the main hall and the area is currently under repair.

Vintage stamp depicting Benjamin Franklin

⑭ National Postal Museum

2 Massachusetts Ave, NE. **Map** 4 E3. **Tel** (202) 633-5555. Ⓜ Union Station. **Open** 10am–5:30pm daily. **Closed** Dec 25. 🍴 🅿️ ♿ Ⓦ postalmuseum.si.edu

Opened by the Smithsonian in 1990, this fascinating museum is housed in the former City

Post Office building. Exhibits include a stagecoach and a postal rail car, showing how mail traveled before modern airmail.

"Mail Call", a permanent exhibition, explores the history of the military postal system. The Philatelic Gallery displays one of the best stamp collections in the world. "Binding the Nation" explains the history of the mail from the pre-Revolutionary era to the end of the 19th century. Other exhibits illustrate how the mail system works and how a stamp is created.

At postcard kiosks, you can address a postcard electronically, see the route it will take to its destination, and drop it in a mailbox on the spot.

Columbus Memorial, sculpted by Lorado Taft, in front of Union Station

THE MALL

In L'Enfant's original plan for the new capital of the United States, the Mall was conceived as a grand boulevard lined with diplomatic residences of elegant, Parisian architecture. L'Enfant's plan was never fully realized, but it is nevertheless a moving sight – this grand, tree-lined expanse is bordered on either side by the Smithsonian museums and features the Capitol at its eastern end and the Washington Monument at its western end. This dramatic formal version of the Mall did not materialize until after World War II. Until then the space was used for everything from a zoo to a railroad terminal to a wood yard.

The Mall forms a vital part of the history of the United States. Innumerable demonstrators have gathered at the Lincoln Memorial and marched to the US Capitol. The Pope said Mass, African-American soprano Marian Anderson sang at the request of first lady Eleanor Roosevelt, and Dr. Martin Luther King, Jr. delivered his famous "I have a dream" speech here. Every year on the Fourth of July (Independence Day), America's birthday party is held on the Mall, with a fireworks display. On summer evenings, teams of locals play softball and soccer on its fields.

Sights at a Glance

Museums and Galleries
1. National Gallery of Art pp60–63
2. National Air and Space Museum pp64–7
3. Hirshhorn Museum
4. Arts and Industries Building
5. National Museum of African Art
6. National Museum of the American Indian pp70–71
7. National Museum of Natural History pp72–3
8. Smithsonian Castle
9. Arthur M. Sackler Gallery
10. Freer Gallery of Art
11. National Museum of American History pp76–8
12. Washington Monument
13. United States Holocaust Memorial Museum pp82–3

Official Buildings
14. Bureau of Engraving and Printing

Monuments and Memorials
15. Jefferson Memorial
17. World War II Memorial
18. Vietnam Veterans Memorial
19. Korean War Veterans Memorial
20. Martin Luther King, Jr. Memorial
21. Franklin D. Roosevelt Memorial
22. Lincoln Memorial

Parks and Gardens
16. Tidal Basin

Restaurants see p184
1. Atrium Café (400 Virginia Ave SW)
2. Atrium Café
3. Cascade Café
4. Mitsitam Café
5. Pavilion Café

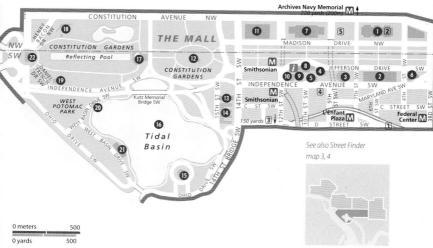

See also Street Finder map 3, 4

For keys to symbols see back flap

Street-by-Street: The Mall

This 1 mile (1.5 km) boulevard between the Capitol and the Washington Monument is the city's cultural heart; the many different museums of the Smithsonian Institution can be found along this green strip. At the northeast corner of the Mall is the National Gallery of Art. Directly opposite is one of the most popular museums in the world – the National Air and Space Museum, a soaring construction of steel and glass. Both the National Museum of American History and the National Museum of Natural History, on the north side of the Mall, also draw huge numbers of visitors.

❼ ★ National Museum of Natural History
The central Rotunda was designed in the Neo-Classical style and opened to the public in 1910.

❽ Smithsonian Castle
The main information center for all Smithsonian activities, this building once housed the basis of the collections found in numerous museums along the Mall.

❾ Arthur M. Sackler Gallery
This extensive collection of Asian art was donated to the nation by New Yorker Arthur Sackler.

12TH STREET NW

MADISON DRIVE NW

JEFERSON DRIVE SW

Washington Monument

⓫ ★ National Museum of American History
From George Washington's uniform to this electric streetcar, US history is documented here.

❺ National Museum of African Art
Founded in 1965 and situated underground, this museum houses a comprehensive collection of ancient and modern African art.

❿ Freer Gallery of Art
Asian art, including this 13th-century Chinese silk painting, is a highlight, in addition to a superb Whistler collection.

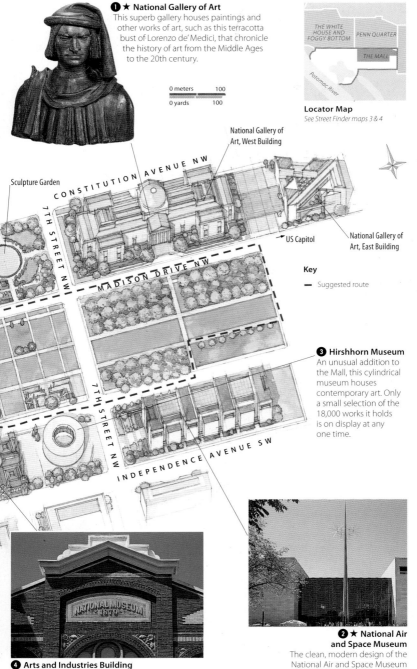

❶ ★ National Gallery of Art
This superb gallery houses paintings and other works of art, such as this terracotta bust of Lorenzo de' Medici, that chronicle the history of art from the Middle Ages to the 20th century.

0 meters 100
0 yards 100

Locator Map
See Street Finder maps 3 & 4

THE WHITE HOUSE AND FOGGY BOTTOM

PENN QUARTER

THE MALL

Potomac River

National Gallery of Art, West Building

Sculpture Garden

CONSTITUTION AVENUE NW

7TH STREET NW

MADISON DRIVE NW

← US Capitol

National Gallery of Art, East Building

Key
— Suggested route

❸ Hirshhorn Museum
An unusual addition to the Mall, this cylindrical museum houses contemporary art. Only a small selection of the 18,000 works it holds is on display at any one time.

7TH STREET NW

INDEPENDENCE AVENUE SW

❹ Arts and Industries Building
This masterpiece of Victorian architecture was originally built to contain exhibits from the Centennial Exposition in Philadelphia.

❷ ★ National Air and Space Museum
The clean, modern design of the National Air and Space Museum echoes the technological advances in aviation illustrated by the spectacular exhibits inside.

❶ National Gallery of Art

In the 1920s, American financier and statesman Andrew Mellon began collecting art with the intention of establishing a new art museum in Washington. In 1936 he offered his collection to the country and offered also to provide a building for the new National Gallery of Art. Designed by architect John Russell Pope, the Neo-Classical building was opened in 1941. Other collectors followed Mellon's example and donated their collections to the Gallery, and by the 1960s it had outgrown the West Building. I.M. Pei designed the innovative East Building, which was opened in 1978. The building was paid for by Andrew Mellon's son and daughter.

★ **Ginevra de' Benci**
This depiction of a thoughtful young Florentine girl by Leonardo da Vinci (c.1474) is his only painting in the US.

The Alba Madonna
Painted c.1510 by Raphael, this work is considered one of the major achievements of the Renaissance.

West Garden Court

Micro Gallery

Sculpture Garden

Ground Floor

★ **Woman with a Parasol – Mme Monet and her Son**
(1875) This painting by Claude Monet of his wife hangs in the West Building.

Portrait of a Young Man and His Tutor
This charming work by French artist Nicolas de Largillierre (1656–1746) was painted in 1685.

NATIONAL GALLERY OF ART | **61**

The giant mobile that hangs
in the middle of the central
courtyard of the East Building was
one of Alexander Calder's last
commissions, completed in 1976.

Main Floor

East Garden Court

Founders Room

East
Building

Concourse
Level

VISITORS' CHECKLIST

Practical Information
West Building Constitution Ave
between 4th St & 7th St, NW; East
Building 4th St between Madison
Drive and Constitution Ave, NW
(East wing closed for renovation).
Map 4 D4. **Tel** (202) 737-4215.
🇼 **nga.gov**
Open 10am–5pm Mon–Sat,
11am–6pm Sun. **Closed** Jan 1,
Dec 25. 📷 call (202) 842-6247.
🏠♿📷🚫📖🅿♿
Children's activities: call (202) 789-
3030 or (202) 842-6176.

Transport
Ⓜ Archives/Navy Memorial,
Judiciary Sq., Smithsonian.
🚌 32, 34, 36, 70.

Gallery Guide
*The National Gallery of Art is divided into
two main buildings. The West Building, shown
here, features European paintings and sculptures
from the 13th to the 19th centuries, including
American works, a substantial Impressionist
collection, and Sculpture Gallery. The East
Building features modern art. An underground
concourse connects the two buildings.*

**Mother of Pearl and
Silver: The Andalusian**
(c.1888–1900) James
McNeill Whistler's
portrait of his sister-in-
law evokes a sombre,
Spanish mood.

Key to Floor Plan

◻ 13th–15th-century Italian art

◻ 15th–16th-century Netherlands
and German art

◻ 16th-century Italian and Spanish art

◻ 17th-century Dutch and Flemish art

◻ 17th–18th-century Spanish, Italian,
and French art

◻ 18th–19th-century Spanish and French art

◻ 19th-century French art

◻ American paintings

◻ British paintings

◻ Sculpture, Decorative Arts,
Drawings and Prints

◻ Special exhibitions

◻ Non-exhibition space

Exploring the National Gallery of Art

The National Gallery's West and East Buildings are an unusual pair. The West Building, designed by John Russell Pope, is stately and Classical, with matching wings flanking its rotunda. Built of Tennessee marble, it forms a majestic presence on the Mall. Its collection is devoted to Western art from the 13th to the early 20th century. The East Building, completed in 1978, occupies a trapezoidal plot of land adjacent to the West Building. The triangular East Building is as audacious as the West one is conservative, but together they are harmonious. The interior of the East Building is a huge, fluid space, with galleries on either side housing works of modern art. The Sculpture Garden, adjacent to the West Building, has a fountain area that becomes an ice rink in winter.

Detail of *Christ Cleansing the Temple* (c.1570), by El Greco

Giotto's *Madonna and Child*, painted between 1320 and 1330

13th- to 15th-century Italian Art

The Italian galleries house paintings from the 13th to 15th centuries. The earlier pre-Renaissance works of primarily religious themes illustrate a decidedly Byzantine influence.

The Florentine artist Giotto's *Madonna and Child* (c.1320–30) shows the transition to the Classical painting of the Renaissance. *Adoration of the Magi*, painted around 1480 by Botticelli, portrays a serene Madonna and Child surrounded by worshipers in the Italian countryside. Around the same date Pietro Perugino painted *The Crucifixion with the Virgin, St. John, St. Jerome and St. Mary Magdalene*. Andrew Mellon bought the triptych from the Hermitage Gallery in Leningrad. Raphael's *The Alba Madonna* of

1510 was called by one writer "the supreme compositional achievement of Renaissance painting." Leonardo da Vinci's *Ginevra de' Benci* (c.1474–8) is thought to be the first ever "psychological" portrait (ie. one depicting emotion) to be painted.

16th-century Italian and Spanish Art

This collection includes works by Tintoretto, Titian, and Raphael. The 1500s were the height of Italian Classicism. Raphael's *St. George and the Dragon* (c.1506) typifies the perfection of technique for which this school of artists is known. Jacopo Tintoretto's *Christ at the Sea of Galilee* (c.1575/1580) portrays Christ standing on the shore while his disciples are on a storm-tossed fishing boat. The emotional intensity of the painting and the role of nature in it made Tintoretto one of the greatest of the Venetian artists.

17th- to 18th-century Spanish, Italian, and French Art

Among the 17th- and 18th-century European works are Jean-Honoré Fragonard's *Diana and Endymion* (c.1753–6), which was heavily influenced by Fragonard's mentor, François Boucher. El Greco's *Christ Cleansing the Temple* (pre-1570) demonstrates the influence of the 16th-century Italian schools. El Greco ("The Greek") signed his real name, Domenikos Theotokopoulos, to the panel.

17th-century Dutch and Flemish Art

This collection holds a number of Old Masters including works by Rubens, Van Dyck, and Rembrandt. An example of Rembrandt's self-portraits on display, which he painted in oils in 1659, ten years before his death.

Oil painting, *Diana and Endymion* (c.1753), by Jean-Honoré Fragonard

Several paintings by Rubens in this section testify to his genius, among them *Daniel in the Lions' Den* (c.1615). This depicts the Old Testament prophet, Daniel, thanking God for his help during his night spent surrounded by lions. In 1617, Rubens exchanged this work for antique marbles owned by a British diplomat. Rubens also painted *Deborah Kip, Wife of Sir Balthasar Gerbier, and her Children* (1629–30). Not a conventional family portrait, the mother and her four children seem withdrawn and pensive, suggesting unhappiness and perhaps even foreboding tragedy. Van Dyck painted Rubens's first wife, *Isabella Brant* (c.1621) toward the end of her life. Although she is smiling, her eyes reveal an inner melancholy.

19th-century French Art

This is one of the best Impressionist collections outside Paris. Works on display include Paul Cézanne's *The Artist's Father Reading "L'Evénement"* (1866), Auguste Renoir's *A Girl with a Watering Can* (1876), *Four Dancers* (c.1899) by Edgar Degas, and Claude Monet's *Woman with a Parasol – Madame Monet and Her Son* (1875) and *Palazzo da Mula, Venice* (1908). Post-Impressionist works include Seurat's pointillist *The Lighthouse at Honfleur* (c.1886), in which thousands of dots are used to create the image, and Van Gogh's *Self Portrait*. The latter was painted in St Rémy in 1889 when he was staying in an asylum and shows his mastery at capturing character and emotion. Toulouse-Lautrec's painting, *Quadrille at the Moulin Rouge* (1892), depicts a dancer provocatively raising her skirts above her ankles.

Geometric skylights in the plaza between the West Building to the East Building

American Painting

This important collection of American artists shows evidence of European influence, but in themes that are resolutely American. James McNeill Whistler's *Mother of Pearl and Silver: The Andalusian* (1888–1900) has a European sophistication. Mary Cassatt left America for exile in Europe and was heavily influenced by the Impressionists, especially Degas. *Boating Party* (1893–4) is an

Miss Mary Ellison by Mary Cassatt (1880)

example of one of her recurrent themes: mother and child. *Children Playing on a Beach* (1884) is also a good example of her child paintings, and *Miss Mary Ellison* of her portraiture. Winslow Homer's *Breezing Up (A Fair Wind)* (1873–6) is a masterpiece by the American Realist. His painting is a charming depiction of three small boys and a fisherman.

Modern and Contemporary Art

The enormous East Building houses modern and contemporary art. I.M. Pei's "H"-shaped building contains a vast atrium which is edged by four balconies and adjacent galleries. Architecturally, this space provides a dramatic focus and spatial orientation for visitors to the East Building.

Centered in the atrium is *Untitled*, a vast red, blue, and black creation by Alexander Calder. It was commissioned in 1972 for the opening of the museum in 1978. At the entrance to the East Building is Henry Moore's bronze sculpture *Knife Edge Mirror Two Piece* (1977–8).

Also in the East Building are a research center for schools, offices for the curators, a library, and a large collection of drawings and prints.

Both the East and West buildings also host traveling exhibits. These are not limited to modern art, but have included the art of ancient Japan, American Impressionists, and the sketches of Leonardo da Vinci. The East Building's galleries are currently closed for renovation.

Sculpture Garden

Located across the street from the West Building at 7th Street, the elegant Sculpture Garden holds 17 sculptures. The late 20th-century works include pieces by Louise Bourgeois, Roy Lichtenstein, and Joan Miró. Although different, the sculptures do not compete with each other because they are spread out. Transformed into an ice rink in winter and a venue for free jazz concerts in summer, the garden functions both as an outdoor gallery and as a pleasant oasis within the city. The pavilion houses a year-round café.

➋ National Air and Space Museum

The Smithsonian's National Air and Space Museum opened in 1976. The soaring architecture of the building on the Mall, designed by Hellmuth, Obata, and Kassabaum, is well suited to the airplanes, rockets, balloons, and space capsules of aviation and space flight. A second site, the Steven F. Udvar-Hazy Center, located near Dulles International Airport, opened in 2003 to celebrate the 100th anniversary of the Wright brothers' first powered flight. The museum is the largest air and space museum complex in the world and is home to the retired Discovery space shuttle.

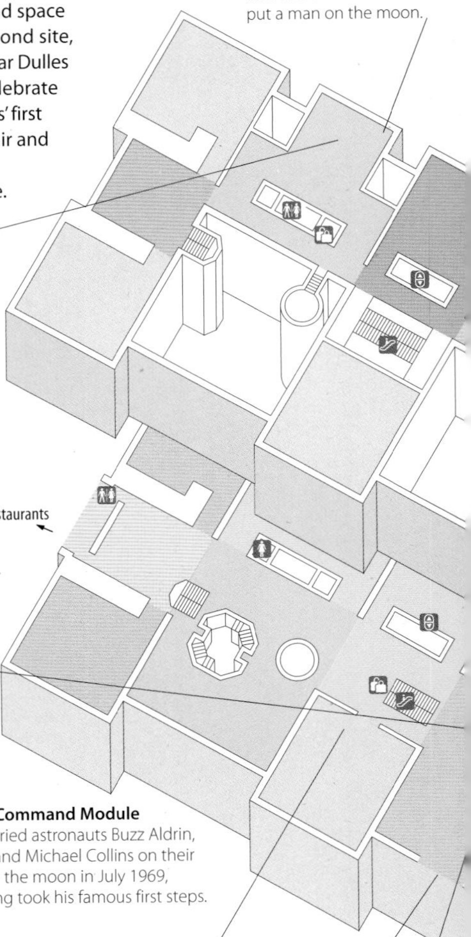

Apollo to the Moon
Full of artifacts, this exhibit tells the story of how the United States put a man on the moon.

Restaurants

Skylab Orbital Workshop
This was an orbiting workshop for sets of three-person crews, who conducted research experiments.

★ Apollo 11 Command Module
This module carried astronauts Buzz Aldrin, Neil Armstrong, and Michael Collins on their historic mission to the moon in July 1969, when Neil Armstrong took his famous first steps.

Lockheed Martin IMAX® Theater

Mall Entrance

Key to Floor Plan

- Milestones of Flight
- Exploring the Moon
- Aviation in World Wars I and II
- The Space Race Barron Hilton
- Pioneers of Flight
- Other exhibitions
- Explore the Universe
- Temporary exhibition space
- Wright Brothers
- Developments in Flight

★ Spirit of St. Louis
At the age of 25, pilot Charles Lindbergh made the first solo transatlantic flight in this plane, landing in France on May 21, 1927.

★ **1903 Wright Flyer**
This exhibit, along with others in the Wright Brothers and the Invention of the Aerial Age gallery, show the accomplishments of Orville and Wilbur Wright.

Albert Einstein Planetarium

Supermarine Spitfire MK. VII
With more than 20,351 Spitfires built, these planes saw service on every major front and successfully defended England against Germany in WWII.

Second Floor

★ **Amelia Earhart's Red Vega**
Amelia Earhart was the first woman to make a solo transatlantic flight. She succeeded in her red Lockheed Vega, five years after Charles Lindbergh.

America by Air
Located near the museum store, this exhibit outlines the fascinating history of America's airline industry and its effect on the nation and the world.

Flight simulators

Milestones of Flight
Many of the firsts in both aviation and space travel are on display in this gallery.

First Floor

Gallery Guide

The first floor houses many themed displays, as well as the Lockheed Martin IMAX® theater and the Museum Store. The lofty second-floor ceilings show exhibits and models demonstrating the history of flight from the early days to the space age.

Exploring the National Air and Space Museum

The National Air and Space Museum on the Mall has a massive exhibition space of 23 galleries. The most visited museum in the world, it has to cope not only with millions of visitors but also with the range and sheer size of its artifacts, which include hundreds of rockets, planes, and spacecraft. In 2003 the museum opened a sister exhibition space: a huge new state-of-the art facility, the Steven F. Udvar-Hazy Center, located near Dulles Airport. Now with two sites, more of NASM's historic collections are on display for the public to enjoy.

The Boeing F4B Navy fighter

Milestones of Flight

Entering the National Air and Space Museum from the Mall entrance, first stop is the soaring **Milestones of Flight** gallery, which gives an overview of the history of flight. The exhibits in this room are some of the major firsts in aviation and space technology, as they helped to realize man's ambition to take to the air.

The gallery is vast, designed to accommodate the large aircraft – many of which are suspended from the ceiling – and spacecraft. Some of these pioneering machines are surprisingly small, however. Charles Lindbergh's *Spirit of St. Louis*, the first aircraft to cross the Atlantic with a solo pilot, was designed with the fuel tanks ahead of the cockpit so Lindbergh had to use a periscope to look directly ahead. John Glenn's Mercury spacecraft, Friendship 7, in which he orbited the earth, is smaller than a sports car.

Near the entrance to the gallery is a moon rock – a symbol of man's exploration of space. Also in this gallery is the Apollo 11 Command Module, which carried the first men to walk on the moon. The Wright brothers' *Flyer* (in gallery 209) was the first plane to sustain powered flight on December 17, 1903, at Kitty Hawk, North Carolina.

Developments in Flight

Travelers now take flying for granted – it is safe, fast, and, for many, routine. The National Air and Space Museum, however, displays machines and gadgets from an era when flight was new and daring. The **Pioneers of Flight** gallery celebrates the men and women who have challenged the physical and psychological barriers faced when leaving the earth. Adventurer Cal Rogers was the first to fly across the United States, but it was not non-stop. In 1911 he flew from coast to coast in less than 30 days, with almost 70 landings. His early biplane is one of the exhibits. (Twelve years later, a Fokker T-2 made the trip in less than 27 hours.) Amelia Earhart was the first woman to fly the Atlantic, just five years after Charles Lindbergh. Her red Lockheed Vega is displayed. Close by is *Tingmissartoq*, a Lockheed Sirius seaplane belonging to Charles Lindbergh. Its unusual name is Inuit for "one who flies like a bird." Some of the greatest strides in aviation were made in the period between the two world wars, celebrated in the **Golden Age of Flight** gallery. The public's intense interest in flight resulted in races, exhibitions, and adventurous exploration. Here a visitor can see planes equipped with skis for landing on snow, with short wings for racing, and a "staggerwing" plane on which the lower wing was placed ahead of the upper.

The propeller-driven Douglas DC-3 aircraft in the America by Air gallery

Rockets on display in the Space
Race gallery

The F4B Navy fighter, used by
US Marine Corps squadrons,
was developed between the
world wars and is on display in
the **Sea-Air Operations** gallery.
Flight then progressed from
propeller propulsion to jets.
The **Jet Aviation** gallery has the
first operational jet fighter, the
German Messerschmitt Me 262A,
Lulu Belle, the prototype of the
first US fighter jet, was used in
the Korean War of 1950–53.

America by Air traces the
development of commercial air-
travel, from the air mail age to
the "glass cockpit," and beyond.
This is a fun, family-friendly
gallery with hands-on exhibits.

Aviation in World Wars I and II

One of the most popular parts
of the museum is the **World
War II Aviation** gallery, which
has planes from the Allied and
the Axis air forces. Nearby is an
example of the Japanese
Mitsubishi A6M5 Zero Model
52, which was a light, highly
maneuverable fighter plane.

The maneuverability of the
Messerschmitt Bf 109 made
it Germany's most successful
fighter. It was matched, and
in some areas surpassed, by
the Supermarine Spitfire of the
Royal Air Force, which helped
to win control of the skies over
Britain in 1940–41.

The Space Race

The animosity that grew
between the United States and
the Soviet Union after World
War II manifested itself in the
Space Race. America was taken
by surprise when the Soviets
launched Sputnik 1 on
October 4, 1957. The US
attempt to launch their first
satellite proved a spectacular
failure when the Vanguard
crashed in December 1957. The
satellite is on display here.

In 1961, Soviet cosmonaut
Yuri Gagarin became the first
person to orbit the earth. The
Americans countered with
Alan Shepard's manned space
flight in Freedom 7 later the
same year. The first space walk
was from the Gemini IV capsule
by American astronaut Edward
H. White in 1965.

On July 20, 1969,
the race reached a
climax when the
world watched as
Neil Armstrong walked
on the moon. His
original spacesuit from
the Apollo 11 mission is
on display. Other exhibits
from the Space Race include
the Skylab 4 command module,
and Gemini VII, a two-person
spacecraft that successfully
orbited the earth in 1965.

Gemini IV capsule

The Space Hall gallery shows
the result of the final détente
between the superpowers
with the Apollo-Soyuz Test
Project. This was a purposefully
collaborative space mission
meant to symbolize a new
era of cooperation.
It was the last
Apollo flight.
When the American
Apollo module
docked along-
side the Soviet
Soyuz space-
craft in 1975,
it was the
start of the
end of the
Space Race.

Progress in Air and Space Technology

Mankind's fascination with
flight is in part a desire to see
the earth from a great distance
and also to get closer to other
planets. In the Independence
Avenue lobby is artist Robert
T. McCall's interpretation of
the birth of the universe, the
planets, and astronauts
reaching the moon.

The Hubble Telescope,
launched from the *Discovery*
shuttle in April 1990, provides
pictures of extremely distant
astronomical objects.
Launched in 1964,
the Ranger lunar
probe also took
high-quality pictures
of the moon, and then
transmitted them to
Cape Canaveral.
**Moving Beyond
Earth** gives an insight
into recent human spaceflight
and future possibilities. A space
shuttle model and other launch
vehicle models, as well as
astronaut gear, are on display.
Visitors can also experience
aspects of spaceflight through
interactive computer kiosks.

The spacesuit worn by Apollo astronauts in 1969

Fountain in the central plaza of the Hirshhorn Museum

❸ Hirshhorn Museum

Independence Ave and 7th St, SW.
Map 3 C4. **Tel** (202) 633-1000.
Ⓜ Smithsonian, L'Enfant Plaza.
Open 10am–5:30pm daily (Sculpture Garden: 7:30am–dusk).
Closed Dec 25. 🖥 ♿ 📷 🏪
Ⓦ hirshhorn.si.edu

When the Hirshhorn Museum was still in its planning stages, S. Dillon Ripley, then Secretary of the Smithsonian Institution, told the planning board that the building should be "controversial in every way" so that it would be fit to house contemporary works of art.

The Hirshhorn certainly fulfilled its architectural mission. It has been variously described as a doughnut or a flying saucer, but it is actually a four-story, not-quite-symmetrical cylinder. It is also home to one of the greatest collections of modern art in the United States.

The museum's benefactor, Joseph H. Hirshhorn, was an eccentric, flamboyant immigrant from Latvia who amassed a collection of 6,000 pieces of contemporary art. Since the museum opened in 1974, the Smithsonian has built on Hirshhorn's original donation, and the collection now consists of 3,000 pieces of sculpture, 4,000 drawings and photographs, and approximately 5,000 paintings. The works of art are arranged chronologically. The main, lower floor displays newly acquired work. It is also home to the "Black Box," a space dedicated to film, video, and other digital works by emerging international artists. The second floor hosts temporary exhibitions, of which there are at least three a year. These are usually arranged thematically, or as tributes to individual artists, such as Lucien Freud, Alberto Giacometti, or Francis Bacon. The third floor houses the permanent collection, which includes works by artists such as Alexander Calder, Arshile Gorky, Willem de Kooning, and John Singer Sargent. In addition, visitors should not miss the outdoor sculpture garden, across the street from the museum. It includes pieces by Alexander Calder, Auguste Rodin, Henri Matisse, and many others.

During nice weather the sculpture garden is a pleasant place for an alfresco lunch. Pack a picnic or grab a bite from the many vendors on Constitution or Independence Avenues.

❹ Arts and Industries Building

900 Jefferson Drive, SW. **Map** 3 C4.
Tel (202) 633-1000. Ⓜ Smithsonian.
Closed to the public. ♿ 📷
Ⓦ si.edu

The ornate, vast galleries and the airy rotunda of the splendid Victorian Arts and Industries Building were designed by Montgomery Meigs, architect of the National Building Museum *(see p105)*. The Arts and Industries Building was extraordinary because of its expanse of open space and abundance of natural light.

The museum served a wide-range of functions after its completion on March 4, 1881. In its opening year, it was the site of President James A. Garfield's inaugural ball; it also displayed artifacts from Philadelphia's 1876 Centennial Exposition, including a steam train; later, it was home to a collection of the First Ladies' gowns, as well as Lindbergh's famous airplane the *Spirit of St. Louis*, before these exhibits were moved to other Smithsonian museums on the Mall. A working carousel is located in front of the building, on the Mall (closed in winter).

Concerns over its deteriorating condition led to the building's closure in 2004, but it has since benefitted from a $25 million renovation project. However, despite the completion of this renovation, the date of reopening is undecided.

Arts and Industries Building's fountain

The Hirshhorn Museum's sculpture garden, a green space in which to contemplate pieces by Calder, Rodin, Matisse, and others

Tribal masks at the National Museum of African Art

❺ National Museum of African Art

950 Independence Ave, SW. **Map** 3 C4.
Tel (202) 633-4600. **M** Smithsonian.
Open 10am–5:30pm daily.
Closed Dec 25. 🎫 ♿ 🏛 🚻
W nmafa.si.edu

Washington's National Museum of African Art is one of the most peaceful spots on the Mall. Perhaps because it is mostly underground, with a relatively low above-ground presence, it is often missed by visitors. The entrance pavilion, situated in the Enid A. Haupt Garden directly in front of the Smithsonian Castle, leads to three subterranean floors, where the museum shares space with the adjacent Ripley Center and the Arthur M. Sackler Gallery *(see pp74–5)*.

The museum was founded in 1964 by Warren Robbins, a former officer in the American Foreign Service (he was a cultural attaché and public affairs officer), and was the first museum in the US to concentrate entirely on the art and culture of the African continent. It was first situated in the home of Frederick Douglass *(see p147)*, on Capitol Hill. For several years Robbins had to finance the museum himself, gradually acquiring more space in the form of a collection of town houses near the original building. Eventually financial support was forthcoming as

the importance of the collection was recognized. The Smithsonian Institution acquired Robbins' collection in 1979, and the works were finally moved to their current home on the Mall in 1987.

The 9,000-piece permanent collection includes both modern and ancient art from Africa, although the majority of pieces date from the 19th and 20th centuries. Traditional African art of bronze, ceramics, and gold are on display, along with an extensive collection of masks. There is also a display of *kente* cloth from Ghana – brightly colored and patterned cloth used to adorn clothing as a symbol of African nationalism. The Eliot Elisofon Photographic Archives (Eliot Elisofon was a famous photographer for *Life* magazine) contain 300,000 prints and some 120,000 ft of edited and unedited film footage, as well

A Benin bronze head at the NMAA

as videos and documentaries on African art and culture. The museum now also holds 525 pieces of the Walt Disney-Tishman African Art Collection. The Warren M. Robbins Library has approximately 32,000 books in its collection, mainly on African art, history, and culture. The library, however, also has children's literature and videos. It is open to the public by appointment only.

To display its vast archive of exhibits, the museum runs a rolling program of themed exhibitions. It also hosts performing arts events featuring dance, music, and the spoken word. Year-round there is a full calendar of educational tours, lectures, and workshops, including many for children. At the bi-monthly Music of Africa workshop, children over six can play African musical instruments and learn about different rhythms and playing techniques.

History of the Mall

In September, 1789, French-born Pierre L'Enfant (1754–1825) was invited by George Washington to design the capital of the new United States. While the rest of the city developed, the area planned by L'Enfant to be the Grand Avenue, running west from the Capitol, remained swampy and undeveloped. In 1850, landscape gardener Andrew Jackson Downing was employed to develop the land in accordance with L'Enfant's plans. However, the money ran out, and the work was abandoned. At the end of the Civil War in 1865, President Lincoln, eager that building in the city should progress, instructed that work on the area should begin again, and the Mall began to take on the park-like appearance it has today. The addition of many museums and memorials in the latter half of the 20th century established the Mall as the cultural heart of Washington. It is undergoing further renovation to live up to its name as "America's Front Yard."

The Mall stretching down from the Capitol

❻ National Museum of the American Indian

Built from Minnesota Kasota limestone, the National Museum of the American Indian was established in collaboration with Native American communities throughout the western hemisphere. It is the only national museum dedicated to the Native peoples of the Americas, and is the eighteenth museum of the Smithsonian Institution. The original collections of artifacts were assembled by George Gustav Heye (1874–1957), a wealthy New Yorker, at the turn of the 20th century. The exhibitions showcase the spiritual and daily lives of diverse peoples and encourage visitors to look beyond stereotypes.

★ **Our Peoples**
American Indians, including the Blackfeet and Kiowa, tell their own stories and histories, focusing on both the destruction of their culture and their resilience.

George Heye (1874–1957)
Collector and world traveler George Gustav Heye and his wife, Thea, accompanied a Zuni delegation in New York c.1923.

★ **Lelawi Theater**
In this circular theater a spectacular multimedia presentation is shown every 15 minutes. "Who We Are" highlights the diversity of American Indian life from the Arctic, to the Northwest Coast, to Bolivia.

★ **Our Universes**
Eight groups of American Indians, from the Santa Clara Pueblo in New Mexico to the Lakota in South Dakota, share their world views, philosophies of creation, and spiritual relationship with nature.

Window on Collections: Many Hands, Many Voices
Over 3,500 objects are on display, including dolls, beaded objects, and artwork.

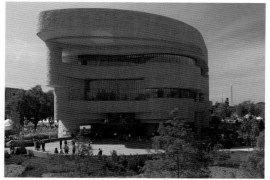

Exterior of Museum
The museum's curvilinear limestone exterior gives it a natural, weathered effect. It is set in a landscape of flowing water, hardwood forest, meadowland, and croplands, to reflect the American Indian's connection to the land.

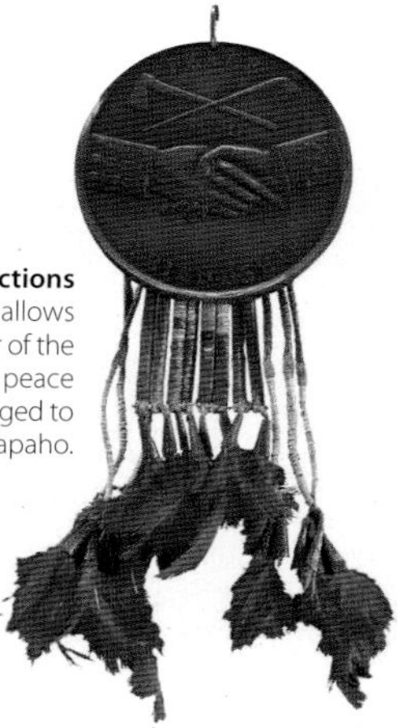

Window on Collections
Interactive technology allows for a self-guided tour of the exhibits. Shown here is a peace medal that once belonged to Powder Face, an Arapaho.

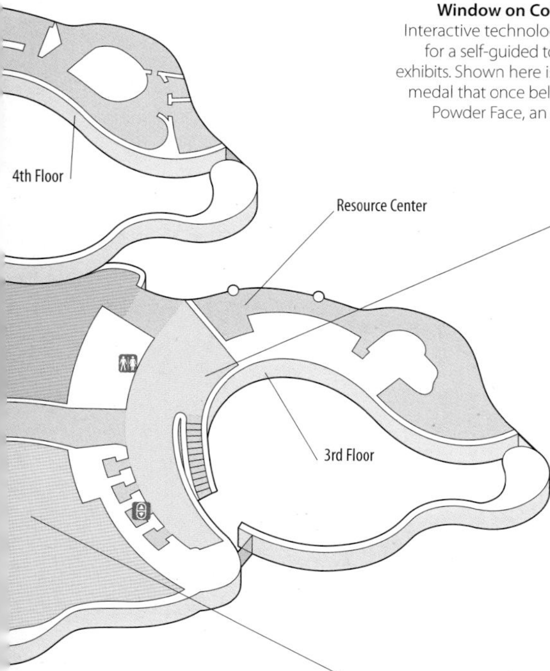

4th Floor

Resource Center

3rd Floor

Key to Floor Plan
- Our Peoples
- Window on Collections
- Our Universes
- Lelawi Theater
- Education classrooms
- Contemporary Gallery
- Our Lives

Gallery Guide
Begin your visit with the "Who We Are" multimedia presentation at the Lelawi Theater (4th floor). The three permanent exhibitions on this level are "Our Universes," "Our Peoples." While "Our Lives" and "Window on Collections" are on the 3rd floor. On the ground level is a shop and the Mitsitam café.

Our Lives
Examines the lives and identities of Native Americans and the consequences of legal policies that determine who is an American Indian. Here Fritz Scholder (b.1937) explores "nativeness" in this work *The American Indian.*

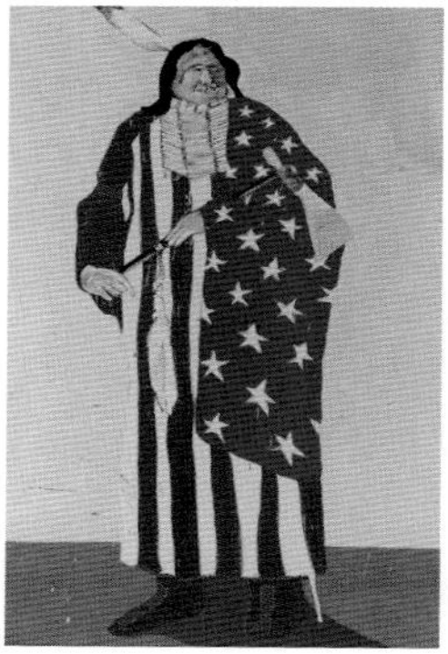

❼ National Museum of Natural History

The National Museum of Natural History, which opened in 1910, preserves artifacts from the earth's diverse cultures and collects samples of fossils and living creatures from land and sea. Visiting the museum is a vast undertaking, so sample the best of the exhibits and leave the rest for return visits. The O. Orkin Insect Zoo, with its giant hissing cockroaches and large leaf-cutter ant colony, is popular with children, while the Dinosaur Hall delights young and old. The stunning Hall of Mammals displays 274 specimens, and looks at how they adapted to changes in habitat and climate over millions of years.

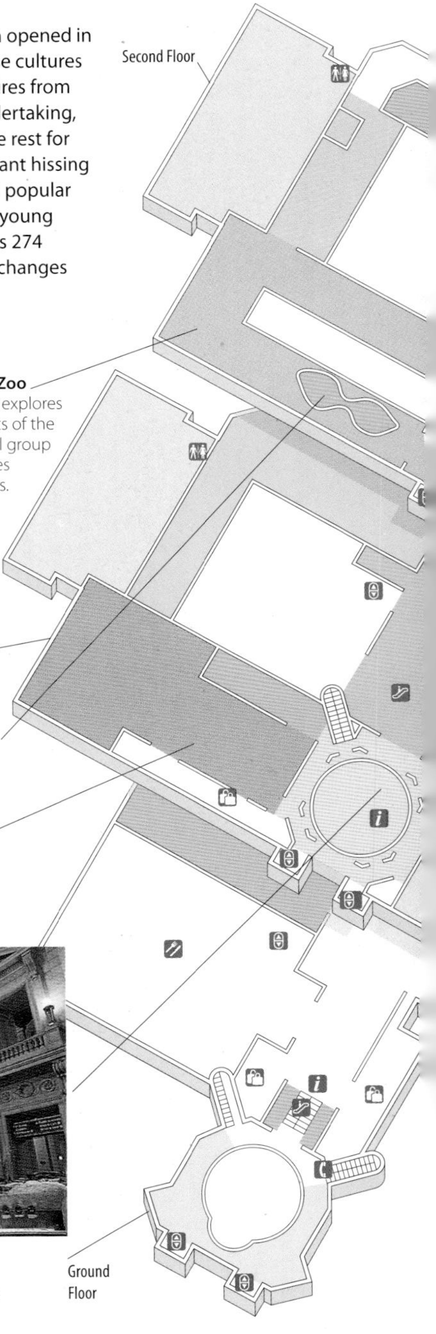

Second Floor

★ O. Orkin Insect Zoo
This popular exhibit explores the lives and habitats of the single largest animal group on earth and features many live specimens.

First Floor

Butterflies and Plants: Partners in Evolution
This permanent exhibition, which includes live butterflies, innovatively combines traditional and experiential learning.

The Kenneth E. Behring Family Hall of Mammals has 22,500 sq ft (2,090 sq m) of displays explaining the diversity of mammals.

African Elephant
The massive African Bush Elephant is one of the highlights of the museum. It is the centerpiece of the Rotunda and creates an impressive sight as visitors enter the museum.

Ground Floor

★ **Hope Diamond**
At 45.52 carats, the Hope Diamond is the largest deep blue diamond in the world and is famed for its stunning clarity and color. It is more than one billion years old and belonged to King Louis XIV of France in the 17th century.

The Johnson IMAX® Theater

★ **Sant Ocean Hall**
Marine specimens and models, high-definition videos, unique exhibits and the latest technology allow visitors at Sant Ocean Hall to explore the past, present, and future of the ocean.

Gallery Guide
The first floor's main exhibitions feature mammals and marine life from different continents. Dinosaurs and myriad cultural exhibits are also displayed on this level. The Gems and Minerals collection and the O. Orkin Insect Zoo are on the second floor.

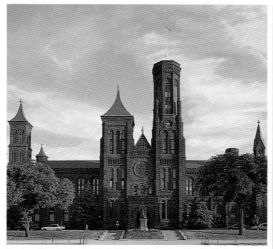

The elegant Victorian façade of the Smithsonian Castle, viewed from the Mall

❽ Smithsonian Castle

1000 Jefferson Drive, SW. **Map** 3 C4.
Tel 633-1000. Ⓜ Smithsonian.
Open 8:30am–5:30pm daily.
Closed Dec 25. 🎫 ♿ 📷 🅦 si.edu

This ornate Victorian edifice served as the first home of the Smithsonian Institution, and was also home to the first Secretary of the Smithsonian, Joseph Henry, and his family. A statue of Henry stands in front of the building.

Constructed of red sandstone in 1855, the Castle was designed by James Renwick, architect of the Renwick Gallery

The tomb of James Smithson

(see p115) and St Patrick's Cathedral in New York. It is an outstanding example of the Gothic Revival style. Inspired also by 12th-century Norman architecture, the Castle has nine towers and an elaborate cornice. Today it is the seat of the Smithsonian administration and houses its Information Center. Visitors can visit the Crypt Room and see the tomb of James Smithson, who bequeathed his fortune to the United States. The South Tower Room was the first children's room in a Washington museum. The ceiling and colorful wall stencils that decorate the room were restored in 1987.

Outside the castle is the Smithsonian rose garden, filled with beautiful hybrid tea roses. The garden was a later addition that now connects the Castle to the equally ornate Arts and Industries Building (see p68).

❾ Arthur M. Sackler Gallery

1050 Independence Ave, SW.
Map 3 C4. **Tel** 633-1000.
Ⓜ Smithsonian. **Open** 10am–5:30pm daily. **Closed** Dec 25. 🎫 12:15pm.
♿ 📷 📄 🅦 asia.si.edu

Dr. Arthur M. Sackler, a New York physician, started collecting Asian art in the 1950s. In 1982, he donated more than 1,000 artifacts, along with $4 million in funds, to the Smithsonian Institution to establish this museum. The Japanese and Korean governments also contributed $1 million each toward the cost of constructing the building, and the museum was completed in 1987.

The entrance is a small pavilion at ground level that leads down to two subterranean floors of exhibits. The Sackler's 3,000-piece collection is particularly rich in Chinese works, and highlights include a stunning display of Chinese bronzes and jades, some dating back to 4000 BC. There are also 7th-century ceramics from the Ming dynasty and an extensive range of sculpture from India and southeast Asia.

Over the years the gallery has built on Arthur Sackler's original collection. In 1987 it acquired the

James Smithson (1765–1829)

Although he never once visited the United States, James Smithson, English scientist and philanthropist, and illegitimate son of the first Duke of Northumberland, left his entire fortune of half a million dollars to "found at Washington, under the name of the Smithsonian Institution, an establishment for the increase and diffusion of knowledge among men." However, this was only if his nephew and heir were to die childless. This did happen and hence, in 1836, Smithson's fortune passed to the government of the United States, which did not quite know what to do with such a vast bequest. For 11 years Congress debated various proposals, finally agreeing to set up a government-run foundation that would administer all national museums. The first Smithson-funded collection was shown at the Smithsonian Castle in 1855.

James Smithson

10th-century Indian sculpture of the goddess Parvati in the Arthur M. Sackler Gallery

impressive Vever Collection from collector Henri Vever, which includes such items as Islamic books from the 11th to the 19th centuries, 19th- and 20th-century Japanese prints, Indian, Chinese, and Japanese paintings, and modern photography. The gallery also hosts international traveling exhibitions of Asian art from museums such as the Louvre in Paris.

The Sackler is one of two underground museums in this area; the other is the National Museum of African Art (see p69), which is part of the same complex. The Sackler is also connected by underground exhibition space to the Freer Gallery of Art. The two galleries share a director and administrative staff as well as the Meyer Auditorium, which hosts dance performances, films, and chamber music concerts. There is also a research library in the Sackler devoted to Asian art.

⑩ Freer Gallery of Art

Jefferson Drive and 12th Street, SW. **Map 3** C4. **Tel** 633-1000. Ⓜ Smithsonian. **Open** 10am–5:30pm daily. **Closed** Dec 25. ♿ 📷 🆆 **asia.si.edu**

The Freer Gallery of Art is named after Charles Lang Freer, a railroad magnate who donated his collection of 9,000 pieces of American and Asian art to the Smithsonian, and funded the building of a museum to house the works. Freer died in 1919 before the

building's completion. When the gallery opened in 1923 it became the first Smithsonian museum of art.

Constructed as a single-story building in the Italian Renaissance style, the Freer has an attractive courtyard with a fountain at its center. There are 19 galleries, most with skylights that illuminate a superb collection of Asian and American art. Since Freer's original donation, the museum has tripled its holdings. In the Asian Art collection are examples of Chinese, Japanese, and Korean art, including sculpture, ceramics, folding screens, and paintings. The gallery also has a fine selection of Buddhist sculpture, and painting and calligraphy from India.

There is a select collection of American art in the Freer as well, most of which shows Asian influences. Works by the artists Childe Hassam (1859–1935), John Singer Sargent (1865–1925), and Thomas Wilmer Dewing (1851–1938) are all on display. The most astonishing room in the museum is James McNeill Whistler's "The Peacock Room." Whistler (1834–1903) was a friend of Freer's who

Detail of a screen by Thomas Wilmer Dewing

encouraged his art collecting. Whistler painted a dining room for Frederick Leyland in London, but Leyland found that it was not to his taste. Freer purchased the room in 1904; it was later moved to Washington and installed here after his death. In contrast to the subtle elegance of the other rooms, this room is a riot of blues, greens, and golds. Whistler's painted peacocks cover the walls and ceiling.

In order to modernize its climate control system and renovate the auditorium, the Freer will remain closed for a period of 18 months, starting January 2016. Some of the galleries will be returned to the original aesthetic created by architect Charles Platt. During the closure, the 25,000 artifacts in the collection can be viewed online (visit www.open.asia.si.edu). The adjacent Sackler galleries will remain open, as will the library and archives. The museum's research component will be moved to the Smithsonian's support facility in Maryland. Visitors should note that concerts and other events usually held at the museum, will be hosted at the Sackler or other Smithsonian venues.

The attractive courtyard of the Freer Gallery of Art

⓫ National Museum of American History

The National Museum of American History preserves a collection of artifacts from the nation's past. Among the 3 million holdings are the First Ladies' gowns, a 280-ton steam locomotive, the National Quilt Collection, and the original Star-Spangled Banner that flew over Fort McHenry in 1814. The museum's west wing will be under renovation until 2017. Some galleries may be closed and exhibits may be moved around.

Second Floor

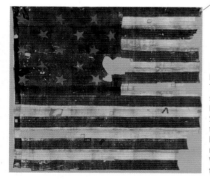

★ **The First Ladies**
Always a popular exhibition, this is a selection of gowns worn by America's First Ladies, such as this floral chine dress worn by Frances Cleveland, a fashion icon in the late 1800s.

Mall Entrance

★ **Star-Spangled Banner**
This flag is the symbol of America. It inspired Francis Scott Key to write the lyrics that became the US national anthem. Visitors can view the flag through a window wall.

Key to Floor Plan

- ☐ Transportation and Technology
- ☐ Science and Innovation
- ☐ American Ideals
- ☐ American Lives
- ☐ American Wars and Politics
- ☐ Entertainment, Sports, and Music
- ☐ Non-exhibition space

On the Water: Stories from Maritime America
Visitors can explore the history of maritime America through documents, objects, stories, audiovisual programs, and interactive exhibits.

Lincoln's Top Hat

Lincoln was wearing this hat when he was assassinated on April 14,1865 while at Ford's Theatre. It has a molded paper base that is embedded with shaved fur fibers.

Third Floor

★ **The Price of Freedom: Americans at War**
A fascinating look at the ways in which wars have shaped American history, from the Colonial era to the present day, including this famous painting by Louis M. D. Guillaume, *The Surrender of the Arm of Northern Virginia* (1867).

Constitution Avenue Entrance

On the Water: Stories from Maritime America

★ **America on the Move**
This first floor exhibition allows visitors to travel back in time through the history of transport in America, including this famous Ford Model T, bicycles, trains, and more.

First Floor

Gallery Guide

The first floor features the transportation and science exhibits. Highlights of the second floor include the Star-Spangled Banner. The third floor offers an eclectic selection including the American Presidency: A Glorious Burden, The First Ladies exhibit, and military displays.

Exploring the National Museum of American History

The collections at the National Museum of American History are very diverse. Whether you head straight for the First Ladies' gowns or spend time viewing the collections of money, medals, musical instruments, and presidential artifacts, planning is the key to a successful visit. The museum is gradually being transformed with the continuing renovation of the 120,000 sq ft (11,148 sq m) west exhibition wing. The center core and east wing remain open to the public.

The museum's modern façade on Madison Drive

First Floor

Stories on Money explores the museum's collection of American coinage and currency. The exhibition "America's Money" examines the changes from Colonial America to the Gold Rush, and the present day, focusing on the renaissance of American coinage.

"The Power of Liberty" exhibit features an array of coins from the United States and around the world, depicting Liberty and the female freedom movement. The exhibition consists of 1.5 million objects, including a Colonial shilling from 1690 and a unique $20 gold coin from 1849.

America on the Move is the museum's largest single exhibition and tells the story of how trains, streetcars, and automobiles have shaped American lives. Exhibits include the locomotive that pulled Franklin D. Roosevelt's funeral train, a 40-ft (12-m) section of pavement from the legendary Route 66, a 1903 Winton, Ford's Model T, and a Hot Rod.

On the Water: Stories from Maritime America is an 8,000-sq-ft (743-sq-m) exhibition chartering American maritime history and exploring life and work on the nation's waterways. The exhibits on display build on the Smithsonian's unparalleled National Watercraft Collection of rigged ship models, patent models, documents, and images to bring the sights, sounds, and stories from the oceans, inland rivers, and coastal communities to museum visitors.

The maritime influence on American history is one of the most compelling chapters in the national story. Maritime trade established major cities, created connections between people and places and opened the continent. From 18th-century sailing ships, 19th-century steamboats and fishing craft to today's mega-containerships, America's maritime connections are shown through interactive displays, documents, and film.

Elsewhere on the first floor visitors can explore **Lighting a Revolution**, which looks at electricity and electrical invention in the 20th century, and illuminates the differences in the process of invention between Thomas Edison's time and our own.

For those with an interest in all things mechanical, the **Power Machinery Hall** is a must. This exhibition features examples of the machines that made America a world leader in industrial production, and contains models and actual examples of engines, turbines, pumps, and more. Perhaps the most famous machine of all is the **John Bull Locomotive** in the East Wing, the oldest operative self-propelled locomotive in the world. **Spark!Lab** invites families to participate in activities that blend traditional science, technology, engineering, and mathematics (STEM), with art and creativity.

Second Floor

American Stories showcases the historic and cultural journey of American history through more than 100 objects from the museum's vast collection, including Dorothy's ruby

1950 Buick Super sedan displayed in America on the Move

The kitchen of 16 Elm Street, rebuilt in the museum as it was in the 1940s

slippers, the rarely displayed walking stick used by Benjamin Franklin, Abraham Lincoln's gold pocket watch, Muhammad Ali's boxing gloves, and a fragment of Plymouth rock.

Through a chronological look at the people, inventions, issues, and events that shaped the American experience, American Stories serves as an introduction to American history.

The West Wing also contains **Within These Walls…** This exhibition tells the story of American history through the domestic lives of the families who lived at 16 Elm Street in Ipswich, Massachusetts, from the mid-1760s to 1945. This extraordinary house saw American colonists forging a new way of living, the birth of a revolution, community activists united against slavery, a family on the home front in World War II, and more.

On the second floor visitors can also explore a series of "artifact walls", 275 ft (84 m) of glass fronted cases lining the museum's center core. The walls highlight such things as anniversaries, new acquisitions, and research projects undertaken by the museum. One example is an artifact wall installation on Celia Cruz, known as the Queen of Salsa. Her glass case exhibits wigs, shoes, and one of her Grammy

Awards – essentially a visual biography of her colorful life.

In the East Wing of the second floor, visitors can see the **Star-Spangled Banner** that flew over Fort McHenry in 1814 and inspired Francis Scott Key to write the lyrics that were later to become the national anthem. Also on the second floor is an exhibit on African-American history and culture. Here the role of visual images in the fight for civil rights and racial justice is explored.

Teddy Bear, dating from 1903

Third Floor

One of the museum's most popular exhibits, where fashion meets history: **The First Ladies** is a collection of gowns worn by some of the nation's most iconic presidential wives. The collection includes Michelle Obama's white chiffon gown worn to the 2009 inaugural ball. It was made by a relatively unknown designer, Jason Wu.

The largest exhibition on this floor is **The Price of Freedom: Americans at War** in the East Wing. It

explores the nation's military history, from the French and Indian War in the 1750s to recent conflicts in Afghanistan and Iraq. The exhibition features a restored Vietnam-era Huey helicopter, uniforms from the Civil War, a World War II jeep, and General Colin Powell's battle dress uniform from Operation Desert Storm.

The gunboat *Philadelphia* is located on the third floor. Sunk by the British in 1776, the 54-ft (16-m), 29-ton timber boat rested on the bottom of Lake Champlain until it was found and recovered in 1935.

The American Presidency: A Glorious Burden displays over 400 objects that represent the lives and office of the presidency. Artifacts include the portable desk on which Thomas Jefferson wrote the Declaration of Independence, and the top hat worn by President Lincoln the night he was shot.

Also here is a delightful teddy bear. The name of the bear was inspired by President Theodore "Teddy" Roosevelt, who, while out hunting one day, refused to shoot a bear cub that had been captured for him. A cartoon appeared in the *Washington Post* the next day, which inspired the production of a range of bears, named Teddy Bears.

Office of War information poster

⑫ Washington Monument

Constructed of 36,000 pieces of marble and granite, the Washington Monument remains one of the most recognizable monuments in the capital. Funds for this tribute to the first president of the United States initially came from individual citizens. A design by Robert Mills was chosen, and construction began in 1848. When the money ran out, the building work stopped for 25 years. Then, in 1876, President Ulysses S. Grant approved an act authorizing the completion of the project. (A slight change in the color of stone marks the point where construction resumed.) The Monument has 897 steps to the top. In August 2011 the monument was damaged by an earthquake but has since been fully restored.

VISITORS' CHECKLIST

Practical Information
Independence Ave at 17th St, SW.
Map 2 F5 & 3 B4.
Tel (202) 426-6841; (202) 347-5114.
W nps.gov/wamo
Book free timed tickets at:
W recreation.gov
Open 9am–5pm (Memorial Day–
Labor Day: to 10pm; last tour
15 mins before closing). ♿ 🅿️

Transport
M Smithsonian. 🚌 13, 52.

Viewing window

Elevator taking visitors to top

The Marble Capstone
The capstone weighs 3,300 pounds (2,000 kg) and is topped by an aluminum pyramid. Restoration of the monument was carried out in 1934 as part of President Roosevelt's public works project (see p25).

The Original Design
Although the original design included a circular colonnade around the monument, lack of funds prohibited its construction.

The two-tone stonework indicates the point at which construction stopped in 1858 and then began again in 1876.

Commemorative stones inside the monument are donations from individuals, societies, states, and nations.

50 flagpoles surrounding the monument represent each state

View of the Monument
The gleaming white stone of the restored monument makes it clearly visible from almost all over the city. The views from the top of the monument across Washington are stunning.

The foundation of the monument is more than 36 ft (10 meters) deep. The width of the base of the shaft is 55 ft (17 meters).

The colonnaded, domed Jefferson Memorial, housing the bronze statue

⓭ United States Holocaust Memorial Museum

See pp82–3.

⓮ Bureau of Engraving and Printing

14th and C St, SW. **Map** 3 B5.
Tel 1-877-874-4114. Ⓜ Smithsonian.
🕘 8:30am–3:30pm Mon–Fri (Apr–Aug: 8:30am–7:30pm). **Closed** Week after Christmas, Federal hols. ♿ 📷
Ⓦ **moneyfactory.gov**

Until 1863, individual banks were responsible for printing American money. A shortage of coins and the need to finance the Civil War led to the production of standardized bank notes, and the Bureau of Engraving and Printing was founded. Initially housed in the basement of the Treasury Building *(see p114)*, the bureau was moved to its present location in 1914. It prints over $140 billion a year, as well as stamps, federal documents, and White House invitations. Coins are not minted here, but in a federal facility in Philadelphia.

The 40-minute tour includes a short film, and a walk through the building to view the printing processes and checks for defects. Also on display are bills that are out of circulation, counterfeit money, and a special $100,000 bill. The Visitor Center has a gift shop, videos, and exhibits.

⓯ Jefferson Memorial

South bank of the Tidal Basin.
Map 3 B5. **Tel** (202) 426-6841.
Ⓜ Smithsonian. **Open** 24 hours daily.
Closed Dec 25. Interpretive talks & Interpretive tours: 10am–11pm hourly. ♿ 📷 Ⓦ **nps.gov/thje**

Thomas Jefferson *(see p168)* was a political philosopher, architect, musician, book collector, scientist, horticulturist, diplomat, inventor and the third American president, from 1801 to 1809. He also played a significant part in drafting the Declaration of Independence in 1776.

The idea for the memorial came from President Franklin Delano Roosevelt, who felt that Jefferson was as important as Lincoln. Designed by John Russell Pope, this Neo-Classical memorial was dedicated in 1943 and covers an area of 2.5 acres (1 ha). At the time, metal was strictly rationed

Statue of Jefferson

so the standing statue of Jefferson had to be cast in plaster. After World War II, the statue was recast in bronze and the plaster version was moved.

Etched on the walls of the memorial are Jefferson's words from the Declaration of Independence and other writings. The statue of Jefferson is 19 ft (6 m) high and weighs 10,000 lbs. It shows him looking towards the White House.

⓰ Tidal Basin

Boathouse: 1501 Maine Ave, SW.
Map 2 F5 & 3 A5. Ⓜ Smithsonian.
Paddle-boats: **Tel** (202) 479-2426.
Open Mar–Oct: 10am–6pm. ♿
Ⓦ **tidalbasinpaddleboats.com**

The Tidal Basin was built in 1897 to catch the overflow from the Potomac River and prevent flooding. In 1912, hundreds of cherry trees, given by the Japanese government, were planted along the shores of the man-made lake. However, during the two weeks when the cherry trees bloom (between mid-March and mid-April) chaos reigns around the Tidal Basin. The area is filled with cars and busloads of people photographing the sight. The only way to avoid this gridlock is to see the blossoms at dawn. The Tidal Basin reverts to a relatively quiet park after the blossoms have fallen and the hordes depart. Paddle-boats can be rented from the boathouse on Maine Avenue.

The banks of the Tidal Basin, with Jefferson Memorial in the distance

⑬ United States Holocaust Memorial Museum

The US Holocaust Memorial Museum, opened in 1993, bears witness to the systematic persecution and murder in Europe of six million Jews and others deemed undesirable by the Third Reich, including homosexuals and the disabled. The exhibition space ranges from the intentionally claustrophobic to the soaringly majestic. The museum contains 2,500 photographs, 1,000 artifacts, 53 video monitors, and 30 interactive stations that contain graphic and emotionally disturbing images of violence, forcing visitors to confront the horror of the Holocaust. While Daniel's Story is suitable for children of eight years and up, the permanent exhibition is not recommended for the under 12s.

★ Hall of Remembrance
The Hall of Remembrance houses an eternal flame that pays homage to the victims of the Holocaust.

Second Floor

★ Daniel's Story
This exhibit, aimed at children between the ages of eight and 12, tells the history of the Holocaust from the point of view of an eight-year-old Jewish boy in 1930s Germany.

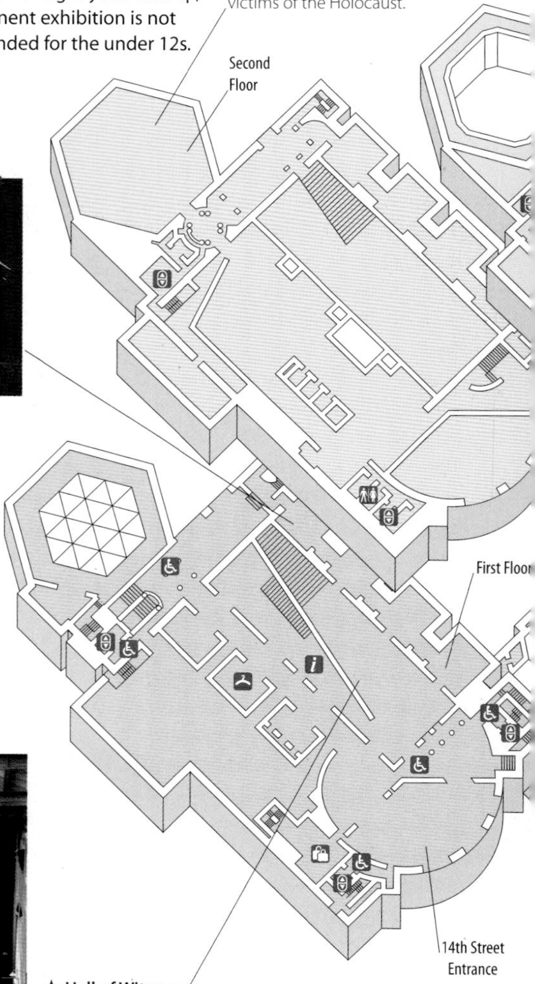

First Floor

Key to Floor Plan

- ☐ Concourse Level
- ☐ First Floor
- ☐ Second Floor
- ☐ Third Floor
- ☐ Fourth Floor

14th Street Entrance

★ Hall of Witness
The soaring central atrium features the Hall of Witness. The Museum aims to preserve the memory of those who died.

The Nazi Assault
On April 1, 1933 the boycott announced by the National Socialist party began. This placard at the Jewish Tietz store in Berlin reads, "Germans, defend yourselves! Do not buy from Jews."

VISITORS' CHECKLIST

Practical Information
100 Raoul Wallenburg Place, SW.
Map 3 B4. **Tel** (202) 488-0400.
🅦 ushmm.org
Open 10am–5:30pm daily (Apr–mid-Jun: to 6:30pm). **Closed** Dec 25 & Yom Kippur. Mar–Aug: timed pass required. Obtain either same day from ticket desk (first-come-first-served basis) or in advance from the website. ♿
🛇 📷 💻 ⛔

Transport
Ⓜ Smithsonian.
🚌 13 (Pentagon shuttle).

Fourth Floor
Documenting the early years of the Nazi regime, these exhibits expose the ruthless and methodical persecution of the Jews.

Third Floor
The third floor permanent exhibits are devoted to the "Final Solution," the killing of 11 million "undesirable" people. Artifacts include a boxcar used to carry prisoners to the concentration camps.

Children's Tile Wall
Children painted over 3,000 tiles on this memorial to commemorate the lives of the one-and-a-half million children murdered in the Holocaust.

Gallery Guide
The Holocaust Museum is meant to be experienced, not just seen. Starting from the top, footage, artifacts, photographs, and testimonies of survivors can be seen from the fourth to the second floors. The first floor has an interactive display, and the Concourse Level houses the Children's Tile Wall.

Concourse Level

The National WWII Memorial looking east towards the Washington Monument

⓱ National WWII Memorial

17th St, NW, between Constitution Ave & Independence Ave. **Map** 2 F5. **Tel** (202) 426-6841. Ⓜ Smithsonian or Federal Triangle. **Open** 9:30am–11:30pm daily. **Closed** Dec 25. ♿
Ⓦ nps.gov/nwwm The online Registry of Remembrances: Ⓦ wwiimemorial.com

Sixteen million Americans served in World War II, and of them, 400,000 died. The 4,000 gold stars, the "Field of Stars," on the Freedom Wall commemorate these war dead, and in front of the wall is the inscription: "Here We Mark the Price of Freedom." Millions more ordinary citizens contributed in some way to the war effort. The National World War II Memorial on the National Mall honors their service and sacrifice.

The establishment of the memorial, however, was not without controversy as to both location and scale. After a bill was first introduced in 1987 it took a further six years before the legislation made its way through Congress. President Clinton signed the bill into law on May 25, 1993 and then there followed a great debate over where it should be located. The Rainbow Pool site was chosen in October 1995 with the condition that the east-west vista from the Washington Monument to the Lincoln Memorial be preserved. Further delays followed because the Commission of Fine Arts criticized the mass and scale of the initial plans and asked that further consideration be given to preserving the vista. Work finally began in 2001.

Design and construction was awarded to the firm of Leo A. Daly, and the design architect

Ceremonial entrance shield

was Friedrich St. Florian (former dean of Rhode Island School of Design).

Two 43 ft (13 m) pavilions stand on either side of the Rainbow Pool, marking the north and south entrances, and represent the Atlantic and Pacific theaters of war. Fifty-six granite pillars, one for each of the country's states and territories during that time, are adorned with bronze wreaths of oak leaves and wheat, which symbolize the nation's agricultural and industrial strength. Bas-relief panels created by sculptor Ray Kaskey line both sides of the 17th St entrance. They depict the many contributions Americans made to the war effort: from enlistment and embarkation to the Normandy landings, from Rosie the Riveter to medics in the field.

Words spoken by presidents and generals are inscribed throughout the memorial, including these by General Douglas MacArthur marking the war's end: "Today the guns are silent…The skies no longer rain death – the seas bear only commerce – men everywhere walk upright in the sunlight. The entire world is quietly at peace."

The memorial was officially opened to the public in April 2004 and on May 29 some 150,000 people, many of them veterans, joined in the dedication ceremony.

The Freedom Wall lined with 4,000 stars commemorating the US war dead

⑱ Vietnam Veterans Memorial

21st St & Constitution Ave, NW.
Map 2 E4. **Tel** (202) 426-6841.
Ⓜ Smithsonian. **Open** 24 hours daily.
Ⓒ 10am–11pm daily on the hour.
♿ Ⓦ **nps.gov/vive**

Maya Lin, a 21-year-old student at Yale University, submitted a design for the proposed Vietnam Veterans Memorial as part of her architecture course. One of 1,421 entries, Maya Lin's design was simple – two triangular black walls sinking into the earth at an angle of 125 degrees, one end pointing to the Lincoln Memorial, the other to the Washington Monument. On the walls would be inscribed the names of more than 58,000 Americans who died in the Vietnam War, in chronological order, from the first in 1959 to the last in 1975. Since the names are not in alphabetical order, there is a book listing all the names that correspond to a panel.

Lin received only a B grade on the course, but she won the competition. Her design has become one of the most moving monuments on the Mall. Veterans and their families leave tokens of remembrance – soft toys, poems, pictures, and flowers – at the site of the fallen soldier's name.

To mollify those opposed to the abstract memorial, a statue of three soldiers, sculpted by Frederick Hart, was added in 1984. Further lobbying led to the Vietnam Women's Memorial, erected close by in 1993.

The Vietnam Women's Memorial

⑲ Korean War Veterans Memorial

21st St & Independence Ave, SW.
Map 2 E5. **Tel** (202) 426-6841.
Ⓜ Smithsonian, Foggy Bottom.
Open 24 hours daily. ♿
Ⓦ **nps.gov/kwvm**

The Korean War Veterans Memorial is a controversial tribute to a controversial war. Although 1.5 million Americans served in the conflict, war was never officially declared. It is often known as "The Forgotten War." Intense debate preceded the selection of the memorial's design. On July 27, 1995, the 42nd anniversary of the armistice that ended the war, the memorial was dedicated. Nineteen larger-than-life stainless steel statues, a squad on patrol, are depicted moving

Names on the wall at the Vietnam Veterans Memorial

towards the American flag as their symbolic objective. Their ponchos are a reminder of the war's notoriously miserable weather conditions. On the south side is a polished black granite wall etched with the images of more than 2,400 veterans. An inscription above the Pool of Remembrance reads: "Our nation honors her sons and daughters who answered the call to defend a country they never knew and a people they never met."

⑳ Martin Luther King, Jr. Memorial

1964 Independence Ave, SW.
Map 2 E5. **Tel** (202) 483-3373.
Ⓜ Smithsonian, Foggy Bottom.
Open 9am–10pm daily. ♿
Ⓦ **mlkmemorial.org**

Set among the famous cherry blossom trees of the Tidal Basin *(see p81)* is the Martin Luther King, Jr. Memorial. The Mall's first memorial to an African-American, dedicated on August 26, 2011, commemorates the life and work of Dr. King. Designed by Chinese sculptor Lei Yixin, the memorial consists of two massive stone tablets – one features excerpts from King's speeches, while the other shows the figure of Martin Luther King emerging from the stone. The choice of a non-American sculptor proved controversial, as did King's somewhat stern expression.

The poignant statues of the Korean War Veterans Memorial

㉑ Franklin D. Roosevelt Memorial

Franklin Roosevelt once told Supreme Court Justice Felix Frankfurter, "If they are to put up any memorial to me, I should like it to be placed in the center of that green plot in front of the Archives Building. I should like it to consist of a block about the size of this," pointing to his desk. It took more than 50 years for a fitting monument to be erected, but Roosevelt's request for modesty was not heeded. Opened in 1997, this memorial is a mammoth park of four granite open-air rooms, one for each of Roosevelt's terms, with statuary and waterfalls. The president, a polio sufferer, is portrayed in a chair, with his dog Fala by his side.

The statue of Roosevelt by Neil Estern, is one of the memorial's most controversial elements as it shows the disabled president sitting in a wheelchair hidden by his Navy cape.

A relief of Roosevelt's funeral cortège was carved into the granite wall by artist Leonard Baskin. It depicts the coffin on a horse-drawn cart, followed by the crowds of mourners walking behind.

KEY

① **The fourth room** honors Roosevelt's life and legacy. A statue of his wife, Eleanor, stands in this room.

② **Third room**

③ **Second room**

④ **The first room** commemorates FDR's first term and includes a bas-relief of his inaugural parade.

⑤ **The Visitor Center** includes an information area and a bookstore. The wheelchair that FDR used after he had polio is also on display.

Dramatic waterfalls cascade into a series of pools in the fourth room. The water reflects the peace that Roosevelt was so keen to achieve before his death.

VISITORS' CHECKLIST

Practical Information
West Basin Drive, SW. **Map** 3 A5.
Tel (202) 426-6841.
W nps.gov/fdrm
Open 24 hours daily.
Closed Dec 25. ♿ 📷
Interpretive programs and talks.

Transport
Ⓜ Smithsonian and 25-minute
walk. 🚌 13.

**Breadline, a sculpture of
figures** waiting in the
breadline, by George Segal,
recalls the hard times of the
Great Depression, during which
Roosevelt was elected and
reelected three times.

President Roosevelt
initiated the New Deal
in the 1930s to create
jobs and provide
immediate relief during
the Great Depression:
"…treating the task as
we would treat the
emergency of war."

㉒ Lincoln Memorial

Constitution Ave, between French
& Bacon Drives. **Map** 2 E5. **Tel** (202)
426-6841. Ⓜ Smithsonian, Foggy
Bottom, and 20-minute walk.
Open 24 hours daily. ♿ 📷 Call (202)
747-3420 to listen to interpretive
programs. **W** nps.gov/linc

Many proposals were made for a
memorial to President Abraham
Lincoln. One of the least
promising was for a monument
on a swampy piece of land to
the west of the Washington
Monument. Yet this was to
become one of the most awe-
inspiring sights in Washington.
Looming over the Reflecting
Pool is the seated figure of
Lincoln in his Neo-Classical
"temple" with 36 Doric columns,
one for each state at the time
of Lincoln's death.

Before the monument could
be built in 1914, the site had to
be drained. Solid concrete piers
were poured for the foundation
so that the building could be
anchored in bedrock. Architect
Henry Bacon realized that the
original 10 ft (3 m) statue by
Daniel Chester French would
be dwarfed inside the building,
so it was nearly doubled in size.
As a result, it had to be carved
from 28 blocks of white marble.

Engraved on the south
wall is Lincoln's Gettysburg
Address *(see p165)*. Above it is
a mural painted by Jules Guerin
depicting the angel of truth
freeing a slave. Dr. Martin Luther
King, Jr.'s famous address, "I Have
a Dream" *(see p99)*, was given
from the steps of the memorial.

Lincoln Memorial, reflected in the still
waters of the pool

PENN QUARTER

Bordered by the Capitol to the east and the White House to the west, Washington's Penn Quarter was the heart of the city at the start of the 20th century. F Street, the city's first paved road, bustled with shops, bars, newspaper offices, and churches, as well as horses and carriages. Penn Quarter was also an important residential neighborhood. The upper classes kept elegant homes, while middle-class merchants lived above their shops. By the 1950s suburbia had lured people away, and in the 1980s Penn Quarter was a mixture of boarded-up buildings and discount shops. The 1990s saw a dramatic change and the beginnings of regeneration, as the Verizon Center attracted new restaurants and stores.

Sights at a Glance

Museums and Galleries

- **5** Newseum
- **12** National Museum of Women in the Arts
- **13** Carnegie Library Building
- **17** Smithsonian American Art Museum and the National Portrait Gallery pp100–103
- **18** International Spy Museum
- **21** National Building Museum

Statues and Fountains

- **1** Mellon Fountain
- **8** Benjamin Franklin Statue

Historic and Official Buildings

- **2** National Archives
- **6** Ronald Reagan Building
- **7** Old Post Office
- **10** Willard Hotel
- **11** National Theatre
- **14** Ford's Theatre
- **15** Martin Luther King Memorial Library
- **19** Verizon Center

Districts, Streets, and Squares

- **4** Pennsylvania Avenue
- **9** Freedom Plaza
- **16** Chinatown

Memorials

- **3** US Navy Memorial
- **20** National Law Enforcement Officers Memorial

☐ **Restaurants** *see pp184–5*

1 Acadiana
2 Austin Grill
3 Brasserie Beck
4 Carmines
5 Chipotle
6 District Chophouse & Brewery
7 District of Pi
8 Fogo de Chao
9 Full Kee
10 Graffiato
11 Jaleo
12 Luke's Lobster
13 Merzi
14 Oceanaire
15 Old Ebbitt Grill
16 Oyamel
17 Paul Bakery
18 Poste
19 Proof
20 Rasika
21 Rosa Mexicano
22 The Source
23 Teaism
24 Zaytinya

See also Street Finder map 3, 4

| 0 meters | | 500 |
| 0 yards | | 500 |

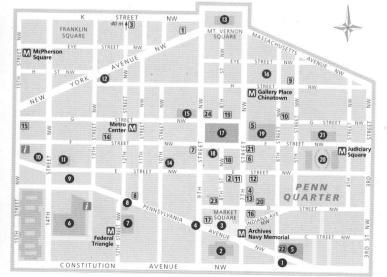

◀ The flag-festooned Old Post Office

For keys to symbols *see back flap*

Street-by-Street: Penn Quarter

By the mid-20th century, Pennsylvania Avenue, the main route for presidential inaugural parades, had become tawdry and run down. It is now a grand boulevard worthy of L'Enfant's original vision. Pennsylvania Avenue links the White House to the US Capitol and is home to some of the city's main sights. Opposite the US Navy Memorial is the US National Archives, housing original copies of the Constitution and the Declaration of Independence. To the east are the Mellon Fountain and the National Gallery of Art. The Ronald Reagan Building was the site of the 1999 NATO summit.

❹ ★ Pennsylvania Avenue
Part of L'Enfant's original plan for the city, Pennsylvania Avenue was the first main street to be laid out in Washington. The thoroughfare reflects the architect's grandiose plans.

❽ Benjamin Franklin Statue
This inventor, statesman, writer, publisher, and man of genius is remembered as "printer, philosopher, philanthropist, patriot".

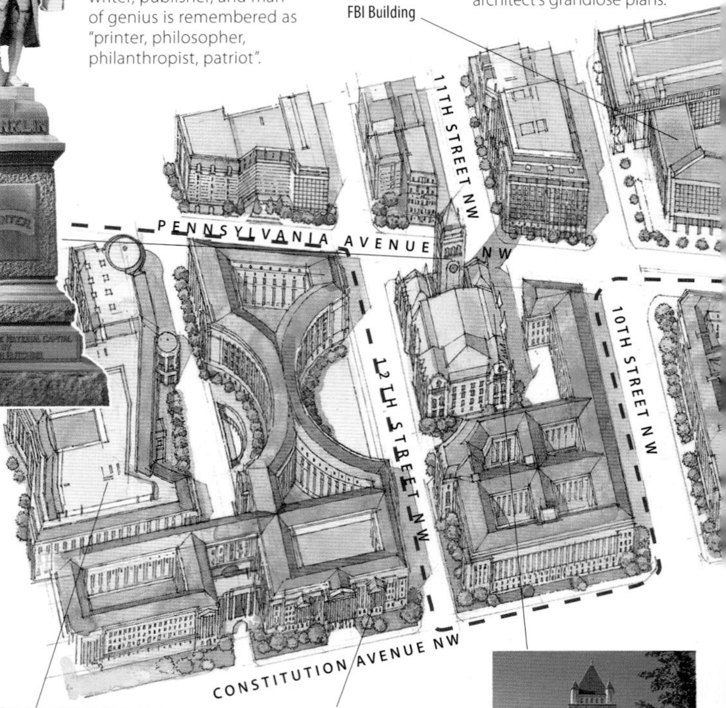

FBI Building

PENNSYLVANIA AVENUE NW

11TH STREET NW

10TH STREET NW

12TH STREET NW

CONSTITUTION AVENUE NW

Interstate Commerce Commission

❼ Old Post Office
This granite building was completed in 1899 and was the city's first skyscraper. The elegant clock tower measures 315 ft (96 m) in height. The building is in the process of becoming an international hotel.

❻ Ronald Reagan Building
Built in 1997, this impressive edifice echoes the Classical Revival architecture of other buildings in the Federal Triangle.

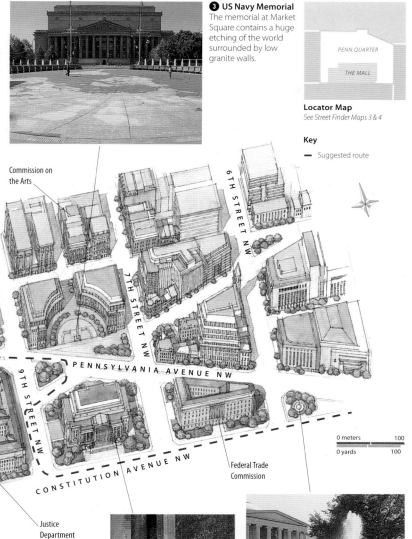

3 US Navy Memorial
The memorial at Market Square contains a huge etching of the world surrounded by low granite walls.

Locator Map
See Street Finder Maps 3 & 4

Key
— Suggested route

Commission on the Arts

6TH STREET NW

7TH STREET NW

9TH STREET NW

PENNSYLVANIA AVENUE NW

CONSTITUTION AVENUE NW

Federal Trade Commission

Justice Department

0 meters 100
0 yards 100

2 ★ National Archives
The Rotunda houses the National Archives' most precious documents, known as the "Charters of Freedom," including the Bill of Rights. A copy of England's Magna Carta is also on display.

1 Mellon Fountain
Located by the National Gallery of Art's West Building, this fountain is named after Andrew Mellon, an industrialist and art collector who founded the gallery in the 1930s.

The cascading water of the Classical-style Mellon Fountain

❶ Mellon Fountain

Constitution Ave & Pennsylvania Ave, NW. **Map** 4 D4. Ⓜ Archives-Navy Memorial.

Situated opposite the National Gallery of Art *(see pp60–63)*, this fountain commemorates the man who endowed the gallery with its collection. Andrew Mellon was Secretary of the Treasury and a financier and industrialist. At his death, his friends donated $300,000 to build the fountain, which was dedicated on May 9, 1952.

The three bronze basins with their cascades of water were inspired by a fountain seen in a public square in Genoa, Italy. On the bottom of the largest basin, the signs of the Zodiac are engraved in bas-relief. The Classical lines of the fountain echo the architectural style of the National Gallery of Art West Building.

❷ National Archives

7000 Constitution Ave, between 7th St & 9th St, NW. **Map** 3 C4. **Tel** 1-866-272-6272. Ⓜ Archives-Navy Memorial/Penn Quarter. **Open** Mar 15–Labor Day: 10am–7pm daily; Sep–Mar: 10am–5:30pm daily. **Closed** Sun, Thanksgiving, Dec 25. 📷 🎦 ♿ 🚺 **archives.gov**

In the 1930s, Congress recognized the need to preserve the country's paper records before they deteriorated, were lost or were destroyed. The National Archives building, created for this purpose, was designed by John Russell Pope, architect of the National Gallery of Art and the Jefferson Memorial; it opened in 1934. This impressive library houses the most important historical and legal documents in the United States.

Statue outside the US National Archives

On display are all four pages of the Constitution of the United States, as well as the Declaration of Independence, the Bill of Rights, and a 1297 copy of the Magna Carta, which is on indefinite loan from Ross Perot.

Also in the National Archives are millions of documents, photographs, motion picture film, and sound recordings going back over two centuries. There is enough material, in fact, to fill around 250,000 filing cabinets. The National Archives and Records Administration (NARA) are charged with cataloging, managing, and conserving all this material. Much of the Archives' information is now stored on computer. A permanent exhibition, "Public Vaults," offers people an interactive opportunity to explore a representative sample of the Archives' vast collection. The National Archives is of great importance as a research center. The Central Research Room is reserved for scholars, who can order copies of rare documents for study purposes. Copies of military records, immigration papers, slave transit documents, death certificates, and tax information are also available.

The impressive Neo-Classical façade of the National Archives Building

The Constitution of the United States

In 1787, delegates from the 13 original American states convened in the city of Philadelphia to redraft the Articles of Confederation *(see p20)*. It soon became clear that an entirely new document was required, rather than a revised one. Weeks of debate grew into months, as delegates drafted the framework for a new country. Cooperation and compromise finally led to the creation of the Constitution, a document that outlines the powers of the central government and the makeup of Congress. One of the main issues, how to elect the representatives, was finally determined to be by direct voting by the people. Once signed, the new Constitution was sent to the states for review. Federalists and anti-Federalists debated fervently over its content in pamphlets, speeches, and articles. In the end, the majority of states ratified the Constitution, giving up some of their power in "order to form a more perfect union."

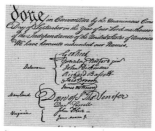
The Preamble of the Constitution of the United States

Signing of the Constitution

After many months of debate by the delegates to the Federal Convention, the Constitution was completed and signed by 39 of the 55 state delegates on September 17, 1787, at Assembly Hall in Philadelphia. The oldest delegate was 81-year-old Benjamin Franklin. James Madison, another signatory, played a major role in achieving the ratification of the new Constitution during the two years after it was signed.

James Madison

Signatures on the US Constitution

The Constitution Today

The seven articles of the Constitution (of which the first three lay out the principles of government; see pp30–31) still determine the laws of the United States. In addition there are Amendments. The first ten form the Bill of Rights, which includes such famous issues as the right to bear arms and the freedom of religion and of speech.

Swearing Allegiance
The pledge of allegiance to the flag was written in 1892 to mark the 400th anniversary of Columbus's discovery of America. Today it is recited daily by schoolchildren and by immigrants taking up American citizenship.

Public Demonstration
Citizens demonstrate their right to free speech by protesting against the Persian Gulf War.

A view down tree-lined Pennsylvania Avenue toward the US Capitol

❸ US Navy Memorial

Market Square, Pennsylvania Ave between 7th St & 9th St, NW. **Map** 3 C3. Ⓜ Archives-Navy Memorial/Penn Quarter. 🚇 Naval Heritage Center: 701 Pennsylvania Ave, NW. **Tel** (202) 737-2300. **Open** 9:30am–5pm daily. **Closed** Jan 1, Thanksgiving, Dec 25. 📷 Ⓦ navymemorial.org

The memorial to the US Navy centers on the statue of a single sailor. Sculpted in bronze by Stanley Bleifeld in 1990, the figure provides a poignant tribute to the men and women who have served the US Navy.

The sculpture stands on a vast map of the world – the outlines of the countries are laid into the ground and protected by low walls. Four waterfalls and a group of flagpoles complete the memorial. There are free summer concerts by military bands in the square. Behind the memorial is the **Naval Heritage Center**, with historical exhibits and portraits of famous naval personnel, including John F. Kennedy. A free film "At Sea," is shown at 10am, noon, and 2pm.

The lone sailor of the US Navy Memorial

❹ Pennsylvania Avenue

Pennsylvania Ave. **Map** 3 A2 to 4 D4. Ⓜ Federal Triangle, Archives-Navy Memorial.

When architect and urban designer Pierre L'Enfant drew up his plans in 1789 for the capital city of the new United States, he imagined a grand boulevard running through the center of the city, from the presidential palace to the legislative building. For the first 200 years of its history, however, Pennsylvania Avenue fell sadly short of L'Enfant's dreams. In the early 19th century it was simply a muddy footpath through the woods. Paved in 1833, it became part of a neighborhood of boarding houses, shops, and hotels.

During the Civil War, the area deteriorated quickly into "saloons, gambling dens, lodging houses, quick-lunch rooms, cheap-jack shops, and catch penny amusement places" according to the *Works Progress Administration Guide to Washington*. When President John F. Kennedy's inaugural parade processed down Pennsylvania Avenue in 1961, Kennedy took one look at "America's Main Street" with its shambles of peep shows, pawn shops, and liquor stores and said, "It's a disgrace – fix it." This command by Kennedy provided the impetus to re-evaluate the future of Pennsylvania Avenue.

Almost 15 years later, Congress established the Pennsylvania Avenue Development Corporation – a public and private partnership that developed a comprehensive plan of

Presidential Inaugural Parades

The tradition of inaugural parades to mark a new president's coming-to-office started in 1809, when the military accompanied President James Madison from his Virginia home to Washington, DC. The first parade to include floats was held in 1841 for President William Henry Harrison. In 1985, freezing weather forced Ronald Reagan's inaugural ceremony indoors to the Capitol Rotunda. A record crowd of approximately 1.8 million attended the 2009 parade for Barack Obama. The Army Band traditionally leads the procession down Pennsylvania Avenue from the US Capitol to the White House.

President Franklin D. Roosevelt's third inaugural parade in 1941

The multistory building housing the Newseum

revitalization. Today, Pennsylvania Avenue is a clean, tree-lined street. Parks, memorials, shops, theaters, hotels, museums, and assorted government buildings border the street on either side, providing a suitably grand and formal setting for all future presidential inaugural parades.

❺ Newseum

555 Pennsylvania Ave, NW. **Map** 4 D4. **Tel** 888-639-7386. Ⓜ Archives-Navy Memorial. **Open** 9am–5pm daily. **Closed** Jan 1, Thanksgiving, Dec 25. ☑ ⓺ ⓐ ⓐ Ⓦ **newseum.org**

This award-winning interactive news and media museum is housed in a beautiful building with a balcony that affords splendid views of the city. The Newseum features seven levels, 14 galleries, and 15 theaters that explore how and why news is made. The galleries span five centuries of news history and include up-to-the-second technology and hands-on exhibits. The gallery of Pulitzer Prize-winning photographs is one of the highlights. Among the iconic images on display are the 1945 photograph documenting the raising of the US flag after the Battle of Iwo Jima and a 1969 photograph portraying the execution of a prisoner in Saigon, Vietnam. Other galleries deal with the history of the Berlin Wall and the events of 9/11. There is also an interactive newsroom where visitors can play the role of a reporter or broadcaster, and a moving memorial to journalists

who have lost their lives in the line of duty. On the front of the building is an inscription of the First Amendment listing the five freedoms – religion, speech, press, assembly, and petition.

❻ Ronald Reagan Building

1300 Pennsylvania Ave, NW. **Map** 3 B3. **Tel** (202) 312-1300. Ⓜ Federal Triangle. **Open** 5am–2am daily. **Closed** Federal hols. ⓐ 11am Mon, Wed & Fri from 14th St entrance (to book ahead call 312-1647). Visitor Center: **Tel** 289-8317. ☑ ⓐ ⓺ Ⓦ **itcdc.com**

The Ronald Reagan Building is a modern 3.1 million sq ft (280,000 sq m) limestone structure that appears Classical

on the outside and modern on the inside. Completed in 1997, it was the most expensive federal building project ever undertaken. Designed by Pei Cobb Freed & Partners, architects of the US Holocaust Memorial Museum *(see pp82–3)* and the National Gallery of Art's East Wing, the building houses a mix of federal, trade, and public spaces. It is named after President Ronald Reagan, who authorized the construction in the late 1980s.

On the east end of the atrium is the largest neon sculpture in North America – "Route Zenith," a creation of Keith Sonnier. Outside the building is the Oscar Straus Memorial

Sculpture from the Oscar Straus Memorial Fountain

Fountain, with sculpture by Adolph Alexander Weinman.

In summer the four-acre Woodrow Wilson Plaza, graced by sculptures by such artists as Martin Puryear and Stephen Rodin, is the venue for free concerts from noon to 1:30pm every weekday.

The Ronald Reagan Building houses a large food court of quality fast food, including Japanese, Middle Eastern, Mexican, and classic American deli and sandwich shops. There are also plenty of coffee shops.

Mock-Classical entrance to the immense Ronald Reagan Building

Façade of the Old Post Office

❼ Old Post Office

1100 Pennsylvania Ave, NW. **Map** 3 C3. **Tel** (202) 219-1103. Ⓜ Federal Triangle. **Open** Mar–Aug: 9am–8pm Mon–Sat, 10am–6pm Sun; Sep–Feb: 9am–5pm Mon–Sat, 10am–6pm Sun. **Closed** Jan 1, Thanksgiving, Dec 25 (closed for renovation until 2016). 🖼 tower only (call 606-8691). ♿ ▫ 📷 🆆 **nps.gov.opot**

Built in 1899, the Old Post Office was Washington's first skyscraper. Soaring 12 stories above the city, it was a fireproof model of modern engineering with a steel frame covered in granite. The huge interior had 3,900 electric lights and its own generator, the first one to be used in the city. Its fanciful Romanesque architecture was fashionable at the time it was built, and the breathtaking hall, with its glass roof and balconies, remains a spectacular mixture of light, color, and gleaming metal.

In the 15 years following its construction, the Post Office became an object of controversy. Its turrets and arches, once praised by critics, were derided. The *New York Times* newspaper said the building looked like "a cross between a cathedral and a cotton mill." Government planners thought the Post Office building clashed with the Neo-Classical architecture that dominated the rest of Washington. When the postal system moved its offices in 1934, there seemed to be no reason to keep the architectural relic. Only a lack of funds during the Great Depression of the 1930s *(see p25)* prevented the Old Post Office from being torn down.

The building was occupied intermittently by various government agencies until the mid-1960s, when its decrepit condition again drew a chorus in favor of demolition. A Washington preservation group, Don't Tear It Down, promoted the historical significance of the Old Post Office, and it was spared once more.

The renovated building housed a complex of shops and restaurants, commonly known as the Old Post Office Pavilion, until its purchase in 2013 by business magnate Donald Trump, who is renovating the area once again. It is scheduled to reopen in 2016.

❽ Benjamin Franklin Statue

Pennsylvania Ave & 10th St, NW. **Map** 3 C3. Ⓜ Federal Triangle.

Donated by publisher Stilson Hutchins (1839–1912), it was unveiled by Benjamin Franklin's great-granddaughter in 1889. The words "Printer, Philosopher, Patriot, Philanthropist" are inscribed on the four sides of the statue's pedestal in tribute to this man of diverse talents. Postmaster general, writer, and scientist, Benjamin Franklin was also a key member of the committee that drafted the 1776 Declaration of Independence. As a diplomat to the court of Louis XVI of France, he went to Versailles in 1777 to gain support for the American cause of independence from Britain. Franklin returned to France in 1783 to negotiate the Treaty of Paris that ended the American Revolution *(see p20)*.

❾ Freedom Plaza

Pennsylvania Ave between 13th St & 14th St, NW. **Map** 3 B3. Ⓜ Federal Triangle, Metro Center.

Freedom Plaza was conceived as part of a Pennsylvania Avenue redevelopment plan in the mid-1970s. Designed by Robert Venturi and Denise Scott Brown, and completed in 1980, the plaza displays Pierre L'Enfant's original plan for Washington in black and white stone embedded in the ground. Around the edge are engraved quotations about the new city from Walt Whitman and President Wilson, among others.

Freedom Plaza provides a dramatic entry to Pennsylvania Avenue *(see pp94–5)*. On the north side of the plaza, where

The large-scale reproduction of L'Enfant's city plans, Freedom Plaza

Pennsylvania Avenue leads into E Street, are the **Warner Theatre** and the **National Theatre**. South of the plaza is the Beaux Arts **District Building** (housing government employees). The Freedom Plaza is a popular site for festivals and political protests.

⑩ Willard Hotel

1401 Pennsylvania Ave, NW.
Map 3 B3. **Tel** (202) 628-9100, 800-827-1747. Ⓜ Metro Center. ♿
Ⓦ intercontinental.com

There has been a hotel on this site since 1816. Originally called Tennison's, the hotel was housed in six adjacent two-story buildings. Refurbished in 1847, it was managed by hotel keeper Henry Willard, who gave his name to the hotel in 1850. Many famous people stayed here during the Civil War (1861–65), including the writer Nathaniel Hawthorne, who was covering the conflict for a magazine, and Julia Ward Howe who wrote the popular Civil War standard *The Battle Hymn of the Republic*. The word "lobbyist" is sometimes claimed to have been coined because it was known by those seeking favors that President Ulysses S. Grant went to the hotel's lobby to smoke his after-dinner cigar.

The present 330-room building, designed by the architect of New York's Plaza Hotel, Henry

Peacock Alley, one of the Willard Hotel's luxuriously decorated corridors

Hardenbergh, was completed in 1904. It was the most fashionable place to stay in the city until the end of World War II, when the surrounding neighborhood fell into decline. For 20 years it was boarded up and faced demolition. A coalition, formed of preservationists and the Pennsylvania Avenue Development Corporation, worked to restore the Beaux Arts building, and it finally reopened in renewed splendor in 1986.

No other hotel can rival the Willard's grand lobby, with its 35 different kinds of marble, polished wood, and petal-shaped concierge station. There is a style café, a bar, and a restaurant called The Willard Room.

⑪ National Theatre

1321 Pennsylvania Ave, NW. **Map** 3 B3.
Tel (202) 628-6161, 800-447-7400.
Ⓜ Metro Center, Federal Triangle.
♿ Ⓦ nationaltheatre.org

The National Theatre is the sixth theater to occupy this site and the oldest cultural institution in the city. The current building dates from 1922 and hosts Broadway-bound productions and touring groups. Known as an "actor's theater" because of its excellent acoustics, the National is said to be haunted by the ghost of 19th-century actor John McCullough, killed by a fellow actor and buried under the stage. There are free performances for children every Saturday at 9:30am and 11am.

The Federal Triangle

The Federal Triangle is bounded by 15th Street, Constitution Avenue, Pennsylvania Avenue, and E Street NW and is composed of 10 government buildings, including the Department of Commerce, the Old Post Office, the Department of Justice, the National Archives, the Labor Building, and others. Except for the National Archives and the Ronald Reagan Building, the public has limited access to these buildings. Taken as a whole (although they were not built at the same time) the Federal Triangle has been called "one of the greatest building projects ever undertaken." The first phase of the project started with the original seven buildings including the Post Office Pavillion, Internal Revenue, Justice, Archives, Commerce, Post Office Department, and the Apex building. The completion of the project was halted because of the Depression and was not completed until the Ronald Reagan Building opened in 1998. The Federal Triangle borrows heavily from Classical Revival architecture, but several buildings show the influence of social realism in their friezes. Especially notable are the Labor Building and National Archives.

National Archives

⓬ National Museum of Women in the Arts

1250 New York Ave, NW. **Map** 3 C3.
Tel (202) 783-5000, 800-222-7270.
Ⓜ Metro Center. **Open** 10am–5pm
Mon–Sat, noon–5pm Sun.
Closed Jan 1, Thanksgiving, Dec 25.
🎟 for groups (call 783-7996). 🅿 ♿
🖥 📷 🌐 nmwa.org

This museum of women's art houses works that span five centuries, from the Renaissance to the present day. The collection was started in the 1960s by Wilhelmina Holladay and her husband, who gathered paintings, sculpture, and photography from all over the world.

The museum operated out of the Holladays' private residence for several years, until it acquired a more permanent home in this Renaissance Revival landmark building, formerly a Masonic Temple. The collection has as its highlights masterpieces by female American artists. Some of the outstanding works on display are from the 19th century include *The Bath* (1891) by Mary Cassatt and *The Cage* (1885) by Berthe Morisot. Among the works by 20th-century artists are Elizabeth Cutlett's *Singing their Songs* (1992) and *Self-Portrait Between the Curtains, Dedication to Trotsky* (1937) by Mexican artist Frida Kahlo. The museum shop sells a range of gifts, also created by women.

Impressive exterior of the National Museum of Women in the Arts

to the building. The state-of-the-art Kiplinger Research Library and Reading Room houses extensive collections of historic materials, including rare publications, prints, maps, photographs, manuscripts, and memorabilia. There are also lectures, workshops, and videos. Washington Perspectives, an overview exhibit, features a giant map of the city set into the floor.

Painting of John Wilkes Booth poised to shoot Abraham Lincoln

⓭ Carnegie Library Building

801 K St (Mount Vernon Sq), NW.
Map 3 C2. **Tel** (202) 393-1420.
Ⓜ Gallery Place–Chinatown,
Mt Vernon Sq. Kiplinger Research
Library: **Tel** 383-1829. **Open** 10am–
5pm Tue–Sat. **Closed** Jan 1, Jul 4,
Thanksgiving, Dec 25. ♿ 🖥 📷
🌐 historydc.org

The Carnegie Library Building was once Washington's central library. It hosts various events and exhibitions, and in 2003 the Washington Historical Society moved its headquarters

⓮ Ford's Theatre

511 10th St between E St & F St, NW.
Map 3 C3. **Tel** (202) 426-6924.
Ⓜ Gallery Place-Chinatown, Metro
Center. **Open** 9am–5pm daily (except
matinee or rehearsal days – call
ahead). ♿ Petersen House:
Closed Dec 25. **Open** 9:30am–5:30pm
daily with free timed ticket. **Closed**
Dec 25. 📷 🌐 fordstheatre.org

John T. Ford, a theatrical producer, built this small jewel of a theater in 1863. Washington was a Civil War boomtown, and the theater, located in the thriving business district,

enjoyed great popularity. The fate of the theater was sealed, however, on April 14, 1865, when President Abraham Lincoln was shot here by John Wilkes Booth while watching a performance. Across the road from the theater, **Petersen House**, where the wounded president died the next morning, has been preserved as a museum.

After the tragedy, people stopped patronizing the theater, and Ford was forced to sell the building to the federal government a year later. It was left to spiral into decay for nearly a century until the government decided to restore it to its original splendor.

The theater now stages small productions. The Presidential Box is permanently decorated in Lincoln's honor.

Exterior of Ford's Theatre, site of the shooting of President Lincoln

⑮ Martin Luther King Memorial Library

901 G St at 9th St, NW. **Map** 3 C3.
Tel (202) 727-0321. Ⓜ Gallery Place–
Chinatown, Metro Center. **Open** noon–
9pm Mon–Tue, 9:30am–5:30pm Wed–
Sat, 1–5pm Sun. **Closed** Federal hols.
Ⓚ Ⓦ dclibrary.org/mlk

Washington's Martin Luther King Memorial Library is the only example of the Modernist architecture of Ludwig Mies van der Rohe in the city. A prominent figure in 20th-century design, van der Rohe finalized his plans for the library shortly before his death in 1969. It was named in honor of Dr. Martin Luther King Jr. when it opened in 1972, replacing the out dated Carnegie Library as the city's central public library.

Architecturally, the building is a classic example of van der Rohe's theory of "less is more." It is an austere, simple box shape with a recessed entrance lobby. Inside, there is a mural depicting the life of Dr. Martin Luther King Jr., the leader of the Civil Rights Movement, painted by artist Don Miller.

The library sponsors concerts and readings, as well as children's events, and is due to undergo a 200-million dollar restoration program.

The "Friendship Archway" spanning H Street in the heart of Chinatown

⑯ Chinatown

5th St to 8th St & H St to I St,
NW. **Map** 3 C3 & 4 D3. Ⓜ Gallery
Place-Chinatown.

The small area in Washington known as Chinatown covers just six square blocks. Formed around 1930, it has never been very large and today houses about 500 Chinese residents. The area was reinvigorated with the arrival of the adjacent Verizon Center *(see p104)* in 1997. H Street is particularly lively, with many shops and a selection of good restaurants.

The "Friendship Archway," a dramatic gateway over H Street at the junction with 7th Street, marks the center of the Chinatown area. Built in 1986, it was paid for by Washington's sister city, Beijing, as a token of esteem, and is based on the architecture of the Qing Dynasty (1649–1911). Its seven roofs, topped by 300 painted dragons, are balanced on a steel and concrete base, making it the largest single-span Chinese arch in the world. It is lit up at night.

During the Chinese New Year celebrations in late January or early Febuary, the area comes alive with a parade, dragon dances, and live musical performances *(see p41)*.

Dr. Martin Luther King, Jr.

A charismatic speaker and proponent of Mahatma Gandhi's theories of non-violence, Dr. Martin Luther King, Jr. was a black Baptist minister and leader of the civil rights movement in the United States.

Born in Atlanta, Georgia in 1929, King's career in civil rights began with the 1955 Montgomery, Alabama bus boycott – a protest of the city's segregated transit system. The movement escalated to protests at schools, restaurants, and hotels that did not admit black people. King's methods of non-violence were often met with police dogs and brutal tactics.

The culmination of the movement was the March on Washington on August 28, 1963, when 200,000 people gathered at the Lincoln Memorial in support of civil rights. The highlight of this event was King's "I Have a Dream" speech, calling for support for the movement. A direct result was the passing by Congress of the civil rights legislation in 1964, and King was awarded the Nobel Peace Prize the same year. In 1968 he was assassinated in Memphis, Tennessee, triggering riots in 100 American cities, including Washington.

Dr. King speaking at the Lincoln Memorial

⑰ Smithsonian American Art Museum and the National Portrait Gallery

Nowhere in Washington is the city's penchant to copy Greek and Roman architecture more obvious than in the former US Patent Office Building, now the home of the Smithsonian American Art Museum and the National Portrait Gallery (NPG). The wonderfully ornate 1836 building was converted into the twin museums in 1968. The American Art Museum contains a permanent collection of works by more than 7,000 American artists. The NPG is America's family album, featuring paintings, photographs, and sculptures of famous Americans. The two museums are joined by a glass covered courtyard.

Façade of the building, housing the main entrance to both galleries

★ Achelous and Hercules

This painting (1947) by Thomas Hart Benton (1889–1975) is a mythological analogy of early American life. Interpreted in many ways, it is widely accepted that Hercules represents man taming the wild, then enjoying the results of his labors.

KEY

① **An African-American** is depicted climbing over a fence into the idealized equality of America.

② **Hercules** tries to capture the bull.

③ **Achelous**, the river god, appears as a bull being wrestled by Hercules, representing the struggle of the American people.

④ **Hercules** is about to break off the bull's horn.

⑤ **The horn** is transformed into a cornucopia, or horn of plenty, symbolizing America as a land of abundance and opportunity.

⑥ **The man** working in the field represents the people of America, enjoying the fruits of the land after laboring.

★ Among the Sierra Nevada, California
Albert Bierstadt painted this Western landscape in 1867–8. He was later criticized by some for not offering a topographically correct view of the West.

Mary Cassatt
This portrait by Edgar Degas, painted c.1882, depicts his fellow artist Mary Cassatt playing cards.

John Singleton Copley
This self-portrait of the artist, who was largely known for his depictions of others, was painted c.1780.

"Casey" Stengel
This bronze sculpture of the baseball great was created by Rhoda Sherbell in 1981 from a 1965 cast.

VISITORS' CHECKLIST

Practical Information
Smithsonian American Art Museum: 8th St & F St, NW.
Map 3 C3.
Tel (202) 633-7970.
W americanart.si.edu
Open 11:30am–7pm daily.

National Portrait Gallery: 8th St & F St, NW.
Map 3 C3.
Tel (202) 633-8300.
W npg.si.edu
Open 11:30am–7pm daily.

Transport
M Gallery Place-Chinatown.

★ Manhattan
This 1932 oil painting by Georgia O'Keeffe was created for an exhibition at New York's Museum of Modern Art. It portrays her vision of the city's architectural landscape.

Mah-to-he-ha, Old Bear, A Medicine Man
This vibrant painting by George Caitlin dates from 1832. Native Americans were a popular choice of subject matter for this artist.

In the Garden
This charming depiction of the poet Celia Thaxter is by the artist Childe Hassam and was painted in 1892.

Exploring the Smithsonian American Art Museum

The Smithsonian American Art Museum was established in 1829 and is the first federal art collection. It began with gifts from private collections and art organizations that existed in Washington, DC before a bequest from British scientist James Smithson enabled the foundation of the Smithsonian Institution "for the increase and diffusion of knowledge" in 1846. The museum is a center for America's cultural heritage, with more than 42,000 artworks spanning 300 years.

19th-century and Early 20th-century Art

Some of the highlights in this collection from the last two centuries are the Thomas Moran Western landscapes and those of Albert Bierstadt. This subject matter can be seen in *Among the Sierra Nevada, California* (1867–8), Bierstadt's evocative depiction of the landscape.

Many of the American artists such as Albert Pinkham Ryder, Winslow Homer, and John Singer Sargent, were contemporaries to the Impressionists. Homer's *High Cliffs, Coast of Maine* (1894) is a dramatic meeting of land and sea. Seascapes were also a popular subject for Ryder. *Jonah*, painted c.1885, illustrates the Bible story of Jonah and the whale, depicting Jonah floundering in the sea during a storm, overlooked by God. The museum holds hundreds of paintings of Native Americans, many of them works by George Caitlin. This was also a popular subject for Charles Bird King and John Mix Stanley. American Impressionists are also well represented in the museum, including Mary Cassatt, William Merritt Chase, John Henry Twachtman, and Childe Hassam. Hassam's paintings, inspired by the French Impressionists, are refreshing yet tranquil. The calm seascape of *The South Ledges, Appledore* (1913) is typical of his style.

American Modernists

The enormous canvases of the Modernists provide a dramatic contrast to the landscapes and portraits of the 19th and 20th centuries. Franz Kline's black slashes on a white canvas in *Merce C* (1961), which was inspired by his involvement with dancer Merce Cunningham, are the antithesis of the delicacy of the Impressionists. Kenneth Noland's geometrical compositions resemble firing targets. Other Modernists here include Georgia O'Keeffe, Robert Rauschenberg, and David Hockney.

American Folk Art

The collection of American folk art includes some truly amazing pieces of work, created from a wide range of materials. James Hampton's *Throne of the Third Heaven of the Nations' Millennium General Assembly* (c.1950–64) is one of the star pieces in the collection.

Robert Rauschenberg's *Reservoir* (1961), mixed media on canvas

Contemporary Art

Roy Lichtenstein's 6.5-ton (5,900-kg) sculpture *Modern Head* (1989) greets visitors at the main entrance to the museum, and reflects the Smithsonian's dedication to the acquisition of modern and contemporary works. Inside are works by Jenny Holzer, Nam June Paik, and Edward Kienholz, among others. Karen LaMonte's *Reclining Dress Impression with Drapery* (2009) is a glorious, almost luminous, life-size sculpture in rippling cast glass.

Luce Foundation Center

The three-story Luce Foundation Center for American Art holds about 3,300 artworks from the museum's collection. The items on display include paintings and sculptures, contemporary craft objects, folk art, and jewelry.

Throne of the Third Heaven of the Nations' Millennium General Assembly by James Hampton

Exploring the National Portrait Gallery

The National Portrait Gallery keeps generations of remarkable Americans in the company of their fellow citizens. The gallery's mission is to collect and display images of "men and women who have made significant contributions to the history, development and culture of the people of the United States." Through the visual and performing arts, the lives of leaders such as George Washington and Martin Luther King, Jr., artists such as George Gershwin and Mary Cassatt, and activists such as Rosa Parks and Sequoyah are celebrated.

Ronald Reagan, an oil on canvas by Henry C. Casselli, Jr. painted in 1989

Overview of the Collection

The National Portrait Gallery illuminates America's family album, magnificently combining history, biography, and art in its collections. The portraits are fascinating not only because they reveal their subjects but also because they illustrate the times in which they were produced. There are more than 20,000 images in the permanent collection, which includes paintings, photographs, sculptures, etchings, and drawings. Both heroes and villains are represented. Portraits taken from life sittings are favored by the gallery.

Portrait of Pocahontas by an unidentified artist

The Great Hall

The third-floor Great Hall is a crazy quilt of tiles and ceiling medallions. A frieze showing the evolution of technology in America also runs around the room. Once a display area for new inventions, it is a reminder of the building's past as the Patent Office.

20th-Century Americans

The National Portrait Gallery's collection is not limited to the political history of the country. There is also a large collection of portraits of American people notable for their achievements in the arts, sports, or in the country's religious or cultural history. Athletes include the famous baseball player Babe Ruth and baseball manager Casey Stengel. Among figures from the world of entertainment are portraits of actresses Judy Garland, Tallulah Bankhead, and Mary Pickford. John Wayne also features among the Hollywood stars, as do Buster Keaton, Clark Gable, and James Cagney. There are also bronze busts of the poet T.S. Eliot and the humorist Will Rogers. Religious leaders, business magnates, pioneers in women's rights and civil rights (such as Dr. Martin Luther King, Jr.), explorers, and scientists are portrayed in a whole range of media, including oils, clay, and bronze. There are also many photographic portraits, including some of Marilyn Monroe, which were taken during a morale-boosting visit the actress made to soldiers during the Korean War.

America's Presidents

In 1857, Congress commissioned George Peter Alexander Healy to paint portraits of the presidents. The chronologically ordered portrayal of all of the country's leaders remains the heart of the National Portrait Gallery's exhibitions.

Two portraits of George and Martha Washington are featured prominently in the Portrait Gallery. The most famous portrait of George Washington is Gilbert Stuart's "Landsdowne", painted from life in 1796. Abraham Lincoln posed for photographer Alexander Gardener several months before he was assassinated (see p98).

The exhibition also features modern-day presidents, such as Bill Clinton and George W. Bush. Shepard Fairey's iconic portrait of Barack Obama, an image seen throughout the latter's presidential campaign, is also here.

Diana Ross and The Supremes, photographed by Bruce Davidson in 1965

The unique and innovative International Spy Museum

⓲ International Spy Museum

800 F St, NW. **Map** 3 C3. **Tel** (202) 393-7798, EYE-SPY-U. Ⓜ Gallery Place-Chinatown, Metro Center. **Open** Apr–Oct: 9am–7pm; Nov–Mar: 10am–6pm. **Closed** Jan 1, Thanksgiving, Dec 25. ⚅ ▢ ⚅ ⚅ group tours by reservation. Ⓦ **spymuseum.org**

The Spy Museum is the first museum in the world devoted to international espionage. Its huge collection includes the German Enigma cipher machine from World War II, a Soviet shoe transmitter, a wristwatch camera, and a lipstick pistol, displayed in a variety of themed exhibits. A visit to the museum begins with a film on the real life of a spy, revealing what motivates people to enter this clandestine world. The "School for Spies" exhibit displays over 200 artifacts used by spies to disguise and protect themselves during operations. "The Secret History of Histories" traces the art of spying from biblical times

World War II cipher machine, essential for breaking enemy codes

to the early 20th century. "Spies Among Us" examines the making and breaking of codes during World War II. Other permanent exhibits such as "Weapons of Mass Disruption" explore technology and cyber attacks, while "War of the Spies" looks at espionage from the Cold War to the present day, featuring spy planes, listening and tracking devices, and the lives of spies, such as Aldrich Ames and Robert Hanssen.

⓳ Verizon Center

601 F St, NW. **Map** 4 D3. **Tel** (202) 628-3200. Ⓜ Gallery Place-Chinatown. Team Store: **Open** 10am–5:30pm daily (later on event days). ⚅ for National Sports Gallery. ⚅ ⚅ ⚅ Ⓦ **verizoncenter.com**

Opened in 1997, the Verizon Center is a sports and entertainment complex that houses many shops and restaurants.

The 20,000-seat Verizon stadium is the home of Washington's basketball teams, the Wizards (men's team), Georgetown Hoyas, and the Mystics (women's), as well as the ice hockey team, the Capitals. The presence of the complex has revived the surrounding area beyond recognition. Half of the arena's seats are below ground level, in a vast but harmonious structure. It hosts rock concerts as well as sports events and exhibitions.

Penn Quarter Renaissance

During the 1990s, Washington's Penn Quarter was transformed from a derelict historic area to prime real estate. The construction of the Verizon Center and renewed appreciation for the restoration of dilapidated Victorian buildings helped to accelerate this process. As a result of losing its shabby image, Penn Quarter also lost many of the artists who carved studios out of the high-ceilinged, low-rent spaces, but their influence can still be seen in the large number of art galleries and exhibitions in the area. Some of the non-profit organizations and small businesses that leased offices in the big, aging buildings were forced to relocate due to an increase in rent. Soaring prices also closed a number of traditional Chinese restaurants around the Verizon Center, which have been replaced by upscale eateries. Today Penn Quarter is a safer area for those on foot, with a buzzing selection of nightly activities available, including sports events, theater shows, concerts, and lively restaurants.

A contemporary office building linking two Victorian façades on 7th Street

Majestic lion statue alongside a marble wall at the police memorial

⑳ National Law Enforcement Officers Memorial

E St, NW, between 4th St & 5th St, NW. **Map** 4 D3. **Tel** (202) 737-3400. Ⓜ Judiciary Square. Visitor Center: 605 E St, NW. **Open** 9am–5pm Mon–Fri, 10am–5pm Sat, noon–5pm Sun. **Closed** Jan 1, Thanksgiving, Dec 25. Ⓓ Ⓖ Ⓕ Ⓦ nleomf.org

Dedicated by President George Bush in 1991, the National Law Enforcement Officers Memorial honors the 18,600 police officers who have been killed since the first known death in 1792. Spread over three acres in the center of Judiciary Square, the memorial's flower-lined pathways are spectacular in springtime. The names of the fallen officers are inscribed on marble walls. Each path is guarded by a statue of an adult lion shielding its cubs, symbolic of the US police force's protective role.

㉑ National Building Museum

401 F St at 4th St, NW. **Map** 4 D3. **Tel** (202) 272-2448. Ⓜ Judiciary Square, Gallery Place-Chinatown. **Open** 10am–5pm Mon–Sat, 11am–5pm Sun. **Closed** Jan 1, Thanksgiving, Dec 25. Ⓐ Ⓒ Ⓖ Ⓓ Ⓕ Ⓦ nbm.org

It is fitting that the National Building Museum, dedicated to the building trade, should be housed in the architecturally audacious former Pension Bureau building. Civil War General Montgomery C. Meigs saw Michelangelo's Palazzo Farnese on a trip to Rome and decided to duplicate it as a Washington office building, albeit twice as big and in red brick as opposed to the stone masonry of the Rome original.

Completed in 1887, the building is topped by a dramatic terracotta frieze of the Civil War measuring 3 ft (1 m) in height. The daring exterior of the building is matched by its flamboyant interior. The vast concourse, measuring 316 ft by 116 ft (96 m by 35 m), is lined with balconies containing exhibitions. The roof is supported by huge columns, constructed of brick, plastered, and faux-painted to give the appearance of marble. The Great Hall has been the impressive venue for many presidential balls.

In 1926 the Pension Bureau relocated to different offices, and there was a move to demolish Meigs' building. Instead it was occupied by various government agencies for a time and was even used as a courthouse.

The building was eventually restored, and in 1985 opened in renewed splendor as the National Building Museum. A privately owned collection, the museum has a display on the architectural history of the city – "Washington: Symbol and City." It includes an excellent illustration of Pierre L'Enfant's original plans for the capital, as well as other photographs, models, and interactive exhibits demonstrating how the city grew and changed. The temporary exhibits in the museum often highlight controversial issues in design and architecture. There is a small café in the courtyard, and a gift shop. For children under six, the "Building Zone" offers some hands-on fun including giant LEGO blocks, bulldozers, and a playhouse.

Ornamental plinth in the grounds of the museum

The splendid, colonnaded Great Hall in the National Building Museum

THE WHITE HOUSE AND FOGGY BOTTOM

The official residence of the President, the White House is one of the most distinguished buildings in DC and was first inhabited in 1800. Although burned by the British during the War of 1812, most of today's building remains as it was planned. Other buildings surrounding the White House are worth a visit, such as the

Daughters of the American Revolution building and the Corcoran Gallery. East of the White House is the Foggy Bottom area, which was built on swampland. Notable edifices here include the Kennedy Center, the State Department building, and the notorious Watergate Complex, focus of the 1970s Nixon scandal.

Sights at a Glance

Galleries
5 Renwick Gallery
7 Corcoran Gallery of Art

Squares
3 Lafayette Square
17 Washington Circle

Historic Buildings
4 Hay-Adams Hotel
6 Eisenhower Old Executive Office Building
8 Octagon Museum
9 Daughters of the American Revolution
15 George Washington University
18 Watergate Complex

Official Buildings
1 The White House pp110–13
2 Treasury Building
10 Organization of the American States
11 Department of the Interior

12 Federal Reserve Building
13 National Academy of Sciences
14 State Department

Performing Arts Center
19 Kennedy Center pp120–21

Church
16 St. Mary's Episcopal Church

Restaurants see pp185–7
1 Ancora
2 Aroma
3 Bayou
4 Blue Duck Tavern
5 The Bombay Club
6 Café Lombardy
7 City Bites
8 Firefly
9 Founding Farmers
10 Georgia Brown's
11 Johnny Rockets
12 Marcel's
13 McFadden's
14 One Fish, Two Fish
15 Potbelly Sandwich Shop
16 The Public Bar
17 Rasika West End
18 Roof Terrace Restaurant
19 Vidalia
20 Westend Bistro

See also Street Finder maps 2, 3

0 meters 500
0 yards 500

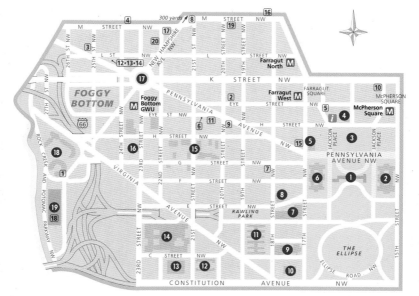

The south portico of The White House

For keys to symbols see back flap

Street-by-Street: Around The White House

The area surrounding the White House is filled with grand architecture and political history, and the vistas from the Ellipse lawn are breathtaking. It is worth spending a day exploring the area and seeing some of its buildings, such as the Treasury Building with its statue of Alexander Hamilton (the first Secretary of the Treasury) and the Eisenhower Old Executive Office Building. The buildings of the Daughters of the American Revolution (DAR) and the Organization of the American States (OAS) both offer the visitor an insight into the pride the nation takes in its past.

6 Eisenhower Old Executive Office Building
Although it was poorly received on its completion in 1888, this attractive building now houses staff of the Executive branch.

5 Renwick Gallery
The gallery, is part of the Smithsonian American Art Museum. The inscription above the entrance of the building reads "Dedicated to Art."

8 Octagon Museum
At one time James Madison's home, this building has had a varied history, functioning as a hospital and a school, among other things.

7 ★ Corcoran Gallery of Art
The gallery (closed for renovation) will feature select pieces from the original Corcoran collection and the National Gallery of Art, once it reopens. It will also serve as a space for exhibiting pieces from traveling shows curated by the National Gallery of Art.

9 DAR Building
This beautiful Neo-Classical building is one of three founded by the historical organization, the Daughters of the American Revolution.

Key

— Suggested route

10 OAS Building
The central statue of Queen Isabella of Spain stands in front of this Spanish Colonial-style mansion. Built in 1910, it houses the Organization of American States.

4 Hay-Adams Hotel
Formed by the joining of two town houses, this luxurious hotel has been the scene of political activity since it opened in the 1920s.

Locator Map
See Street Finder maps 2 & 3

3 Lafayette Square
Named after the Marquis de Lafayette, a Revolutionary War hero, this leafy square has at its center this statue of Andrew Jackson, the seventh president, sculpted by Clark Mills.

2 ★ Treasury Building
Widely regarded as the most impressive Neo-Classical structure in the city, this building took over 60 years to complete.

1 ★ The White House
One of the most famous sights in Washington, DC, this has been the President's official residence since the 1800s.

0 meters 100
0 yards 100

❶ The White House

In 1791 George Washington chose this site as the location for the new President's House. Irish-born architect James Hoban was selected to design the building, known as the Executive Mansion. In 1800, President and Mrs. John Adams became the first occupants, even though the building was not yet completed. Burned by the British in 1814, the restored edifice was occupied again in 1817, by James Monroe. In 1901, President Theodore Roosevelt changed the official name of the building to the White House and in 1902 ordered the West Wing to be built. The East Wing was added in 1942 on the instruction of President Franklin D. Roosevelt, completing the building as it is today.

The White House
The official residence of the US president for over 200 years, the White House façade is familiar to millions of people around the world.

★ State Dining Room
Able to seat as many as 140 people, the State Dining Room was enlarged in 1902. A portrait of President Abraham Lincoln, by George P.A. Healy, hangs above the mantel.

KEY

① **The West Terrace** leads to the West Wing and the Oval Office, the President's official office.

② **The Stonework** has been painted over and over to maintain the building's white façade.

③ **Blue Room**

④ **The Green Room** was first used by Thomas Jefferson as a dining room.

⑤ **Treaty Room**

⑥ **The East Room** is used for large gatherings, such as concerts and press conferences.

⑦ **The East Terrace** leads to the East Wing.

★ Red Room
One of three reception rooms on the state floor, the Red Room is furnished in red in the Empire Style (1810–30).

Lincoln Bedroom
President Lincoln used this room as his Cabinet Room. Today it is used as a guest bedroom furnished in Lincoln-era decor.

VISITORS' CHECKLIST

Practical Information
The White House: 1600 Pennsylvania Ave, NW. **Map** 3 B3.
W **whitehouse.gov**
Open 7:30–10am Tue–Sat only for groups with congressional or embassy appointments. Contact Visitor Center for information. **Closed** federal hols and official functions. 📷 obligatory; call (202) 456-7041 for more information.

White House Visitor Center: 1450 Pennsylvania Ave, NW.
Tel (202) 208-1631.
W **nps.gov/whho**
Open 7:30am–4pm daily.
Closed Jan 1, Thanksgiving, Dec 25. 📷 ♿ 📷

Transport
M Federal Triangle.

⑦

⑤ ⑥

④

③

★ **The Vermeil Room**
This yellow room houses six paintings of first ladies, including this portrait of Eleanor Roosevelt by Douglas Chandor.

Diplomatic Reception
This room is used to welcome friends and ambassadors. It is elegantly furnished in the Federal Period style (1790–1820).

White House Architects

After selecting the site, George Washington held a design competition to find an architect to build the residence where the US president would live. In 1792 James Hoban, an Irish-born architect, was chosen for the task. It is from Hoban's original drawings that the White House was initially built and all subsequent changes grew. In 1902 President Teddy Roosevelt hired the New York architectural firm of McKim, Mead, and White to check the structural condition of the building and refurbish areas as necessary. The White House underwent further renovations and refurbishments during the administrations of Truman and Kennedy.

James Hoban, architect of the White House

Exploring the White House

The rooms in the White House are beautifully decorated in period styles and filled with valuable antique furniture, china, and silverware. Hanging on their walls are some of America's most treasured paintings, including portraits of past presidents and first ladies. Those not lucky enough to be granted permission to tour the White House can experience a virtual tour at the White House Visitor Center.

The Library

Originally used as a laundry area, this room was turned into a "gentleman's ante-room" at the request of President Theodore Roosevelt in 1902. In 1935 it was remodeled into a library. Furnished in 1962 in the style of the late Federal period (1800–1820), the library was redecorated in 1962, and then again in 1976. It had its latest update in 2006 when it was painted in classic cream and red tones. Today, it is often used for media tapings.

Portraits of four native-American chiefs, painted by Charles Bird King, are displayed in the library. The chandelier was crafted in the early 1800s and was originally owned by the family of James Fenimore Cooper, author of *The Last of the Mohicans*.

The Vermeil Room

The Vermeil Room is named after the collection of vermeil, or gilded silver, that is on display in the cabinets. On show are 18th-, 19th-, and 20th-century tableware, including pieces crafted by English Regency silversmith Paul Storr (1771–1836) and French Empire silversmith Jean-Baptist Claude Odiot (1763–1850). The collection was bequeathed to the White House in 1958 by Margaret Thompson Biddle.

Several portraits of first ladies hang on the walls: Elizabeth Shoumatoff's painting of Claudia (Lady Bird) Johnson, Aaron Shikler's portrait of Jacqueline Kennedy in her New York apartment, and an unusual painting of Eleanor Roosevelt, caught in various moods, by Douglas Chandor. Also on display are portraits of Lou Hoover, Mamie Eisenhower, Pat Nixon, and Nancy Reagan.

The China Room

Edith Wilson created this room in 1917 to display examples of tableware used in the White House. Today it is used as a reception room. The rich red color scheme is suggested by the stunning portrait of Grace Coolidge, painted in 1924 by Howard Chandler Christy. The Indo-Isfahan rug dates from the early 20th century.

The Blue Room

President James Monroe chose the French Empire-style decor for this magnificent, oval-shaped room in 1817. The Classically inspired furniture and accompanying motifs, such as urns, acanthus leaves, and imperial eagles, typify the style. The settee and seven chairs were created by Parisian cabinetmaker, Pierre-Antoine Bellangé.

A portrait of Thomas Jefferson by Rembrandt Peale, dating from 1800, hangs in this elegant room, along with a portrait of President John Adams, painted in 1793 by artist John Trumball. The Blue Room has always been used as a reception room, except for a brief period during the John Adams administration.

The Red Room

This room was decorated in the Empire style by Jacqueline Kennedy in 1962 and was refurbished in 1971, and again in 2000. Much of the wooden furniture in the room, including the beautiful inlaid round table, was created by cabinetmaker Charles-Honoré Lannuier in his New York workshop. Above the mantel hangs a portrait of Angelica Singleton Van Buren, the daughter-in-law of President Martin Van Buren, which was painted by Henry Inman in 1842. The room is used as a parlor or sitting room; it has also been used for small dinner parties.

The State Dining Room

As a result of the growing nation and its international standing, the size of official dinners in the White House increased. Finally in 1902 the architects McKim, Mead, and White were called in to enlarge the State Dining Room. The plaster and paneling was modeled on the style of 18th-century Neo-Classical English houses. The mahogany dining table was created in 1997. The pieces of French

The red and cream color scheme of the China Room

giltware on the table were bought by President Monroe in 1817.

The dining room was redecorated in 1998, when the Queen Anne-style chairs, which date from 1902, were reupholstered.

The Lincoln Bedroom

Used today as the guest room for the friends and family of the President, the Lincoln Bedroom is decorated in the American Victorian style, dating from around 1860. Used by Lincoln as an office and cabinet room, this room became the Lincoln Bedroom when President Truman decided to fill it with furniture from Lincoln's era. In the center is a 6 ft- (1.8 m-) wide rosewood bed with an 8 ft- (2.5 m-) high headboard. The portrait of General Andrew Jackson next to the bed is said to have been one of President Lincoln's favorites.

The Treaty Room

Beginning with Andrew Johnson's presidency in 1865, the Treaty Room served as the Cabinet Room for 10 presidential Administrations. The room contains many Victorian pieces bought by President Ulysses S. Grant, including the original table used by the Cabinet. The cut-glass chandelier that hangs here was made in Birmingham, England around 1850. The

The White House Visitor Center

The White House Visitor Center has interesting exhibits about the history of the White House and its decor, as well as royal gifts on display. There are also seasonal lectures by renowned speakers on

aspects of history in and out of the White House. The Center has a monthly Living History program with actors portraying historic figures. The gift shop carries an extensive range, including the annual White House Christmas ornament. Tours of the state rooms of the White House are extremely limited at this time. Guided tours can only be booked by special arrangement through a member of Congress or, if a non-US citizen, through an embassy. Requests need to be made at least 30 days in advance.

Façade of the White House Visitor Center

chandelier has 20 arms, each one fitted with a frosted glass globe.

The East Wing

The East Wing houses offices rather than ceremonial rooms. The walls of the Lobby are adorned with portraits of presidents. Both the East Landing and the East Colonnade, which fronts the East Terrace, look out onto the Jacqueline Kennedy Garden. The Terrace, which links the East Wing to the Residence, houses the White House movie theater. It was once Theodore Roosevelt's coatroom.

The interior of the Oval Office, located in the West Wing

The West Wing

In 1902, the West Wing was built by the architectural firm McKim, Mead, and White for a total cost of $65,196. In this wing, the former Fish Room was renamed the Roosevelt Room by President Nixon, in honor of presidents Theodore and Franklin Roosevelt who created this wing. Their portraits still hang in the room.

Also in the West Wing are the Cabinet Room, where government officials meet with the president, and the Oval Office, added in 1909, where the president meets with visiting heads of state. Over the years, many presidents have personalized this room in some way.

The Victorian-era interior of the Treaty Room

The colonnaded portico of the Neo-Classical Treasury Building

❷ Treasury Building

15th St & Pennsylvania Ave, NW.
Map 3 B3. **Tel** (202) 622-2000. Ⓜ
McPherson Square. 🎫 Tours for US
citizens only, by appointment through
congressman. ♿ Ⓦ **treasury.gov**

The site of this massive, four-story Greek Revival building, home to the Department of the Treasury, was chosen by President Andrew Jackson. The grand, sandstone-and-granite edifice was designed by architect Robert Mills, who also designed the Washington Monument *(see p80)*.
A statue of Alexander Hamilton, the first Secretary of the Treasury, stands in front of the southern entrance to the building.

Liberty Bell beside the Treasury

The official guided tour, shows visitors the restored historic rooms, including the 1864 burglar-proof vault, the Andrew Johnson suite (Johnson's temporary office after the assassination of President Lincoln in 1865), and the marble Cash Room.
Between 1863 and 1880, US currency was printed in the basement, and during the Civil War it was used as storage space for food and arms. Today, the building is home to the Department of the Treasury, which manages the government's finances and protects US financial systems.

❸ Lafayette Square

Map 2 F3 & 3 B3. Ⓜ Farragut West, McPherson Square. Ⓦ **nps.gov**

Set behind the White House is Lafayette Square, named after the Marquis de Lafayette (1757–1834), a hero of the American Revolutionary War *(see p20).*
Due to its proximity to the White House, this public park is often the scene of peaceful demonstrations. It is home to 19th-century former mansions and the historic church of St. John's (the "Church of the Presidents"), built in 1816 by Benjamin Latrobe, who designed Decatur House, 748 Jackson Place, which was home to famous figures such as Henry Clay and Martin

Federal-style 19th-century houses overlooking tranquil Lafayette Square

Van Buren, and is open to the public. In the center of the Square is a huge statue of President Andrew Jackson (1767–1845) seated on a horse. Cast in bronze by Clark Mills, it was the first equestrian statue of its size to be built in the US and was dedicated in 1853.
At each of the square's four corners stand statues of men who took part in America's struggle for liberty. The southeast corner has the bronze figure of French compatriot Lafayette. In the southwest corner is a statue of another Frenchman, Jean-Baptiste Donatien de Vimeur, Comte de Rochambeau (1725–1807). This was a gift from France to the American people and accepted by Theodore Roosevelt in 1902. A statue of Polish general, Thaddeus Kosciuszko (1746–1817), who fought with the American colonists in the Revolutionary War, stands in the northeast corner. Baron von Steuben (1730–94), a German officer and George Washington's aide at the Battle of Valley Forge, is honored at the northwest end.

❹ Hay-Adams Hotel

1 Lafayette Square, NW. **Map** 2 F3
& 3 B2. **Tel** (202) 638-6600, 1-800-424-5054. Ⓜ Farragut North, Farragut West. Ⓦ **hayadams.com**

Situated close to the White House, the historic Hay-Adams Hotel is an Italian Renaissance landmark in Washington. Its plush interior is adorned with European and Oriental antiques.
It was originally two adjacent houses, built by Henry Hobson Richardson in 1885, belonging to statesman and author John Hay and diplomat and historian Henry Adams. A popular hotel since its conversion in 1927 by developer Harry Wardman, the exclusive Hay-Adams remains one of Washington's top establishments *(see p179)*, well situated for all the major sights. Afternoon tea and drinks are available in the Lafayette Restaurant.

❺ Renwick Gallery

Pennsylvania Ave at 17th St, NW.
Map 2 F3 & 3 A3. **Tel** (202) 633-
1000. Ⓜ Farragut West.
Open 10am–5:30pm. 🗓 ♿ 🔊
📷 ⓦ americanart.si.edu

Forming part of the Smithsonian American Art Museum *(see p102)*, this red-brick building was designed and constructed by James Renwick Jr. in 1858. It originally housed the art collection of William Wilson Corcoran until this was moved to the current Corcoran Gallery of Art in 1897.

The building was later bought by the Smithsonian. Refurbished and renamed, the Renwick Gallery opened in 1972, primarily to conserve and display the Smithsonian's collection of 20th-century and contemporary American arts, crafts, and design.

In late 2015, the Renwick reopened after a renovation that included the updating of its heating and cooling systems and the control system for digital and electronic work. However, the renovation revealed a few surprises: concealed vaulted ceilings were disclosed after the modern drop ceilings were dismantled. Covered windows were opened to let natural light flow in. The Renwick now has a custom carpet for its grand staircase, designed by French architect Odile Decoq.

With the reopening, the gallery rededicates itself to show-casing American crafts. Its first exhibition, "Wonder", featured large-scale installations on how art is perceived.

The magnificent Renwick Gallery, a fine example of French Empire style

The Renwick, will however, not shed its history completely. In the Octagon Room, Hiram Powers' famous sculpture, *The Greek Slave*, will be displayed as a 3D print, made from a scan of the original plaster model. Permanent exhibitions from the Renwick's collection will be re-installed after mid-2016. Temporary exhibitions are open to the public.

❻ Eisenhower Old Executive Office Building

17th St at Pennsylvania Ave, NW.
Map 2 F4 & 3 A3. Ⓜ Farragut West.
Closed to the public. 📷 Sat. Call (202) 395-5895 to book. ♿
ⓦ nps.gov

Formerly known simply as the Old Executive Office Building, this structure stands on the West side of the White House. It was once the home of the War, Navy, and State Departments. Built over 17 years between 1871 and 1888 by Alfred B. Mullett, its exuberant French Second Empire design, inspired by the 1852 expansion of the Louvre in Paris, generated much criticism at the time.

The building has long been the site of historic events, such as the meeting between Secretary of State Cordell Hull and the Japanese after the bombing of Pearl Harbor.

Today the building houses government agencies, including the White House Office, the Office of the Vice President, and the National Security Council.

Lion statue guarding the Corcoran Gallery

❼ Corcoran Gallery of Art

500 17th St, NW.
Map 2 F4 & 3 A3.
Tel (202) 639-1700.
Ⓜ Farragut West, Farragut North.
Closed for renovation.
📷 🗓 ♿ 🖥 ♿ 🔊 🚻
📷 ⓦ corcoran.org

One of the first fine art museums in the country, the Corcoran Gallery of Art opened in 1874. It outgrew its original home (what is now the Renwick Gallery building) and moved to this massive edifice designed in 1897 by Ernest Flagg. A privately funded art collection, the Corcoran was founded by William Wilson Corcoran – a banker whose main interest was American art.

The Corcoran is undergoing renovation and will reopen as a space for exhibiting pieces from traveling shows curated by the National Gallery of Art, which will display select artworks from the collection. It will also have iconic paintings from the orginal Corcoran collection, such as Frederick Church's magnificent painting *Niagara*, housed in what will be called The Legacy Gallery.

Imposing façade of Eisenhower Old Executive Office Building

❽ Octagon Museum

1799 New York Ave, NW. **Map** 2 F4 & 3 A3. **Tel** (202) 626-7439. Ⓜ Farragut West and Farragut North. **Open** by appointment. **Closed** Jan 1, Thanksgiving, Dec 25. 🅿️ 🎫 1–4pm Thu & Fri. ♿ (first floor only). Ⓦ **theoctagon.org**

Actually hexagonal in shape, the Octagon is a three-story red-brick building, designed in the late-Federal style by Dr. William Thornton (1759–1828), first architect of the US Capitol. The Octagon was completed in 1801 for Colonel John Tayloe III, a rich plantation owner from Richmond County, Virginia, and a friend of George Washington.

When the White House was burned in the War of 1812 against Britain (see p21), President James Madison and his wife, Dolley, lived here from 1814 to 1815. The Treaty of Ghent that ended the war was signed by Madison on the second floor of the house on February 17, 1815.

In the early 1900s, the building was taken over by the American Institute of Architects. The American Architectural Foundation, established in 1970, set up a museum of architecture in the Octagon. The building has been restored to its historically accurate 1815 appearance, and has some original furnishings and fine architectural features, such as a circular entrance hall. Ongoing restoration work and private events cause occasional suspension of tours (check website or call ahead).

The circular main entrance to the attractive Octagon Museum

South portico of the DAR Memorial Continental Hall

❾ Daughters of the American Revolution

1776 D St, NW. **Map** 2 F4 & 3 A3. **Tel** (202) 628-1776. Ⓜ Farragut West. **Open** 9am–4pm Mon–Fri, 9am–5pm Sat. **Closed** 1 week in Jul, Federal hols. 🎫 9am–3pm Sat (book in advance for groups of 5 or more). ♿ Caters for children. Ⓦ **dar.org/museum**

Founded in 1890 as a non-profit organization, the Daughters of the American Revolution (DAR) is dedicated to historic preservation and promoting education and patriotism. In order to become a member, you must be a woman with blood relations to any person, male or female, who fought in or aided the Revolution. There are currently over 160,000 members in 3,000 regional branches throughout the USA and in nine other countries.

The DAR Museum is located in the Memorial Continental Hall, designed for the organization by Edward Pearce Casey and completed in 1910.

The 13 columns in the south portico symbolize the 13 original states of the Union. Entrance to the museum is through the gallery, which displays an eclectic range of pieces from quilts to glassware and china.

The 33 period rooms that form the State Rooms in the museum house a collection of over 50,000 items, from silver to porcelain, ceramics, stoneware, and furniture. Each room is decorated in a unique style particular to an American state from different periods during the 18th and 19th centuries. An attic room filled with 18th- and 19th-century toys will delight children. Also, there is a huge genealogical library, consisting of approximately 125,000 publications.

DAR Museum banners proclaiming Preservation, Patriotism, Education

Fountain in the courtyard of the OAS building

⑩ Organization of American States

17th St & Constitution Ave, NW. **Map** 2 F4 & 3 A4. **Tel** (202) 458-3000. **Open** 9am–5:30pm Mon–Fri. **Closed** Sat & Sun, Federal hols. Art Museum of the Americas: 201 18th St, NW. **Tel** (202) 458-6016. **Open** 10am–5pm Tue–Sun. **Closed** Good Friday, Federal hols. Ⓜ Farragut West. 📷 Call (202) 458-6016. 🔲 **museum.oas.org**

Dating back to the First International Conference of the American States, held from October 1889 to April 1890 in Washington, the Organization of American States (OAS) is the oldest alliance of nations dedicated to reinforcing the peace and security of the continent, and maintaining democracy. The Charter of the OAS was signed in Bogotá, Colombia, in 1948 by the US and 20 Latin American republics. Today there are 35 members. The building houses the Columbus Memorial Library and the **Art Museum of the Americas**, which exhibits 20th-century Latin American and Caribbean art.

⑪ Department of the Interior Building

19th St, between C St & E St, NW. **Map** 2 F4 & 3 A3. **Tel** (202) 208-3100. Ⓜ Farragut West. **Open** 8:30am–4:30pm Mon–Fri (photo ID needed) . ♿ 📷 🔲 **doi.gov/interiormuseum**

Designed by architect Waddy Butler Wood and built in 1935, this huge limestone building is the headquarters of the Department of the Interior. The building has a long central section, with six wings that extend off each side. In total it covers more than 16 acres of floor space, and has 2 miles (3 km) of corridors.

The Department of the Interior was originally formed of only the Departments of Agriculture, Labor, Education, and Energy, but it expanded to oversee all federally owned land across the United States. Visible inside, but only when taking the official guided tour, are 36 murals painted by Native American artists in the 1930s, including one of the singer Marian Anderson performing at the Lincoln Memorial in 1939 (see p87).

Displays in the small **Department of the Interior Museum**, located on the first floor, include an overview of the Department's history, and some intricate dioramas of American wildlife and important historical events, such as the 1929 Kinloch Mine explosion. Also on view are paintings by 19th-century surveyors, and crafts by Native Americans, including a great collection of basketry.

The south façade of the immense Department of the Interior Building

The Tayloe Family

Portrait, in crayon, by Saint Memin of Colonel John Tayloe III

John Tayloe III (1771–1828), a colonel in the War of 1812, was responsible for the construction of the unusual Octagon building. He and his wife Ann, the daughter of Benjamin Ogle (the governor of Maryland), had their primary residence at Mount Airy, an estate and tobacco plantation in Richmond County, Virginia. The Tayloes decided they wanted to build a second house where they could spend the inclement winter seasons. President George Washington, a close friend of Tayloe and his father, was at the time overseeing the building of the US Capitol and was eager for people to move into the new city. The president encouraged Tayloe and his family to choose a plot in Washington rather than in the more popular Philadelphia. The family heeded his advice and the triangular-shaped corner plot for the Octagon was chosen. Tayloe's vast wealth enabled him to employ the services of William Thornton, the original designer of the US Capitol building, and spend a total of $35,000 on the construction of the house.

⑫ Federal Reserve Building

Constitution Ave & 20th St NW.
Map 2 E4 & 3 A4. **Tel** (202) 452-3324.
🎫 of exhibitions: 10am–3:30pm
Mon–Fri. Ⓜ Foggy Bottom. **Open** by appointment. **Closed** Federal hols.
♿ 🌐 federalreserve.gov

Known to most people as "the Fed," this building is home to the Federal Reserve System. This is the US banking system under which 12 Federal Reserve banks in 12 districts across the country regulate and hold reserves for member banks in their districts. Dollar bills are not printed here, however, but at the Bureau of Engraving and Printing *(see p81)*.

The four-story, white marble edifice opened in 1937 and was designed by Paul Philippe Cret, architect for the OAS building *(see p117)* and the Folger Shakespeare Library *(see p50)*. Small art exhibitions are held in the building throughout the year.

The gleaming, white marble exterior of the Federal Reserve Building

Marble eagle above the entrance to "the Fed"

⑬ National Academy of Sciences

2101 Constitution Ave, NW.
Map 2 E4. **Tel** (202) 334-2000.
Ⓜ Foggy Bottom. **Open** 9am–5pm Mon–Fri (ID required). ♿
🌐 nationalacademies.org

Established in 1863, the National Academy of Sciences is a non-profit organization that conducts over 200 studies a year on subjects such as health, science, and technology, and educates the nation by providing news of scientific discoveries. It also holds exhibitions about its mission and on science. Among the past and present Members of the Academy are nearly 200 Nobel Prize winners, most notably Albert Einstein. To be elected as a member is considered a great honor for a scientist.

The three-story white marble building, designed by Bertram Grosvenor Goodhue, was completed in 1924. Inside is a gold dome adorned with portraits of Greek philosophers and panels illustrating various scientists. A 700-seat auditorium hosts a series of free chamber recitals throughout the year. On the building's upper floors are the offices of the National Research Council, the National Academy of Sciences, and the National Academy of Engineering.

Nestled among the trees in front of the Academy is the much-admired bronze statue of Albert Einstein, sculpted by Robert Berks. The same artist created the bust of President John F. Kennedy, which can be seen in the Grand Foyer of the Kennedy Center *(see pp120–21)*. The huge statue of Albert Einstein reaches 12 ft (4 m) in height and weighs 7,000 pounds (4 tons). It was erected in 1979.

⑭ State Department

23rd St & C St, NW. **Map** 2 E4 & 3 A3.
Tel (202) 647-4000. Ⓜ Foggy Bottom-GWU. 🎫 9:30am, 10:30am, & 2:45pm; call (202) 647-3241 or email touroffice@state.gov to book; must show photo ID. **Closed** Federal hols.
♿ 🌐 state.gov

As the oldest executive department of the United States government, established in 1781, the State Department handles all foreign policy.

Covering an expanse of 2.5 million sq ft (232,250 sq m) over four city blocks, the State Department building rises eight stories high. Workplace of the Secretary of State, the State Department, and the United States Diplomatic Corps, the building plays host to some 80,000 guests and 60,000 visitors every year. The State Department's Diplomatic Reception Rooms were lavishly refurbished in the late 1960s, and now contain antiques worth over $90 million.

⑮ George Washington University

2121 I (Eye) St, NW. **Map** 2 E3.
Tel (202) 994-1000. Ⓜ Foggy Bottom-GWU. Lisner and Betts Auditoriums:
Tel (202) 994-6800. 🌐 gwu.edu

Founded in 1821, George Washington University, known as "GW" to many people, is

Sculpture of Albert Einstein outside the National Academy of Sciences

named after the first president of the United States. George Washington is the largest university in Washington, DC. There are nine schools offering both undergraduate and graduate studies. Strong subjects on offer include International Affairs, Business Administration, Medicine, Law, and Political Science.

As a result of its location, the university has many famous alumni, including Colin Powell (US Secretary of State in George W. Bush's administration) and Jacqueline Bouvier (who married John Kennedy) as well as a number of children of past presidents, including Lynda Johnson, Margaret Truman, and D. Jeffrey Carter.

The on-campus Lisner, Morton and Betts auditoriums host a series of plays, dances, lectures, and concerts.

St. Mary's Episcopal Church, built for freed slaves

⓰ St. Mary's Episcopal Church

728 23rd St, NW. **Map** 2 E3. **Tel** (202) 333-3985. Ⓜ Foggy Bottom-GWU. **Open** 9:30am–3pm Mon–Thu. 🕆 10am Sun, 12:10pm Wed. ♿ 🅦 stmarysfoggybottom.org

Opened on January 20, 1887, the red-brick, Gothic St. Mary's Episcopal Church was the first church in Washington to be built specifically for freed slaves.

St Mary's was designed by James Renwick, the architect of the Renwick Gallery (see p115), the Smithsonian Castle (see p74), and St. Patrick's Cathedral in New

York City. The church was placed on the city's register of protected historic buildings in 1972.

⓱ Washington Circle

Map 2 E3. Ⓜ Foggy Bottom-GWU.

One of several circles and squares created by Pierre L'Enfant's original design of the city (see p21), Washington Circle lies at the northern edge of Foggy Bottom. It forms the point where Pennsylvania Avenue and New Hampshire Avenue meet K Street and 23rd Street. The circle boasts an imposing bronze statue of George Washington astride his horse, designed by artist Clark Mills and unveiled in 1860. The statue faces east, looking toward the White House and the US Capitol.

The distinctive curved walls of the infamous Watergate Complex

⓲ Watergate Complex

Virginia Ave between Rock Creek Parkway and New Hampshire Ave, NW. **Map** 2 D3. Ⓜ Foggy Bottom-GWU. ♿

Located next to the Kennedy Center (see pp120–21), on the bank of the Potomac River, the impressive, Italian-designed Watergate Complex was completed in 1971. The four rounded buildings that make up the complex were designed to contain shops, offices, apartments, hotels, and diplomatic missions. The complex is undergoing a massive renovation.

In the summer of 1972 the complex found itself at the center of international news. Burglars, linked to President Nixon, broke into "the offices of the Democratic National Committee, sparking off the Watergate scandal that led to the president's resignation.

The Watergate Scandal

On June 17, 1972, during the US presidential campaign, five men were arrested for breaking into the Democratic Party headquarters in the Watergate Complex. The burglars were employed by the re-election organization of President Richard Nixon, a Republican.

President Nixon addressing the nation while still in office

Found guilty of burglary and attempting to bug telephones, the men were not initially linked to the White House. However, further investigation, led by Washington Post reporters Woodward and Bernstein, uncovered the extent of the President's involvement, including the possession of incriminating tapes and proven bribery. This led to an impeachment hearing, but before Nixon could be impeached, he resigned. Vice-President Gerald Ford succeeded him.

⑲ The Kennedy Center

In 1958, President Dwight D. Eisenhower signed an act to begin fund-raising for a national cultural center that would attract the world's best orchestras, opera, and dance companies to the US capital. President John F. Kennedy was an ardent supporter of the arts, taking the lead in fund-raising for it. He never saw the completion of the center, which was named in his honor. Designed by Edward Durrell Stone, it was opened on September 8, 1971 and houses several huge theaters; the Opera House, the Concert Hall, the Eisenhower Theater, and the Family Theater; on the roof are the Jazz Club, the Terrace Theater (closed for renovation until August 2017), and the Theater Lab.

Don Quixote Statue
This bronze and stone statue by Aurelio Teno was a gift to the center from Spain.

The Eisenhower Theater
This is one of the three main theaters. A bronze bust of President Eisenhower by Felix de Weldon hangs in the lobby.

Millennium Stage
The Millennium Stage provides free performances in the Grand Foyer every evening at 6pm.

KEY

① **East Roof Terrace**

② **The Hall of Nations** houses the flag of every country with which the US has diplomatic relations.

③ **The Concert Hall** is the largest auditorium, seating more than 2,400 people. It is the home of the National Symphony Orchestra.

The Hall of States
The flags of each of the 50 American states, the five US territories, and the District of Columbia hang here.

★ **The Opera House**
The Opera House seats over 2,300 people. The vast chandelier is made of Lobmeyr crystal and was a gift from Austria.

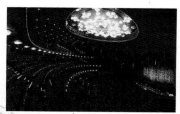

VISITORS' CHECKLIST

Practical Information
New Hampshire Ave & Rock Creek Parkway, NW. **Map** 2 D4.
Tel (202) 467-4600.
W kennedy-center.org
Open 10am–9pm daily; 10am–9pm Mon–Sat, noon–9pm Sun and hols (box office).
🎟 10am–5pm Mon–Fri, 10am–1pm Sat & Sun (call (202) 416-8340). 🚻 📷 ✏ 🍴

Transport
Ⓜ Foggy Bottom. 🚌 80.

★ **Bust of JFK**
Created by sculptor Robert Berks, this bronze bust stands in the Grand Foyer.

The JFK Terrace
This stretches the length of the Center and overlooks the Potomac and has glorious views up and down the river. Quotes by John F. Kennedy are engraved into the marble walls.

★ **The Grand Foyer**
This enormous room stretches 630 ft (192 m) and provides an impressive entrance into the Opera House, the Concert Hall, and the Eisenhower Theater.

GEORGETOWN

Georgetown developed well before Washington, DC. Native Americans had a settlement here, and in 1703 a land grant was given to Ninian Beall, who named the area the Rock of Dumbarton. By the mid-18th century immigrants from Scotland had swelled the population, and in 1751 the town was renamed George Town. It grew rapidly into a wealthy tobacco and flour port and finally, in 1789, the city of Georgetown was formed. The harbor and the Chesapeake and Ohio Canal were built in 1828, and the streets were lined with town houses. The birth of the railroad undercut Georgetown's economy, which by the mid-1800s was in decline. But by the 1950s the cobblestone streets and charming houses were attracting wealthy young couples, and restaurants and shops sprang up on Wisconsin Avenue and M Street. Today Georgetown retains its quiet distinction from the rest of the city, and is a pleasant area in which to stroll for a few hours *(see pp150–51)*.

Sights at a Glance

Historic Buildings
5 Old Stone House
7 Washington Post Office
9 Georgetown University
10 Tudor Place
13 Dumbarton Oaks

Streets, Canals, and Harbors
1 Washington Harbor
2 Wisconsin Avenue
4 Chesapeake and Ohio Canal
6 M Street
8 N Street

Churches and Cemeteries
3 Grace Church
11 Mt. Zion Church
12 Oak Hill Cemetery

Restaurants *see pp187–9*
1 1789
2 Bandolero
3 Booeymonger
4 Café Bonaparte
5 Café Divan
6 Café Milano
7 La Chaumiere
8 Chez Billy Sud
9 Clyde's
10 Das Ethiopian Cuisine
11 El Centro D.F.
12 Farmers Fishers Bakers
13 Filomena
14 Fiola Mare
15 Five Guys
16 Johnny Rockets
17 Kafe Leopold
18 Martin's Tavern
19 Le Pain Quotidien
20 Paolo's
21 Patisserie Poupon
22 Paul
23 Peacock Café
24 Pizzeria Paradiso
25 Sea Catch
26 Sequoia
27 ShopHouse Southeast Asian Kitchen
28 Sweetgreen
29 The Tombs
30 Tony and Joe's Seafood Café
31 Unum

See also Street Finder maps 1–2

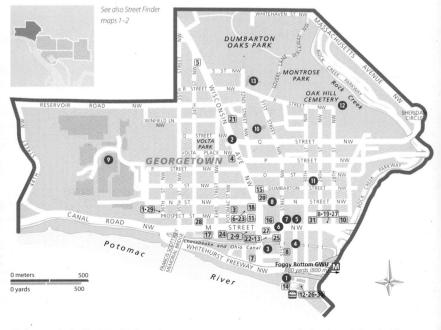

◀ Vine-covered walls of Dumbarton Oaks Summerhouse

For keys to symbols *see back flap*

Fountain at Washington Harbor

❶ Washington Harbor

3000-3020 K St, NW. **Map** 2 D3.

Washington is a city where few architectural risks have been taken. However, the approach used by architect Arthur Cotton Moore for Washington Harbor, which is a combination residential and commercial building on the Potomac River, is unusually audacious.

Moore's creation is a structure that hugs the waterfront and surrounds a semi-circular pedestrian plaza. The architect borrowed motifs from almost every type of design, such as turrets and flying buttresses. The harbor has a pleasant boardwalk, a huge fountain, and tall, columned lampposts. Under the ground are steel gates that can be raised to protect the building from floods. The top floors of the harbor are apartments. On the bottom floors are office complexes, restaurants, and shops. Sightseeing boats dock at the river's edge for trips to Mount Vernon and Alexandria. The spring of 2011 saw severe flooding to the harbor, which caused considerable damage. However, with new floodgates in place, Hurricane Sandy did not damage the waterfront in 2012.

❷ Wisconsin Avenue

Wisconsin Ave. **Map** 1 C2.
Ⓜ Foggy Bottom.

Wisconsin Avenue is one of two main business streets in Georgetown and is home to a wide variety of shops and restaurants. It is also one of the few streets in Washington that pre-dates L'Enfant's grid plan (see p21). It starts at the bank of the Potomac and runs north through Georgetown right to the city line, where it continues as Rockville Pike. On the

❹ The Chesapeake and Ohio Canal

When it was constructed in 1828, the C&O Canal featured an ingenious and revolutionary transportation system of locks, aqueducts, and tunnels that ran along its 184 miles (296 km) from Georgetown to Cumberland, Maryland. With the arrival of the railroad in the late 19th century, the canal fell out of use. It was only as a result of the efforts of Supreme Court Justice William Douglas that the Chesapeake and Ohio Canal was finally declared a protected national park in 1971. Today visitors come to enjoy its recreational facilities and also to study its fascinating transportation system. A 15-mile (20-km) walking and biking trail along the canal connects Georgetown with Great Falls Park (see p166).

Georgetown
The attractive federal houses of Georgetown line the banks of the canal for about 1.5 miles (2 km).

Great Falls
14 miles
←
CANAL ROAD NW
Williamsport
75 miles
Chesapeake and Ohio Canal

The Francis Scott Key Memorial Bridge was named after the the composer of the American national anthem, *The Star-Spangled Banner.*

Potomac

Canal Trips
The towpath trail runs north to Great Falls and historic Williamsport, where boat trips can be taken and costumed guides add colour to the waterside.

junction of Wisconsin Avenue and M Street is the landmark gold dome of PNC Bank (formerly the Riggs National Bank).

During the French and Indian Wars, George Washington marched his troops up the avenue on his way to Pittsburgh to engage the French.

The gold dome of PNC Bank

❸ Grace Church

1041 Wisconsin Ave, NW.
Map 1 C3. **Tel** (202) 333-7100.
Open call office in advance (office open 10am–6pm Mon, Tue, Fri).
W gracedc.org

Built in 1866, Grace Church was designed to serve the religious needs of the boatmen who worked on the Chesapeake and Ohio Canal and the sailors of the port of Georgetown. Set on a tree-filled plot south of the canal and M Street, the Gothic Revival church, with its quaint exterior, is an oasis in Georgetown.

The building has undergone few extensive alterations over the years and has a certain timeless quality. The church's multi-ethnic congregation makes great efforts to reach out to the larger DC community and

Sign for Grace Church

works with soup kitchens and shelters for the homeless. The church also sponsors the "Thank God It's Friday" lunchtime discussion group, and holds a poetry coffee house on the third Tuesday of the month. Classical concerts, including chamber pieces, organ, and piano works, are held here regularly. There is also a popular annual festival devoted to the music of the German composer J.S. Bach.

Rowing on the Canal
Boating is popular on the C&O and is best between Georgetown and Violette's Lock – the first 22 miles (35 km) of the canal.

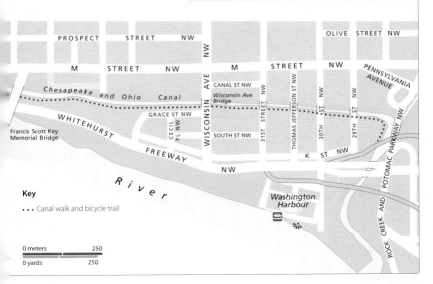

Key

• • • Canal walk and bicycle trail

0 meters 250
0 yards 250

For additional map symbols *see back flap*

🟡 Old Stone House

3051 M St, NW. **Map** 2 D2. **Tel** (202)
426-6851. **Open** noon–5pm daily.
🚌 30, 32, 34, 36, 38. 🎧 call (202)
895-6070. ♿ limited
🌐 nps.gov/olst

The Old Stone House may be
the only building in Washington
that pre-dates the American
Revolution. It was built in 1765
by Christopher Layman, and
the tiny two-story cottage has
a large garden, which is a
welcome respite from the
shops of busy M Street.
    There is a legend that still
persists about the Old Stone
House – that it was the Suter's
Tavern where Washington and
Pierre L'Enfant made their plans
for the city. However, most
historians today now believe
that they met in a tavern located
elsewhere in Georgetown.
    Over the years, the building
has housed a series of artisans,
and in the 1950s it even served
as offices for a used-car
dealership. In 1960 the National
Park Service restored it to its
pre-Revolutionary War appearance. Today park rangers give
talks (noon–5pm) about what
Georgetown would have been
like during the Colonial days.
The Old Stone House is
technically the oldest house in
DC, although The Lindens, which
is now in Kalorama, was built in
the mid-1750s in Massachusetts
and later moved to Washington.

The picturesque Old Stone House

🟡 M Street

M St, NW. **Map** 1 C2.
🚌 30, 32, 34, 36, 38.

One of two main shopping
streets in Georgetown, M Street
is also home to some of the
most historic spots in the city.
On the northeast corner of 30th
and M Streets, on the current
site of a bank, stood Union
Tavern. Built in 1796, the tavern
played host to, among others,
Presidents George Washington
and John Adams, Napoleon's
younger brother Jerome
Bonaparte, author Washington
Irving, and Francis Scott Key, the
composer of the "Star Spangled
Banner." During the Civil War, the
inn was turned into a temporary
hospital where Louisa May
Alcott, the author of *Little
Women,* nursed wounded
soldiers. In the 1930s the tavern
was torn down and replaced
by a gas station. Dr. William
Thornton, architect of the
US Capitol and Tudor Place
(see p128) lived at 3219 M Street.
    On the south side of M Street
is Market House, which has been
the location of Georgetown's
market since 1751. In 1796 a
wood frame market house was
constructed and later replaced
by the current brick market in

Only the two end houses in
this group of fine Federal homes
(numbers 3327–3339) are still in
their original state.

🟡 N Street

N St, NW. **Map** 1 C2. 🚌 30, 32, 34, 36.

N Street is a sampler of
18th-century American Federal
architecture – a style favored by
leaders of the new nation as
being of a more refined design
than the earlier Georgian houses.
    At the corner of 30th and
N Streets is the Laird-Dunlop
House. Today it is owned by
Sally Quinn, the widow of
Benjamin Bradlee, the former
editor of the *Washington Post.*

An excellent example of
a Federal house is the Riggs-
Riley House at 3038 N Street,
once owned by Averill and
Pamela Harriman. At 3041–3045
N Street is Wheatley Row. These
houses were designed to
provide not only maximum light
from large windows but also
maximum privacy as they were
placed above street level.

Known as Wheatley Row,
these three well-designed
Victorian town houses were
built in 1859.

1865. In the 1930s the market became an auto supply store, and in the 1990s the New York gourmet food store Dean and Deluca opened a branch here.

Today M Street is home to a collection of fashionable stores and restaurants. Young buyers shop for alternative music at Hill & Dale Records and alternative clothing at Urban Outfitters. National chainstores such as Banana Republic, Anthropologie, CB2, and Starbucks have branches along M Street. The fashionable Cady's Alley, at 3318 M Street, is a haven of trendy boutiques and high end furnishing stores.

Clyde's restaurant at number 3236 is a Georgetown institution, famous for its "happy hour."

The elegant façade of the Post Office in Georgetown

❼ Washington Post Office, Georgetown Branch

1215 31st St, NW. **Map** 2 D2. 🚌 30, 32, 34, 36. **Open** 9am–5pm Mon–Fri, 9am–2pm Sat.

Built in 1857 as a customhouse, the still-functioning Georgetown Branch of the Washington Post Office is interesting both historically and architecturally. A customhouse was a money-producing venture for the Federal government, and the US government's investment in such an expensive building provides evidence of Georgetown's importance as a viable port for many years. Architect Ammi B. Young, who was also responsible for the design of the Vermont State Capitol building in 1832 and the Boston Custom House in 1837, was called to Washington in 1852. He designed several other Italianate buildings in the capital, but this post office is his finest work. The granite customhouse was converted to a post office when Georgetown's fortunes declined.

The building underwent a renovation in 1997 that increased its accessibility but retained the integrity of Young's simple, functional design.

In 2013, the post office was sold. Today, the space is used for private offices. A small post office station still exists, but the architecturally interesting interior is not accessible to the public.

Attractive houses lining the bustling M Street

The Thomas Beall House (number 3017) was built in 1794 by one of Georgetown's most prominent families. It has since been occupied by the Secretary of War during World War I, and by Jackie Kennedy, who lived here for a year after the death of JFK.

Number 3025–3027, with its raised mansard roof, shows the influence of the French during this period.

The Laird-Dunlop House (number 3014) was built by John Laird who owned many of Georgetown's tobacco warehouses. Laird modeled his home on those in his native Edinburgh. It was subsequently owned by President Lincoln's son, Robert.

Unusual flat roof

❾ Georgetown University

37th St & O St, NW. **Map** 1 B2. **Tel** (202) 687-0100. **Open** varies, depending on university schedule. **W** georgetown.edu

Georgetown University was the first Catholic college to be established in America. Founded in 1789 by John Carroll, and affiliated with the Jesuit Order, the university now attracts students of all faiths from over 100 countries around the world.

The oldest building on the campus is the Old North Building, completed in 1872, but the most recognizable structure is the Healy Building, a Germanic design topped by a fanciful spiral. The university's most famous graduate is President Bill Clinton.

The Gothic-inspired Healy Building, Georgetown University

❿ Tudor Place

1644 31st St, NW. **Map** 1 C2. **Tel** (202) 965-0400. **Open** 10am–4pm Tue–Sat, noon–4pm Sun. **Closed** Jan, Easter Sunday, Memorial Day, Jul 4, Labor Day, Thanksgiving, Dec 24, 25. **W** tudorplace.org

The manor house and large gardens of this Georgetown estate, designed by William Thornton, offer a unique glimpse into a bygone era.

Martha Washington, the First Lady, gave $8,000 to her granddaughter, Martha Custis Peter, and her granddaughter's husband. With the money, they purchased eight acres and commissioned Thornton, the

Stone dog in the garden of Tudor Place

architect of the Capitol *(see pp52–3)*, to design a house. Generations of the Peters family lived here from 1805 to 1984. It is a mystery as to why this stuccoed, two-story Georgian structure with a "temple" porch is called Tudor Place, but it was perhaps illustrative of the family's English sympathies at the time.

The furniture, silver, china, and portraits provide a glimpse into American social and cultural history; some of the pieces on display come from Mount Vernon *(see pp162–3)*.

⓫ Mt. Zion Church

1334 29th St, NW. **Map** 2 D2. **Tel** (202) 234-0148. ⬆ 11am Sun.

This church is thought to have had the first black congregation in DC. The first church, at 27th and P Streets, was a "station" on the city's original Underground Railroad. It provided shelter for runaway slaves on their journey

Altar in Mt. Zion church

north to freedom. The present redbrick building was completed in 1884 after the first church burned down.

Mt. Zion Cemetery, the oldest black burial ground in Washington, is located a short distance away, in the middle of the 2500 block of Q Street.

⓬ Oak Hill Cemetery

3001 R St, NW. **Map** 2 D1. **Tel** (202) 337-2835. **Open** 9am–4:30pm Mon–Fri, 1–4pm Sun (weather permitting). **Closed** Federal hols. **W** oakhillcemeterydc.org

William Wilson Corcoran *(see p115)* bought the land and Congress then established Oak Hill Cemetery in 1849. Today, about 18,000 graves cover the 25-acre site, which is planted with huge oak trees.

Members of some of the city's most prominent families are buried here, their names featuring throughout the city's history, including Magruder, Thomas, Beall, and Marbury.

At the entrance to the cemetery is an Italianate gatehouse that is still used as the superintendent's lodge and office. Northeast of the gatehouse is the Spencer family monument, designed by Louis Comfort Tiffany. The granite low-relief of an angel is signed by Tiffany. Also notable is

The Founding of the United Nations

In 1944, a conference held at the Dumbarton Oaks estate laid the groundwork for establishing the United Nations. President Franklin Roosevelt and the British Prime Minister, Winston Churchill, wanted to create a "world government" that would supervise the peace at the end of World War II. Roosevelt proposed that a conference be held in Washington, but at the time the State Department did not have a room big enough to accommodate all the delegates. As a solution, Robert Woods Bliss offered the use of the music room in his former home, Dumbarton Oaks, for the event.

The structure of the United Nations was settled at the Dumbarton Oaks Conference and then refined at the San Francisco Conference a year later when the United Nations' charter was ratified. The UN Headquarters building, the permanent home of the organization, was built in New York on the East River site after John D. Rockefeller donated $8.5 million toward its construction.

The conference members in the music room of Dumbarton Oaks

the Gothic chapel designed by James Renwick. Nearby is the grave of John Howard Payne, composer of "Home, Sweet Home," who died in 1852. The bust that tops Payne's monument was originally sculpted with a full beard, but Corcoran requested a stonemason to "shave the statue" and so now it is clean shaven.

⓫ Dumbarton Oaks

1703 32nd St, NW. **Map** 2 D2. **Tel** (202) 339-6401 (call ahead to check times). **Open** House: 2–5pm Tue–Sun. Gardens: 2–6pm Tue–Sun (to 5pm Nov–Feb). **Closed** Federal hols. 🎫 gardens only. 📷 for groups call (202) 339-6409. ♿ 🚻 house only. 🌐 **doaks.org**

In 1703, a Scottish colonist named Ninian Beall was granted around 800 acres of land in this area. In later years the land was sold off and in 1801, 22 acres were bought by Senator William Dorsey of Maryland, who proceeded to build a Federal-style brick home here. A year later, financial difficulties caused him to sell it, and over the next century the property changed hands many times.

By the time pharmaceutical heirs Robert and Mildred Woods Bliss bought the run-down estate in 1920, it was overgrown and neglected. The Blisses altered and expanded the house, with the architectural

advice of the prestigious firm McKim, Mead and White (see p111), to meet 20th-century family needs. They engaged their friend, Beatrix Jones Farrand, one of the few female landscape architects at the time, to lay out the grounds. Farrand designed a series of terraces that progress from the formal gardens near the house to the more informal landscapes farther away from it.

Fountain in Dumbarton Oaks

In 1940 the Blisses moved to California and donated the whole estate to Harvard University. It was then converted into a library, research institution, and museum. Many of the 1,400 pieces of Byzantine Art on display were collected by the

Blisses themselves. Examples of Greco-Roman coins, late Roman and early Byzantine bas-reliefs, Egyptian fabrics, and Roman glass and bronzeware are just some of the highlights. In 1962 Robert Woods Bliss donated his collection of pre-Columbian art. In order to house it, architect Philip Johnson designed a new wing, consisting of eight domes surrounding a circular garden. Although markedly different from the original house, a separate wing is well suited to the dramatic art collection it houses, which includes masks, stunning gold jewelry from Central America, and Aztec carvings.

Swimming pool in the grounds of Dumbarton Oaks

FARTHER AFIELD

North of the White House is Dupont Circle, a neighborhood of museums, galleries, and restaurants. The Embassy Row, Kalorama, Adams-Morgan, and Cleveland Park neighborhoods are a walker's paradise, especially for visitors interested in architecture. Arlington, Virginia, across the Potomac River, was one of DC's first suburbs. Arlington National Cemetery was founded in 1864 to honor those who died for the Union. The Pentagon was built 80 years later by Franklin D. Roosevelt and is the area's most famous landmark.

Sights at a Glance

Museums and Galleries

7 African American Civil War Memorial and Museum
10 National Geographic Museum
11 The Phillips Collection
12 14th and U Street NW
17 Mary McLeod Bethune Council House
18 Hillwood Estate Museum
29 Anacostia Museum

Historic Districts, Streets, and Buildings

2 The Pentagon
4 Southwest Waterfront
6 Heurich Mansion
9 Dupont Circle
13 Woodrow Wilson House
14 Embassy Row
15 Kalorama
16 Adams-Morgan
19 Lincoln Theatre

21 *Washington National Cathedral pp144–5*
27 Howard University
28 Frederick Douglass House

Monuments

3 Air Force Memorial
8 Iwo Jima Statue
24 Basilica of the National Shrine of the Immaculate Conception

Parks and Gardens

5 Theodore Roosevelt Island
20 *National Zoological Park pp140–41*
22 Cleveland Park
23 Rock Creek Park
25 National Arboretum
26 Kenilworth Park and Aquatic Gardens

Cemetery

1 *Arlington National Cemetery pp132–3*

Key

- Central Washington
- Greater Washington
- Metro line
- Freeway (motorway)
- Major road
- Minor road
- State Border

0 kilometers   2.5
0 miles   2.5

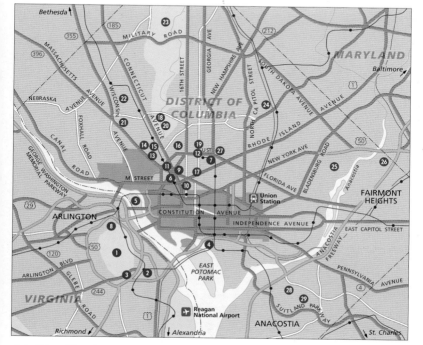

◀ Amphitheater, Arlington National Cemetery

For additional map symbols *see back flap*

❶ Arlington National Cemetery

For 30 years, Confederate General Robert E. Lee (1807–70) lived at Arlington House. In 1861 he left his home to lead Virginia's armed forces, and the Union confiscated the estate for a military cemetery. By the end of the Civil War in 1865, 16,000 soldiers were interred in the consecrated Arlington National Cemetery. Since then, around another 400,000 veterans have joined them. Simple headstones mark the graves of soldiers who died in every major conflict from the Revolution to the present. The focus of the cemetery is the Tomb of the Unknowns, which honors the thousands of unidentified soldiers who have died in battle.

Confederate Memorial
This bronze and granite monument honors the Confederate soldiers who died in the Civil War. It was dedicated in 1914.

Sea of Graves
More than 330,000 service members and their families are buried on the 624 acres of Arlington Cemetery.

0 meters   200
0 yards   200

★ Tomb of the Unknowns
This tomb contains four vaults – for World War I and II, Vietnam, and Korea. Each vault held one unidentified soldier until the Vietnam soldier was identified by DNA analysis and reburied in his home town.

Memorial Amphitheater
This marble amphitheater is the setting of the annual services on Memorial Day (see p38) when the nation's leaders pay tribute to the dead who served their country. It has also hosted many military ceremonies.

★ Arlington House
Once home to Robert E. Lee, this Georgian-Revival house is now a memorial to the general and his family. It is possible to tour the house during cemetery visiting hours.

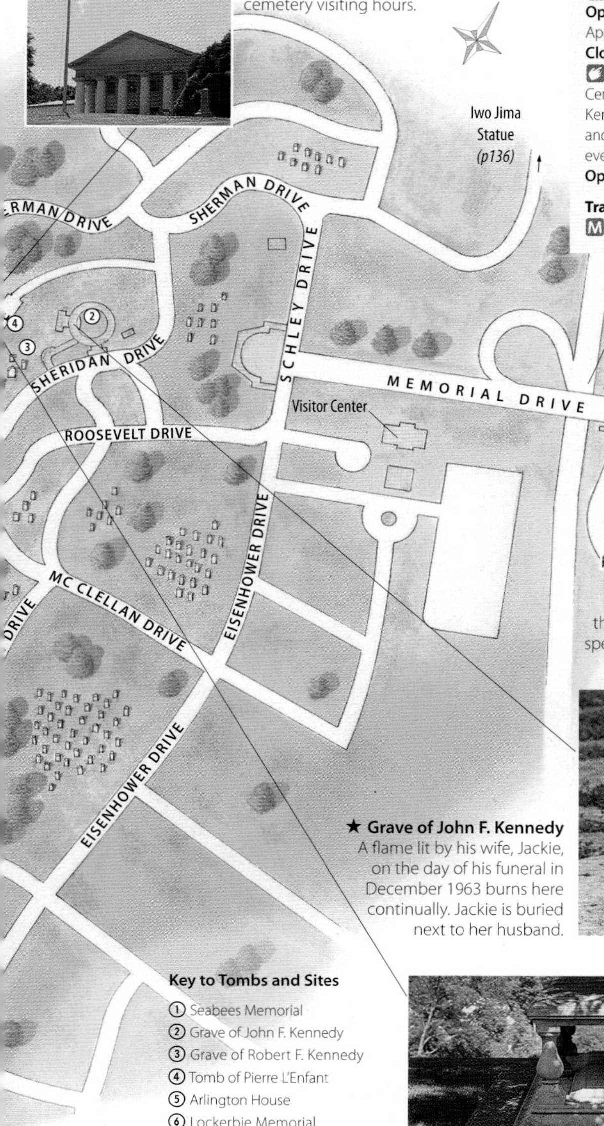

Iwo Jima Statue (p136)

(p136)

VISITORS' CHECKLIST

Practical Information
Arlington, VA. **Tel** 877-907-8585.
W arlingtoncemetery.org;
W anctours.com
Open Oct–Mar: 8am– 5pm daily;
Apr–Sep: 8am–7pm daily.
Closed Dec 25.
ANC Tours leaves the Visitor Center and stops at the John F. Kennedy grave, Arlington House, and Tomb of the Unknowns every 15–30 mins.
Open 8:30am–4:30pm.

Transport
M Arlington National Cemetery.

Main Entrance

MEMORIAL DRIVE

Visitor Center

SHERMAN DRIVE

SHERMAN DRIVE

SCHLEY DRIVE

SHERIDAN DRIVE

ROOSEVELT DRIVE

EISENHOWER DRIVE

MC CLELLAN DRIVE

EISENHOWER DRIVE

Seabees Memorial
This memorial is dedicated to the section of the US Navy that specializes in construction work.

★ Grave of John F. Kennedy
A flame lit by his wife, Jackie, on the day of his funeral in December 1963 burns here continually. Jackie is buried next to her husband.

Key to Tombs and Sites

① Seabees Memorial
② Grave of John F. Kennedy
③ Grave of Robert F. Kennedy
④ Tomb of Pierre L'Enfant
⑤ Arlington House
⑥ Lockerbie Memorial
⑦ Confederate Memorial
⑧ Rough Riders Memorial
⑨ Challenger and Columbia Shuttle Memorials
⑩ Memorial Amphitheater
⑪ Tomb of the Unknowns

Tomb of Pierre L'Enfant
The architect responsible for planning the city of Washington has a suitably grand burial site in the cemetery *(see p69)*.

The Pentagon building's formidable concrete façade

❶ The Pentagon

1000 Defense Pentagon, Hwy 1-395, Arlington, VA. **Tel** (703) 697-1776. Ⓜ Pentagon. Tours by appointment for US citizens only – book online. Ⓦ **pentagon.afis.osd.mil**

President Franklin Roosevelt decided in the early 1940s to consolidate the 17 buildings that comprised the Department of War (the original name for the Department of Defense) into one building. Designed by army engineers, and built of gravel dredged from the Potomac River and molded into concrete, the Pentagon was started on September 11, 1941 and completed on January 15, 1943, at a cost of $83 million. As the world's largest office building, it is almost a city in itself. Yet despite its size, the Pentagon's unique five-sided design is very efficient, and it takes only seven minutes to walk between any two points.

The Pentagon is the headquarters of the Department of Defense, a Cabinet-level organization consisting of three military departments, the Army, Navy, and Air Force, as well as 14 defense agencies. Leading personnel are the Secretary of Defense and the Chairman of the Joint Chiefs of Staff.

On September 11, 2001, the building was damaged in a terrorist attack. A memorial to the 184 people who died in the Pentagon and on Flight 77 was dedicated on September 11, 2008.

❷ Air Force Memorial

Off Columbia Pike. **Tel** (703) 979-0674. Ⓜ Pentagon City & Pentagon. **Open** Apr–Oct: 8am–11pm daily; Nov–Mar: 8am–9pm daily. 🎦 by appt. Ⓦ **airforcememorial.org**

Located on a promontory overlooking the Pentagon, this memorial honors the service and sacrifices of the men and women of the United States Air Force and its predecessor organizations. Central to the bold, graceful design, intended to evoke flight, are three stainless steel spires which soar skyward, the highest reaching 270 ft (82 m). President George W. Bush accepted the Memorial on behalf of the American people in October 2006.

The elegant Air Force Memorial

❸ Southwest Waterfront

Ⓜ Waterfront. Fish Market: **Open** 7:30am–8pm daily. Ⓦ **swdcwaterfront.com**

In the 1960s, urban planners tested their new architectural theories on Washington's southwest waterfront along the Potomac River. Old neighborhoods were torn down, and apartment high-rises put up in their place. Eventually new restaurants developed along the waterfront, and Arena Stage, a regional theater company, built an experimental theater here. The area enjoyed a regeneration, and today is a popular place to eat or just take a stroll, particularly during summer.

A stall at the waterfront's fish market

The fish market here is the oldest in the country. A remnant of the old waterfront culture, it is located off Maine Avenue. Today it is still a thriving business, drawing customers from all over Washington and enjoying its reputation as one of the most vibrant spots in the area. Lobster, crabs, oysters, and all kinds of fresh fish are sold from barges on the river. There are also several good restaurants along the waterfront that specialize in freshly caught local fish and seafood.

The waterfront is currently undergoing a massive renovation that will transform the walkway along the river.

September 11

On September 11, 2001, one of four airplanes hijacked by terrorists was flown into the Pentagon, resulting in huge loss of life and causing the side of the building to collapse. Crews at the Pentagon

worked tirelessly to rebuild the damaged 10 percent of the building (400,000 to 500,000 square feet). It was estimated that repairs would take three years to finish but they were completed in less than a year. The west wall has a dedication capsule and a single charred capstone. A memorial has been erected.

The Pentagon Memorial commemorating the victims of 9/11

when it relocated to the City Museum in the Carnegie Library Building *(see p98)*. The Heurich Mansion is a fine example of an upper-middle-class family house in Washington in the late 1800s.

The ornate carving in Heurich's Beer Hall

❺ Theodore Roosevelt Island

GW Memorial Pkwy, McLean, VA.
Map 1 C4. **Tel** (703) 289-2500.
Ⓜ Rosslyn. **Open** 6am–10pm daily.
☑ by appt only. ☑ nps.gov/this

A haven for naturalists, Theodore Roosevelt Island's 91 acres (37 ha) of marshlands and 2 miles (4 km) of nature trails are home to a variety of wildlife including red-tailed hawks, great owls, groundhogs, and wood ducks, as well as many species of trees and plants. President Theodore Roosevelt (1858–1919), a great naturalist himself, is honored with a 17 ft (5 m) tall memorial in bronze, and four granite tablets, each inscribed with quotes by the president.

The island is just one of several sites that form part of the George Washington Memorial Parkway. Enjoy a quiet stroll or visit one of the parkway's other historical sites. Remember to

carry drinking water, especially during the summer months.

There is a carpark on the George Washington Memorial Parkway (northbound) from where you can access the footbridge leading to the island. Bicycles are not permitted on the island.

❻ Heurich Mansion

1307 New Hampshire Ave, NW.
Tel (202) 429-1894. Ⓜ Dupont Circle.
☑ 10:30am, 1pm & 1:30pm Thu–Sat.
Closed Federal hols. 🎫 donation.
♿ ☑ heurichhouse.org

Brewer Christian Heurich built this wonderful Bavarian fantasy for his family just south of Dupont Circle in 1894. The turreted mansion built in the Romanesque Revival architectural style was home to the Historical Society of Washington, DC until 2003,

❼ African American Civil War Memorial and Museum

Museum: 1925 Vermont Ave,
NW. Memorial: 10th St and
Vermont Ave, NW. **Tel** (202) 667-
2667. Ⓜ U Street. **Open** 10am–
6:30pm Tue–Fri, 10am–4pm Sat
(call for tours), noon–4pm Sun.
☑ afroamcivilwar.org

Opened in January 1999, the African American Museum uses photographs, documents, and audiovisual equipment to explain the still largely unknown story of African Americans' long struggle for freedom. The Museum's permanent exhibition is entitled "Slavery to Freedom; Civil War to Civil Rights." Interactive kiosks bring together historic documents, photographs, and music in a powerful and evocative way. There is also a service for anyone interested in tracing relatives who may have served with United States Colored Troops during the Civil War. At the center of a paved plaza is situated the "Spirit of Freedom," a sculpture by Ed Hamilton, which was unveiled on July 18, 1998. It is the first major art piece by a black sculptor on federal land in the District of Columbia. It stands 10 ft (3 m) tall and features uniformed black soldiers and a sailor poised to leave home.

Statue of President Roosevelt and granite tablets on Theodore Roosevelt Island

The elaborate fountain at the heart of the Dupont Circle intersection

❽ Iwo Jima Statue (US Marine Corps Memorial)

Meade St, between Arlington National Cemetery & Arlington Blvd. **Map** 1 B5. Ⓜ Rosslyn. ♿

The horrific battle of Iwo Jima that took place during World War II was captured by photographer Joe Rosenthal. His Pulitzer Prize-winning picture of five Marines and a Navy Corpsman raising the American flag on the tiny Pacific island came to symbolize in the American psyche the heroic struggle of the American forces in the war against Japan.

This image was magnificently translated into bronze by sculptor Felix DeWeldon and paid for by private donations. The three surviving soldiers from Rosenthal's photograph actually posed for DeWeldon; the other three men, however, had been killed in further fighting on the islands. The Iwo Jima Memorial is dedicated to all members of the Marine Corps who have died defending their country.

A poignant memorial to the men who died in the battle of Iwo Jima

❾ Dupont Circle

Map 2 F2 & 3 A1. Ⓜ Dupont Circle.

This area to the north of the White House gets its name from the fountain and is at the intersection of Massachusetts, Connecticut, and New Hampshire Avenues, and 19th Street, NW. At the heart of this traffic island is the Francis Dupont Memorial Fountain, named for the first naval hero of the Civil War, Admiral Samuel Francis Dupont. Built by his family, the original memorial was a bronze statue that was moved eventually to Wilmington, Delaware. The present marble fountain, which was constructed in 1921, has four figures (which represent the sea, the wind, the stars,

Playing chess in Dupont Circle

and the navigational arts) supporting a marble basin.

The park area around the fountain draws a cross section of the community – chess players engrossed in their games, cyclists pausing at the fountain, picnickers, and tourists taking a break from sightseeing. Do not stray into the Circle after dark as it may not be safe at night.

In the early 20th century the Dupont Circle area was a place of grand mansions. Its fortunes then declined until the 1970s, when Washingtonians began to buy the decaying mansions. The district is now filled with art galleries, bars, restaurants, and bookstores. The old Victorian buildings have been divided into apartments, restored as single family homes, or converted into small office buildings. Dupont Circle is also the center of Washington's gay community. The bars and clubs on the section of P Street between Dupont Circle and Rock Creek Park are the most popular area for gay men and women to meet.

❿ National Geographic Museum

1145 17th St at M St, NW. **Map** 3 B2. **Tel** (202) 857-7700. Ⓜ Farragut North, Farragut West. **Open** 10am–6pm daily. **Closed** Dec 25. ♿ 📷 🌐 nationalgeographic.com/museum

This small museum is located in the National Geographic Society's headquarters, designed by Edward Durrell Stone, the architect behind the Kennedy Center. A series of permanent and temporary exhibitions documents the richness of nature and the diversity of human culture all over the world. Past exhibitions include the "Terra-Cotta Warriors" and an exploration of the Golden Age of the pharaohs.

Auguste Renoir's masterpiece, *The Luncheon of the Boating Party* (1881)

❶ The Phillips Collection

1600 21st St at Q St, NW. **Map** 2 E2 & 3 A1. **Tel** (202) 387-2151. **Ⓜ** Dupont Circle. **Open** 10am–5pm Tue–Sat (to 8:30pm Thu), 11am–6pm Sun. **Closed** Jan 1, Jul 4, Thanksgiving, Dec 25, Federal hols. 🅿️ 📷 11am Fri & Sat. ♿ 💻 📷
Ⓦ phillipscollection.org

This is one of the finest collections of Impressionist works in the world and the first museum devoted to modern art in the United States. Duncan and Marjorie Phillips, who founded the collection, lived in the older of the museum's two adjacent buildings. Following the death of his father and brother in 1917, Duncan Phillips decided to open two of the mansion's rooms as The Phillips Memorial Gallery.

Collector Duncan Phillips (1886–1966)

The couple spent their time traveling and adding to their already extensive collection. During the 1920s they acquired some of the most important modern European paintings, including *The Luncheon of the Boating Party* (1881) by Renoir, for which they paid $125,000 (one of the highest prices ever paid at the time).

In 1930 the Phillips family moved to a new home on Foxhall Road in northwest Washington and converted the rest of their former 1897 Georgian-Revival residence into a private gallery. The Phillips Gallery was then reopened to the public in 1960 and renamed The Phillips Collection. The museum currently has over 3,000 pieces of 19th-, 20th-, and 21st-century American and European art.

The elegant Georgian-Revival building that was the Phillips' home makes for a more intimate and personal gallery than the big Smithsonian art museums. The Phillips Collection is best known for its wonderful selection of Impressionist and Post-Impressionist paintings; *Dancers at the Barre* by Degas, *Self-Portrait* by Cézanne and *Entrance to the Public Gardens in Arles* by Van Gogh are just three examples. The museum also has one of the largest collections in the world of pieces by French artist Pierre Bonnard, including *The Open Window* (1921).

Other great paintings to be seen in the collection include El Greco's *The Repentant Saint Peter* (1600), *The Blue Room* (1901) by Pablo Picasso, and the huge *Ochre and Red on Red* (1954) by Mark Rothko. In addition to the permanent exhibits, the museum supports traveling exhibitions, which start at The Phillips Collection before appearing in galleries around the country. The exhibitions often feature one artist (such as Georgia O'Keeffe) or one particular topic or period (such as the *Twentieth-Century Still-Life Paintings* exhibition).

The Phillips Collection encourages enthusiasts of modern art to visit the museum for a number of special events. On the first Thursday of each month the museum hosts "Phillips after 5." These evenings include gallery talks, live music, and light refreshments, and give people the opportunity to discuss the issues of the art world in a relaxed, social atmosphere. On Sunday afternoons from September through May, a series of concerts are staged in the gallery's Music Room. Running since 1941, these popular concerts are free to anyone who has purchased a ticket to the museum on that day. They range from piano recitals and string quartets to performances by established singers of world renown, such as the famous operatic soprano Jessye Norman.

The museum shop sells merchandise linked to permanent and temporary exhibitions. Books, posters, and prints can be found as well as ceramics, glassware, and other creations by contemporary artists. There are also hand-painted silks and artworks based on the major paintings in the collection.

Entrance to the Public Gardens in Arles (1888), by Vincent Van Gogh

The Lincoln Theater, a late-night entertainment venue on U Street

⓬ 14th and U Street NW

Intersection of 14th and U Street NW. Ⓜ U Street-Cardozo.

The intersection of 14th Street and U Street NW is one of Washington's most vibrant neighborhoods. Until the middle of the 20th century, U Street, once known as Black Broadway, hosted many prominent African American entertainers, including Duke Ellington and Pearl Bailey. They performed at the Lincoln Theater and the Howard Theater as well as in many nightclubs.

Known as Automobile Row, 14th Street was lined with posh car showrooms that displayed expensive wares. But after the assassination of Dr. Martin Luther King in 1968 both 14th Street and U Street burned in the ensuing riots. Businesses fled the area and for decades it was left to drug trafficking and crime. In 1997 the well-respected local company Studio Theatre bought a derelict car showroom and construc-ted a state-of-the-art performance space. Restaurants, high-end apartments, music venues, and bars followed. Today, U and 14th is a thriving corridor for late night entertainment. Of note is the famous Ben's Chili Bowl (1213 U Street NW), a landmark restaurant established in 1958.

⓭ Woodrow Wilson House

2340 S St, NW. **Map** 2 E1. **Tel** (202) 387-4062. Ⓜ Dupont Circle. **Open** 10am–4pm Tue–Sun. **Closed** Federal hols. 🐾 📷 ♿ Ⓦ woodrowwilsonhouse.org

Located in the Kalorama neighborhood, the former home of Woodrow Wilson (1856–1924), who served as president from 1913 to 1921, is the only presidential museum within the District of Columbia.

Wilson led the US through World War I and advocated the formation of the League of Nations, the precursor to the United Nations. Although exhausted by the war effort, Wilson campaigned tirelessly for the League.

In 1919 he collapsed from a stroke and became an invalid for the rest of his life. Many believe that Wilson's second wife, Edith Galt, assumed many of the presidential duties herself (she guided his hand when he signed documents). Unable to leave his sickbed, Wilson saw his dream, the League of Nations, defeated in the Senate. In 1920 he was awarded the Nobel Peace Prize – small consolation for the failure of the League.

Wilson and his wife moved to this town house, designed by Waddy B. Wood, at the end of his

Statue of Churchill, British Embassy

second term in 1921. Edith Galt Wilson arranged for the home to be bequeathed to the nation. Since then the building has been maintained as it was during the President's lifetime, containing artifacts from his life, such as his Rolls-Royce, and reflecting the style of an upper-middle-class home of the 1920s. The house today belongs to the National Trust for Historic Preservation.

⓮ Embassy Row

Massachusetts Avenue. **Map** 2 D1–F2. Ⓜ Dupont Circle. *See also pp148–9.*

Embassy Row stretches along Massachusetts Avenue from Scott Circle toward Observatory Circle. It developed during the Depression when many of Washington's wealthy families were forced to sell their mansions to diplomats, who bought them for foreign missions. Since then, many new embassies have been built, often in the vernacular style of their native country, making Embassy Row architecturally fascinating.

At No. 2315 Massachusetts Avenue, the Embassy of Pakistan is an opulent mansion built in 1908, with a mansard roof (four steep sloping sides) and a rounded wall that hugs the corner.

Farther down the road, at No. 2349, is the Embassy of

An elaborately decorated room in the Georgian Revival Woodrow Wilson House

the Republic of Cameroon, one of the Avenue's great early 20th-century Beaux Arts masterpieces. This romantic, Norwegian chateau-style building was commissioned in 1905 to be the home of Christian Hauge, first Norwegian ambassador to the United States, before passing to Cameroon.

Situated opposite the Irish Embassy stands a bronze statue of the hanged Irish revolutionary Robert Emmet (1778–1803). The statue was commissioned by Irish Americans to commemorate Irish independence.

At No. 2536 is the India Supply Mission. Two carved elephants stand outside as symbols of Indian culture and mythology. In the park in front of the Indian Embassy is an impressive bronze sculpture of Mahatma Gandhi.

The British Embassy, at No. 3100, was designed by Sir Edwin Lutyens in 1928. The English-style gardens were planted by the American wife of the then British ambassador, Sir Ronald Lindsay. Outside the embassy is an arresting statue of Sir Winston Churchill by William M. McVey.

Façade of the Croatian Embassy on Massachusetts Avenue

⓯ Kalorama

Map 2 D1 & 2 E1.
Ⓜ Woodley Park or Dupont Circle.

The neighborhood of Kalorama, situated north of Dupont Circle, is an area of stately private homes and elegant apartment buildings. From its development at the turn of the 20th century as a suburb close to the city center, Kalorama (Greek for "beautiful view") has been home to the wealthy and upwardly mobile. Five presidents had homes here: Herbert Hoover,

The apartments at 2311 Connecticut Avenue, Kalorama

Franklin D. Roosevelt, Warren Harding, William Taft, and Woodrow Wilson. Only Wilson's home served as his permanent post-presidential residence.

Some of the most striking and ornate apartment buildings in Washington are found on Connecticut Avenue, south of the Taft Bridge that crosses Rock Creek Park. Most notable are the Georgian Revival-style Dresden apartments at No. 2126, the Beaux Arts-inspired Highlands building at number 1914, and the Spanish Colonial-style Woodward apartments at No. 2311 Connecticut Avenue. Also worth viewing is the Tudor-style building at No. 2221 Kalorama Road.

The best views of nearby Rock Creek Park (see p143) are from Kalorama Circle at the northern end of 24th Street.

⓰ Adams-Morgan

North of Dupont Circle, east of Rock Creek Park, and south of Mt. Pleasant. **Map** 2 E1 & 2 F1. Ⓜ Dupont Circle or Woodley Park-Zoo/Adams Morgan.

Adams-Morgan was one of the first racially and ethnically diverse neighborhoods in the city. It was given its name in the 1950s when the Supreme Court ruled that Washington must desegregate its educational system, and forced the combination of two schools in the area – Adams (for white children) and Morgan (an all-black school). Packed with

cafés, bookstores, clubs, and galleries, the district is a vibrant and eclectic mix of African, Hispanic, and Caribbean immigrants, as well as white urban pioneers, both gay and straight. People are attracted by the neighborhood's lively streets and its beautiful, and relatively affordable, early 20th-century houses and apartments.

The area has a thriving music scene and, on any night, rap, reggae, salsa, and Washington's indigenous go-go can be heard in the clubs and bars. The cosmopolitan feel of Adams-Morgan is reflected in its wide variety of restaurants (see pp189–90). Cajun, New Orleans, Ethiopian, French, Italian, Caribbean, Mexican, and Lebanese food can all be found along 18th Street and Columbia Road, the two main streets. Although the area is becoming increasingly modern and trendy, its 1950s Hispanic roots are still evident.

The area's cultural diversity is celebrated in September each year with food, music, and dance at the Adams-Morgan Day Festival (see p40).

It should be noted that this area can be dangerous after dark, so be wary if you are walking around at night. Parking, especially on weekends, can be difficult so allow plenty of time if you are traveling by car.

Colorful mural on the wall of a parking lot in Adams-Morgan

⑳ National Zoological Park

Established in 1889 as the Smithsonian's Department of Living Animals and sited on the Mall, Washington's National Zoo moved to its present location in 1891. The park, which covers 163 acres, was designed by Frederick Law Olmsted, the landscape architect responsible for New York's Central Park. Today, the zoo is home to more than 2,000 animals, many of which are endangered. The zoo also runs a number of breeding programs, one of the most successful of which is the Sumatran tiger program.

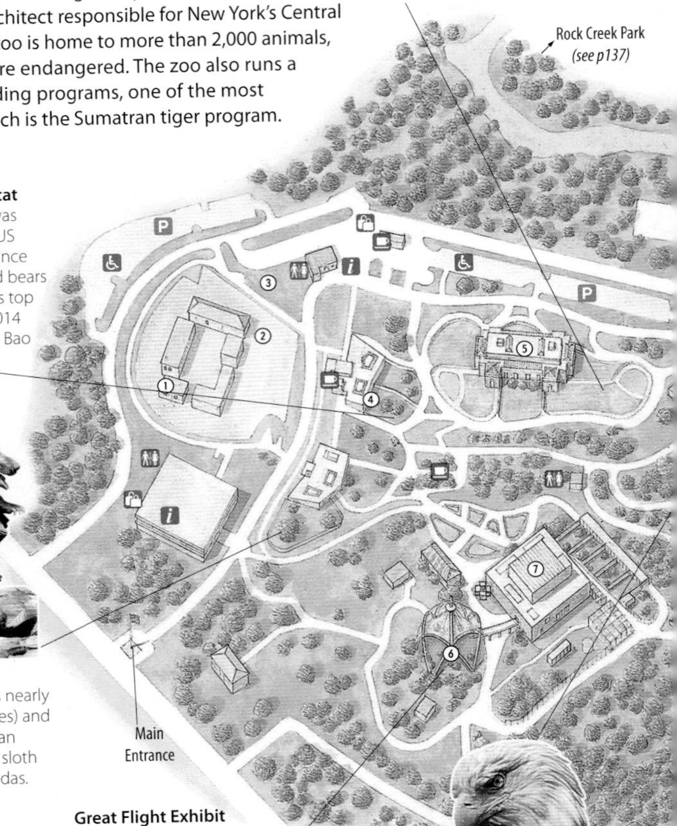

Elephant Trails
This exhibit gives an innovative home with diverse habitats to a small herd of Asian elephants, and is part of a campaign to save this endangered species.

Rock Creek Park
(see p137)

Giant Panda Habitat
The National Zoo was the first zoo in the US to house pandas. Since 1972 these beloved bears have been the zoo's top attraction and in 2014 a new baby panda, Bao Bao, was born.

★ **Asia Trail**
This exhibit covers nearly 6 acres (2.4 hectares) and features seven Asian species, including sloth bears and red pandas.

Main Entrance

Great Flight Exhibit
Endangered species such as the Guam rail and Bali Mynah can be seen here.

Bald Eagle
The only eagle unique to North America, the bald eagle is named for its white head, which appears to be "bald" against its dark body.

Key to Animal Enclosures

① Cheetah Conservation Station
② Zebras
③ Wallabies
④ Giant Panda Habitat
⑤ Elephants
⑥ Great Flight Exhibit
⑦ Bird House
⑧ Golden Lion Tamarins
⑨ American Trail
⑩ Bald Eagles
⑪ Seals and Sea Lions
⑫ Andean Bears
⑬ Amazonia
⑭ Gibbon Ridge
⑮ Great Ape House
⑯ Small Mammal House
⑰ Reptile Discovery Center
⑱ Lemur Island
⑲ Think Tank
⑳ Sumatran Tigers
㉑ Great Cats
㉒ Kids Farm

0 meters   100
0 yards   100

Golden Lion Tamarins
These endangered mammals are protected by an international conservation program, which includes breeding and conservation education.

VISITORS' CHECKLIST

Practical Information
3001 Connecticut Ave, NW.
Tel (202) 673-4800.
Open Apr–Oct: 10am–6pm daily (buildings), 6am–8pm daily (grounds); Nov–Apr: 10am–4:30pm daily (buildings), 6am–6pm daily (grounds).
Closed Dec 25.
call (202) 633-4888.
 nationalzoo.si.edu

Transport
Ⓜ Cleveland Park, Woodley Park-Zoo.

★ Great Ape House
Western Lowland Gorillas – whose males can weigh over 400 pounds (180 kg) – can be seen in the Great Ape House. Other occupants include tree-dwelling orangutans.

★ Komodo Dragons
These rare lizards can grow up to 10 ft (3 m) in length, and weigh up to 200 lbs (90 kg). They are the first to be born in captivity outside Indonesia.

Sumatran Tigers
Native to the Indonesian island of Sumatra, these are the smallest of all surviving tiger subspecies and are excellent swimmers.

Amazonia
This exhibit re-creates the Amazonian habitat. Visitors can see many creatures from poison-dart frogs to giant catfish.

⓱ Mary McLeod Bethune Council House National Historic Site

1318 Vermont Ave, NW. **Map** 3 B1.
Tel (202) 673-2402. Ⓜ McPherson
Square/U Street. **Open** 9am–5pm
Mon–Sat. **Closed** Jan 1, Thanksgiving,
Dec 25. ⓖ plus interactive tour for
children. ⓐ Ⓦ **nps.gov/mamc**

Born in 1875 to two former-
slaves, Mary McLeod Bethune
was an educator and civil and
women's rights activist. In
1904 she founded a college for
impoverished black women in
Florida, the Daytona
Educational and Industrial
School for Negro Girls.
Renamed the Bethune-
Cookman College, it is
still going strong.

In the 1930s,
President Franklin D.
Roosevelt asked her
to be his special
advisor on racial affairs,
and she later became
director of the Division
of Negro Affairs in the
National Youth
Administration. As part
of Roosevelt's cabinet, Bethune
was the first black woman to
obtain a high position in the
US government.

Bethune went on to found
the National Council of Negro
Women, which gives voice to
the concerns of black women.
The Council grew to have a
membership of 10,000, and this

Mary McLeod
Bethune

house on Vermont Avenue was
bought by Bethune and the
Council as its headquarters.

It was not until November
1979, 24 years after
Bethune's death, that
the original Council
House was opened
to the public, with
photographs, manu-
scripts, and other
artifacts from her life on
display. In 1982 the house
was declared a National
Historic Site and was
bought by the National
Park Service.

⓲ Hillwood Estate Museum and Gardens

4155 Linnean Ave, NW. **Tel** (202)
686-5807. Ⓜ Van Ness/ UDC.
Open 10am–5pm Tue–Sun.
Closed Jan, Federal hols. ⓖ ⓕ
ⓐ ⓔ Ⓦ **hillwoodmuseum.org**

Hillwood was owned by
Marjorie Merriweather Post,
and opened to the public in
1977. The Museum contains
the most comprehensive
collection of 18th- and 19th-
century Russian imperial art
to be found outside of Russia,
including Fabergé eggs and
Russian Orthodox icons. It
also has some renowned
pieces of 18th-century French
decorative art. The Gardens
are set within a 25 acre (10 ha)
estate, surrounded by woodlands in the heart of Washington,
and have important collections
of azaleas and orchids.

The stunning interior of the restored Lincoln Theatre

⓳ Lincoln Theatre

1215 U St, NW. **Map** 2 F1.
Tel (202) 888-0050. Ⓜ U Street-
Cardozo. **Open** 10am–6pm Mon–Fri.
Closed Federal hols. ⓖ groups by
appt. ⓐ Ⓦ **thelincolndc.com**

Built in 1922, the Lincoln Theatre
was once the centerpiece of
cultural life for Washington's
downtown African American
community. Like the Apollo
Theater in New York, the
Lincoln presented big-name
entertainment, such as jazz
singer and native Washingtonian
Duke Ellington, Ella Fitzgerald,
and Billie Holiday.

By the 1960s the area around
the theater began to deteriorate;
the 1968 riots turned U Street
into a corridor of abandoned
and burned-out buildings,
and attendance at the theater
dropped dramatically. By the
1970s the theater had closed
down. Then, in the early 1980s
fundraising began for the $10
million renovation. Even the
original, highly elaborate
plasterwork was carefully
cleaned and repaired, and
the theater reopened in 1994.

Today the Lincoln Theatre is
a center for the performing arts,
and one of the linchpins of
U Street's renaissance. The
magnificent auditorium hosts
a program of concerts, stage
shows, and events including the
DC Film Festival *(see p198)*.

⓴ National Zoological Park

See pp140–41.

Entrance to the Mary McLeod
Bethune Council House

㉑ Washington National Cathedral

See pp144–5.

㉒ Cleveland Park

🅜 Cleveland Park.

Cleveland Park is a beautiful residential neighborhood that resembles the picture on a postcard of small-town America. It was originally a summer community for those wanting to escape the less bucolic parts of the city. In 1885, President Grover Cleveland (1885–9) bought a stone farmhouse here as a summer home for his bride.

The town's Victorian summer houses are now much sought after by people wanting to be close to the city but live in a small-town environment. There are interesting shops and good restaurants, as well as a grand old Art Deco movie theater, called the Uptown.

㉓ Rock Creek Park

🅜 Cleveland Park. Rock Creek Park Nature Center: 5200 Glover Rd, NW. **Map** 2 D1–D3. **Tel** (202) 895-6070. 🅜 Friendship Heights. 🚌 E2, E3, E4. **Open** 9am–5pm Wed–Sun. **Closed** Federal hols. 🎫 by appt. 🌐 nps.gov/rocr

Named for the creek that flows through it, Rock Creek Park bisects the city of Washington.

Pierce Mill, the 19th-century gristmill in Rock Creek Park

The Shaw Neighborhood

This neighborhood is named for Union Colonel Robert Gould Shaw, the white commander of an all-black regiment from Massachusetts. He supported his men in their struggle to attain the same rights as white soldiers. Until the 1960s, U Street was the focus of black-dominated businesses and organizations. Thriving theaters, such as the Howard and the Lincoln, attracted top-name performers, and Howard University was the center of intellectual life for black students. The 1968 riots, sparked by the assassination of Dr. Martin Luther King, Jr., wiped out much of Shaw's business district, and many thought the area could never be revived. However, the restoration of the Lincoln Theatre, the renewal of the U Street business district, and an influx of homebuyers renovating historic houses, have all contributed to the rejuvenation. In the part of U Street closest to the U Street-Cardoza metro stop, many fashionable bars and clubs have opened.

Mural in the Shaw neighborhood depicting Duke Ellington

This 1,800-acre stretch of land runs from the Maryland border south to the Potomac River and constitutes nearly five percent of the city. Unlike the crowded lawns of Central Park, Rock Creek Park has a feeling of the wilderness. Although the elk, bison, and bears that used to roam the park have vanished, raccoons, foxes, and deer can still be found here in abundance.

The park was endowed in 1890 and is now run by the National Park Service. In addition to hiking and picnicking, the park has a riding stable and horse trails, tennis courts, and an 18-hole golf course. On Sundays, a portion of Beach Drive – one of the main roads running through the park – is closed to cars to allow cyclists and in-line skaters freedom of the road. The creek

itself is inviting, with little eddies and waterfalls, but visitors are advised not to go into the water because it is polluted.

The **Rock Creek Park Nature Center** is a good place to begin an exploration of the park. It includes a small planetarium, and a 1 mile (1.6 km) nature trail, which is very manageable for children.

Pierce Mill near Tilden Street was an active gristmill, which was restored by the National Park Service in 1936. It was kept working as a visitor exhibit until 1993 when it was deemed unsafe to work any more. There is a barn next to the mill where works by local artists can be bought. The Carter Barron Amphitheater, near 16th Street and Colorado Avenue, stages rock, pop, jazz, and classical concerts, many of them free, during the summer months.

㉑ Washington National Cathedral

The building of the Cathedral Church of Saint Peter and Saint Paul (its official name) began in 1907 and was completed in 1990. The world's sixth-largest cathedral, it dominates the city's skyline and measures 301 ft (94.8 m) from grade to the top of the central tower and 518 ft (158 m) in length – almost the length of two soccer fields. Built with Indiana limestone, the Washington National Cathedral boasts elements typical of Gothic religious architecture, such as soaring vaulting, stained-glass windows, and intricate carvings. The exterior features fanciful gargoyles and dramatic sculpture. The cathedral has been the location of funeral and memorial services for several US presidents. Extensive renovations continue on some parts of the cathedral following an earthquake in 2011.

Exterior
A masterpiece of Gothic-style architecture, the towers of the cathedral dominate the skyline.

★ **Ex Nihilo** Above the center portal is *Ex Nihilo* by artist Frederick Hart. It depicts figures of men and women emerging from the swirling background.

Main Entrance
Three huge Gothic arches dominate the west façade, with pierced bronze gates depicting stories from the book of Genesis.

KEY

① **George Washington Bay**

② **Pilgrim Observation Gallery**

③ **The pinnacles** on the cathedral towers are decorated with leaf-shaped ornaments and topped by elaborately carved finials.

Space Window
Mankind's achievements in science and technology are commemorated in this window with the flight of Apollo 11 and a piece of moon rock.

High Altar
Carved on the high altar are 110 figures, surrounding the central statue of Christ. Encased in the floor in front of the altar is stone from Mt. Sinai.

Children's Chapel
A statue of Jesus as a boy stands by this chapel built to the scale of a six-year-old. There are also motifs of baby and mythical animals.

Nave
From the West Portal to the High Altar, the iconography tells the story of humanity to redemption.

★ **South Rose Window**
The theme of this window by Joseph Reynolds and Wilbur Burnham is "The Church Triumphant."

❷ Basilica of the National Shrine of the Immaculate Conception

400 Michigan at 4th St, NE. **Tel** (202) 526-8300. **M** Brookland-CUA. **Open** Apr 1–Oct 31: 7am–7pm daily; Nov 1–Mar 31: 7am–6pm daily. 🚻 🎫 💻 📷 ♿ 🌐 **nationalshrine.com**

Completed in 1959, this enormous Catholic Church is dedicated to the Virgin Mary. The church was designed in the shape of a crucifix and has many stained-glass windows. The building can seat a congregation of 2,500 people or more.

In the early 1900s, Bishop Thomas Shahan, rector of the Catholic University of America, proposed building a national shrine in Washington. Shahan gained the Pope's support in 1913, and in 1920 the cornerstone was laid. The Great Upper Church was dedicated on November 20, 1959. An unusual and striking combination of Romanesque and Byzantine styles, the shrine boasts classical towers as well as minarets in its design. The basilica's large interior includes a number of chapels, each with a distinctive design of its own.

Visitors can also enjoy the peaceful and extensive Prayer Garden, which covers almost an acre (4,050 sq m).

View down the nave to the Basilica's altar

Entrance to the Chinese Pavilion at the National Arboretum

❷ National Arboretum

3501 New York Ave or 24th St & R St off Bladensburg Rd, NE. **Tel** (202) 245-2726. **M** Stadium Armory, then Metrobus B-2. **Open** 8am–5pm daily. Museum: **Open** 10am–4pm daily. **Closed** Federal hols. 📷 by appt only. 🎫 ♿ limited. 🌐 **usna.usda.gov**

Tucked away in a corner of northeast Washington is the National Arboretum – a center for research, education, and the preservation of trees, shrubs, flowers, and other plants. The many collections here mean that the Arboretum is an ever-changing, year-round spectacle.

The Japanese Garden, which encompasses the National Bonsai and Penjing Museum, has bonsai that are from 20 to 380 years old. The herb garden has ten specialty gardens, where herbs are grouped according to use and historical significance. At the entrance to the garden is an elaborate 16th-century European-style "knot garden," with about 200 varieties of old roses. The National Grove of State Trees has trees representing every state.

❷ Kenilworth Park and Aquatic Gardens

1550 Anacostia Ave, NE. **Tel** (202) 426-6905. **M** Deanswood. **Open** 7am–4pm daily. **Closed** Jan 1, Thanksgiving, Dec 25. 🌐 **nps.gov/keaq/index.htm**

Opened in the late 1800s, this tranquil park offers 12 acres (5 ha) of natural wetland areas and historic ponds filled with

beautiful water lilies and other aquatic plants from around the world. In late summer, the lotus pond is covered with pink blossoms. Abundant wildlife can also be seen, including otters, turtles, frogs, salamanders, and water birds.

❷ Howard University

2400 Sixth St, NW. **Tel** (202) 806-6100. **M** Shaw-Howard. 🌐 **howard.edu**

In 1866 the first Congregational Society of Washington considered establishing a seminary for the education of African-Americans – a school intended for "teachers and preachers." The concept expanded to include a multi-purpose university, and within two years the Colleges of Liberal Arts and Medicine of Howard University were founded, named for General Oliver O. Howard (1830–1909), an abolitionist and Civil War hero who later became a commissioner of the Freedman's Bureau. The impetus for establishing such a university was the arrival of newly freed men from the South who were coming to the North seeking education to improve their lives. The university's charter was enacted by Congress and approved by President Andrew Jackson.

Famous graduates include Thurgood Marshall, who championed desegregation of public schools and was the first African-American Supreme Court Justice, Carter Woodson, Toni Morrison, Ralph Bunche, Stokely Carmichael, and Ossie Davis.

Frederick Douglass (1817–95)

Born a slave around 1818, Frederick Douglass became the leading voice in the abolitionist movement that fought to end slavery in the United States. Douglass was taught to read and write by his white owners. At the age of 20 he fled to Europe. British friends in the anti-slavery movement purchased him from his former masters, and he was at last a free man. For most of his career he lived in New York, where he worked as a spokesman for the abolitionist movement. A brilliant speaker, he was sent by the American Anti-Slavery Society on a lecture tour and won added fame with the publication of his autobiography in 1845. In 1847 he became editor of the anti-slavery newspaper *The North Star*, named after the constellation point followed by escaping slaves on their way to freedom. During the Civil War (*see p23*), Douglass was an advisor to President Lincoln and fought for the constitutional amendments that guaranteed equal rights to freed black people.

Frederick Douglass

❷❽ Frederick Douglass House

1411 W St, SE. **Tel** (202) 426-5961.
Ⓜ Anacostia. **Open** mid-Oct–mid-Apr: 9am–4:30pm daily; mid-Apr–mid-Oct: 9am–5pm daily. **Closed** Jan 1, Thanksgiving, Dec 25. 🎫 📷
♿ call ahead. 🌐 nps.gov/frdo

The abolitionist leader Frederick Douglass lived in Washington only toward the end of his illustrious career. After the Civil War he moved first to a town house on Capitol Hill, and then to Anacostia. In 1877 he bought this white-framed house, named it Cedar Hill, and lived here, with his family, until his death in 1895.

Douglass's widow opened Cedar Hill for public tours in 1903, and in 1962 the house was donated to the National Park Service. Most of the furnishings are original to the Douglass family and include gifts to Douglass from

"The Growlery" in the garden of the Frederick Douglass House

President Lincoln and the writer Harriet Beecher Stowe, author of *Uncle Tom's Cabin* (1852).

In the garden is a small stone building that Douglass used as an alternative study, and which he nicknamed "The Growlery." From the front steps of the house there is a magnificent view across the Anacostia River.

❷❾ Anacostia Museum

1901 Fort Place, SE. **Tel** (202) 633-4820.
Ⓜ Anacostia. **Open** 10am–5pm daily for tours. **Closed** Dec 25.
📷 by appointment only; call (202) 287-3369 or book online.
♿ 🌐 anacostia.si.edu

The full name of this museum is the Anacostia Museum and Center for African-American History and Culture. It is part of the Smithsonian Institution (*see p74*), and is dedicated to increasing public understanding and awareness of the history and culture of people of African descent and heritage living in the Americas.

Basic needs such as housing, transportation, healthcare, and employment were long denied to members of the African-American community, and the Anacostia Museum sponsors exhibits addressing these concerns. Two of its major initiatives have been *Black Mosaic*, a research project on Washington's diverse Afro-Caribbean culture, and *Speak to MY Heart: African American Communities of Faith and Contemporary Life*.

The museum is as much a resource center as it is a space for art and history exhibitions; it has an extensive library and computers for visitors. Its collections include historical objects, documents, videos, and works of art. A nationally traveling exhibit, *Reflections in Black*, traces the history of African-American photography from 1840 to the present.

Façade of Cedar Hill, the Frederick Douglass House

Three Guided Walks

The best way to discover Washington's historic neighborhoods, diverse architecture, parks, and gardens is on foot. The first walk takes you up and down Massachusetts Avenue, past many of the city's larger embassies and grand, imposing mansions into Kalorama, a pretty area that's home to many of the smaller embassies. Afterwards, you may wish to spend more time exploring. You'll find at least one hidden gem; the Embassy area also houses the Phillips Collection *(see p137)* and several art galleries. On the walks through Georgetown and Old Town Alexandria you'll notice that many of the historic buildings you pass are open to the public.

A Closer Look

In Georgetown you could tour Dumbarton Oaks, Tudor Place, or Georgetown University *(see pp122–9)*. In Alexandria you might look inside the churches, the Lyceum (the local history museum), the Lee-Fendall House, Gadsby's Tavern Museum, or the Carlyle House *(see pp160–61)*.

Dumbarton Oaks, Georgetown *(see p129)*

Embassy Row *(see p149)*

Georgetown *(see pp150–51)*

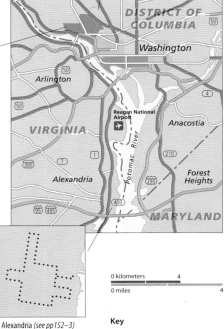

Carlyle House, a Georgian mansion on Fairfax Street, Alexandria *(see p160)*

Alexandria *(see pp152–3)*

Key

• • • Walk route

0 kilometers   4
0 miles   4

A Walk Around Embassy Row

For those fans of eclectic architecture this walk is a fascinating experience. Starting off west from Dupont Circle takes you along Massachusetts Avenue, past many of the larger embassies to the Italian Embassy and then back along Massachusetts Avenue to Kalorama, a quiet residential area where smaller embassies and museums are tucked away in its tree-lined streets.

⑦ Islamic Center's striking minaret

① Ornate Embassy of Indonesia

Walsh McLean (his daughter), who also owned the 44-carat Hope Diamond, which is at the Natural History Museum. Farther on, there's an Italianate palace, now home to the Society of Cincinnati ②, a charitable organization set up by officers who served George Washington. A statue of Civil War General Philip T. Sheridan on his horse greets you at Sheridan Circle ③. Walk around the circle to the left, passing the Irish and Romanian embassies. You'll see the former Turkish Embassy ④, an ornate mansion that boasts a mixture of Romanesque and Turkish styles on the exterior, while inside there are Doric columns, marble floors, mosaic tiles, bronze statues, stained-glass windows, and frescoes. It was built by Washington architect George Oakley Totten, who was inspired by palaces in Istanbul, for wealthy industrialist Edward Hamlin Everett. Known as the "bottle top king" (he obtained the patent for corrugated bottle tops), Everett staged elaborate musical evenings here. As you stroll along Massachusetts Avenue, take a look at the

garden behind the gate of the Japanese Embassy ⑤, a simple and graceful Georgian-Revival building. After crossing the bridge over Rock Creek Park, you reach the Italian Embassy ⑥, a stunning contemporary structure that was designed by Piero Sartogo Architetti in Rome and Leo A. Daly in Washington. Its cantilevered copper eaves are reminiscent of a Renaissance palazzo. Cross Massachusetts Avenue and turn back toward Dupont Circle. Keep walking until you come to the Islamic Center ⑦, a mosque with a 160-ft (48-m) minaret. Wander inside to see the exquisite tiles and carpets. (Head coverings for women are provided.) Turn left on California Street, right onto 24th Street and left onto S Street past the Woodrow Wilson House ⑧ (the unpretentious home of the 28th president). Go right onto 22nd Street, walking down the Spanish Steps to R Street. Turn left on R and right on 21st Street, passing the Phillips Collection ⑨, one of the country's most delightful modern art museums. Turn left on Q Street to make your way back to your start at the Dupont Circle Metro.

At Dupont Circle Metro head northwest on the south side of Massachusetts Avenue. Look for the Indonesian Embassy ①. This Beaux-Arts mansion was built at the turn of the century by an Irish immigrant from Tipperary who made his fortune in the gold mines. The house later became the property of Evalyn

Tips for Walkers

Starting point: Dupont Circle Metro.
Length: 2.5 miles (4 km).
Stopping off points: Choose from one of several good restaurants near the Dupont Circle Metro stop.

Key

• • • Walk route

For additional map symbols *see back flap*

A 90-Minute Walk in Georgetown

Renowned for its beautiful and historic architecture, eclectic shops, and delightful restaurants, Georgetown has it all. Starting in upper Georgetown, this walk takes you along residential streets past grand homes and Federal-style rowhouses, past early churches and cemeteries, parks and river vistas, quiet lanes and crowded streets. The walk ends on M Street in the commercial heart of Georgetown at the oldest house built in the district. Details of many sights mentioned are in the section on Georgetown *(see pp122–9)*.

⑥ Dumbarton House, beautifully designed inside and out

and then left onto 29th Street. Mt. Zion Church ⑧, on your right at 1334, was Washington's first African-American church *(see p128)*. West African influences can be seen in the church's structure, such as its tin ceiling.

At the corner, turn right onto Dumbarton Street, left on 30th Street, and right on N Street, which is full of elegant

Start at Wisconsin Avenue and S Street where you head east and then right on to 32nd Street. Dumbarton Oaks ① at 1703, a Federal-style mansion owned by Harvard University, contains a huge collection of pre-Columbian and Byzantine art, and may be worth returning to explore at length one afternoon *(see p129)*.

Turn left on R Street and right onto 31st Street. Admire Tudor Place ②, designed by the Capitol architect William Thornton on the right *(see p128)*. Turn left onto Avon Lane and left again on Avon Place. Walk across R Street to Montrose Park ③, which has a maze where you might meander, and then return to R Street. Head east and go into Oak Hill Cemetery ④.

James Renwick, architect of New York's St. Patrick's Cathedral, designed the chapel inside *(see p128)*.

Back on R Street, head east to 28th Street. Turn right past Evermay ⑤, a private Georgian manor, built by Scotsman Samuel Davidson in 1792. Turn left on Q Street. On your left, the Federal-style Dumbarton House ⑥, is noted for its beautiful 18th- and 19th-century furnishings. Make a left at the corner on 27th Street. Facing you is the Mt. Zion cemetery ⑦ where African-Americans were buried before the Civil War.

Turning around, walk back on 27th Street until you come to O Street. Turn right onto O Street

Tips for Walkers

Starting point: Wisconsin Ave & S Street. **Length:** 3 miles (5 km).
Getting there: Metro Connection express bus from Foggy Bottom metro stop to Wisconsin Ave & R St, or Circulator bus from Union Station and points along K St NW.

⑪ Smith Row, American Federal-style architecture on N Street

③ Montrose Park, a tranquil space for city relaxation

18th-century architecture. On your right you pass 3017 N Street ⑨, the house where Jackie Kennedy once lived. At Wisconsin Avenue you can take a break at Martin's Tavern (est. 1933) or one of many cafés here. Turn right on Wisconsin and then left onto O Street. Note the old streetcar tracks and St. John's Episcopal Church ⑩ at 3240, once attended by Thomas Jefferson. Turn left on Potomac Street, then right on N Street.

Walk along N Street for several blocks. You'll pass Smith Row ⑪ with its brick Federal-style houses at 3255-63, John and Jackie Kennedy's home ⑫ from 1957 to 1961 at 3307, and Cox's Row ⑬ at 3327-39, built by Colonel Cox, a former

⑭ Georgetown University

merchant and mayor. Farther along N Street is Georgetown University ⑭ (see p128). Turn left on 36th Street to find The Tombs bar, a favorite haunt of students. On Prospect Street ⑮ next to the Car Barn (once used to house trolleys and now part of the university), go down three flights of steep steps (where a scene from The Exorcist was filmed) to M Street, the city's busiest and most colorful street, and the Potomac River.

Cross M Street and turn left, passing the Key Bridge and the Francis Scott Key Park ⑯, named for the author of "The Star-Spangled Banner". Still on M Street, look for the sign to Cady's Alley at 3316, make a right, and go down the steps. Turn left on Cady's Alley ⑰, browse in the high-end home furnishing shops, left again on 33rd Street to return to M Street. Turn right and you may want to stop at Dean & DeLuca ⑱, a lively café and gourmet market built in 1866. Stroll past the Victorian-style Georgetown Park ⑲, a former tobacco warehouse that now houses a variety of shops. Cross Wisconsin Avenue and go along M Street to 31st Street. Turn right then left onto the towpath by the C & O Canal ⑳ for a block, turning right on Thomas Jefferson Street and head toward Washington Harbor ㉑ (see pp124–5). Walk through this large complex of shops to the waterfront. After admiring the magnificent river view, retrace your steps to M Street and visit the Old Stone House ㉒, which dates from pre-Revolutionary days.

Key

• • • Walk route

0 meters 300
0 yards 300

⑳ Passenger barge on the C & O Canal, a reminder of 19th-century shippers

For additional map symbols see back flap

A 90-Minute Walk in Alexandria

Stroll along cobblestone streets to see historic Alexandria, settled in the 18th century. This walk through the Old Town will take you by many historic homes, two of the oldest churches (George Washington attended both of them at one time or another), Gadsby's Tavern, and an old firehouse. The walk ends at the Torpedo Factory, now a thriving art center where over 200 artists exhibit their work. Afterward, go around to the back of the Torpedo Factory for a view of the Potomac River.

② Historic Farmer's Market in Market Square

Start at the Ramsay House Visitor Center ①, once the home of a Scottish merchant and city founder, William Ramsay. Built in 1724, it is the oldest house in Alexandria. Outside Ramsay House, you'll see Market Square ② where farmers have sold their produce for over 250 years. At the corner of Fairfax and King Streets turn left onto South Fairfax Street. Walk past the Stabler-Leadbeater Apothecary Shop ③ *(see p160)*, built in 1792. This was formerly run by Edward Stabler who worked with the "Society for the Relief of People Illegally Held in Bondage" to free enslaved African Americans. Turn left on Prince Street to find

211, which was the former home of Dr. Elisha Cullen Dick, the doctor who attended George Washington on his deathbed. At the corner is the Athenaeum ④, a Greek Revival building dating from 1851, once the Bank of the Old Dominion. Cross Lee Street and continue walking on Prince Street. This block, dubbed Captain's Row ⑤, is still paved with cobblestones and was once home to sea captains and shipbuilders. Turn right on Union Street. You'll pass several art galleries and

catch a glimpse of the river on your left. Turn right on Duke Street to see the Federal-style homes and pretty gardens. Turn left on South Fairfax Street. The Old Presbyterian Meeting House ⑥ *(see p160)*, a brick church built by Scottish settlers in 1775 and rebuilt in 1837 after a fire, is on your right. On George Washington's death the bell of the Old Presbyterian tolled for four days. You'll find the Tomb of the Unknown Soldier of the American Revolution in the churchyard.

Go to the corner of South Fairfax Street and turn right onto Wolfe Street. This cuts through what was once a neighborhood called Hayti, home to many prominent African-American leaders in the early 1800s. Continue until you reach Royal Street. The house at 404 South Royal Street ⑦ is the home of George Seaton, a black

Tips for Walkers

Starting point: The Ramsay House Visitor's Center.
Length: 2.5 m (4 km).
Getting there: Take the Dash bus from the King Street Metro stop to the Ramsay House Visitor's Center.
Stopping Off Points: The Friendship Firehouse is open Fri–Sun. For lunch try Gadsby's Tavern or one of the restaurants on King Street.

① Ramsay House, the oldest building in Alexandria

master carpenter whose mother was freed by Martha Washington. Continue for three blocks. At 604 Wolfe Street is the Alexandria Academy ⑧, built with the support of George Washington and others. This free school was attended by white children before it became a school for African Americans in the first half of the 19th century.

Cross South Washington Street and turn right. After two blocks you'll come to the Lyceum ⑨, a building inspired by a Doric temple, which was originally a library, then a hospital for Union troops during the Civil War, and now a local history museum. A statue of a Confederate soldier, "Appomattox," stands in the center of the Prince and Washington Streets intersection, marking the spot where

⑯ Gadsby's Tavern, where President Jefferson's inaugural banquet was held

troops left Alexandria to join the Confederate army on May 24, 1861. Turn left on Prince Street and walk two blocks to South Alfred Street. Turn right to see the Friendship Firehouse ⑩ at 107. Turn right on King Street where you'll find colorful shops and restaurants. Turn left on Washington Street. Christ Church ⑪ will be on your left. Wander through the historic cemetery and into the church – this is where every year presidents have come to honor George Washington on his birthday. Continue on Washington Street past Lloyd House ⑫, a Georgian home built in 1796, once a station on the underground railroad. After two blocks turn right on Oronoco Street at the Lee-Fendall House ⑬ (see p161). The house, now a museum, was built by Philip Fendall who then married the sister of "Light Horse" Harry Lee (Robert E. Lee's father and a Revolutionary hero). Across the road at 607 Oronoco Street is Robert E. Lee's boyhood home ⑭ (see p160), which is now closed to the public. Alexandria loves

Portrait of Robert E. Lee ⑭

its dogs and they are all welcome at the Olde Towne School of Dogs on the corner of Oronoco and St. Asaph Streets. Turn right on St. Asaph and cross Princess Street with its cobblestones that were laid in the 1790s. Cross Cameron Street and turn left. A replica of the small house built by George Washington in 1769 is at 508 Cameron Steet ⑮.

Turning right on Royal Street, you'll find Gadsby's Tavern ⑯ (see p160), where Jefferson's inaugural banquet was held. Across the street is the City Hall ⑰. Continue on Cameron Street and cross Fairfax Street. The Bank of Alexandria, the city's oldest bank, established in 1792, stands on the corner. Next door is Carlyle House ⑱ (see p160), a Georgian mansion modeled after the Scottish estate Craigiehall. Go around to the rear to see the gardens. Back on Fairfax Street, continue to King Street and turn left. Enjoy the shop windows for two blocks to the Torpedo Factory on Union Street ⑲ (see p161), a dynamic arts center.

Key

••• Walk route

0 meters   300
0 yards   300

FOUNDERS PARK

WATERFRONT PARK

MARKET SQUARE

Potomac River

⑲ The Torpedo Factory, with riverview studios, art galleries, and an archeology museum

Waterfalls at Great Falls Park, Virginia ▶

EXCURSIONS BEYOND WASHINGTON, DC

EXCURSIONS BEYOND WASHINGTON, DC

Within a half-day's drive of Washington lies enough history and natural beauty to satisfy the most insatiable sightseer. Alexandria and Williamsburg are a must for history buffs, while Chesapeake Bay and the islands of Chincoteague and Assateague offer a wealth of natural beauty. This area of Virginia and Maryland, along with parts of West Virginia and Pennsylvania, has been at the center of 400 years of turbulent American history.

Founded in 1623, Jamestown was the first permanent English settlement in America. In the 18th century, Williamsburg became the capital of Virginia and the first colony to declare independence from England. Today, Williamsburg is a living museum of the Colonial era.

The cultural influence of Europe is clearly seen in the architecture of this region. The two presidents largely responsible for crafting the character of the early republic lived in Virginia – George Washington at Mount Vernon, and Thomas Jefferson at Monticello. These homes reveal the lives their occupants led, at once imaginative, agrarian, inventive, comfortable – and, like many wealthy landowners, relying on slavery.

Cities and towns throughout the area have attractive historic districts that are a welcome contrast to the modern commercial strips on their outskirts.

Annapolis, for example, is a pleasant Colonial and naval port city. Baltimore also has a diverse charm, combining working-class neighborhoods and Old World character, and the town of Richmond blends the Old South's Victorian gentility with the luxuries of modern life.

Civil War battlefields are spread over the map as far as Gettysburg and tell the war's painful story with monuments, museums, cemeteries, and the very contours of the land itself.

The 105-mile (170-km) Skyline Drive through Shenandoah National Park, situated west of DC, makes the beautiful Blue Ridge Mountains accessible to hikers, cyclists, and drivers alike. To the east of the city, the Chesapeake Bay region attracts sailors and fishermen, as well as seafood lovers who can indulge in the delicious local specialty – blue crabs.

Mount Vernon Bike Trail

◀ Colorful clapboard house in Annapolis, Maryland

Exploring Beyond Washington, DC

Just minutes outside the bustling center of Washington is a striking and varied area of mountains, plains, and historic towns. To the west are Virginia's Blue Ridge Mountains, the setting for Shenandoah National Park. To the south is the Piedmont, an area of gently rolling hills that supports the vineyards of Virginia's burgeoning wine industry. To the east, the Chesapeake Bay divides Maryland almost in two, and to the south it travels the length of the Virginia coastline. To the north is the big port city of Baltimore, with its pleasant waterfront promenade, shops, museums, and stunning National Aquarium.

The Philadelphia Brigade Monument at Gettysburg

A re-created fort in Jamestown

Sights at a Glance

For additional map symbols *see back flap*

The dramatic Bearfence Mountain, part of Shenandoah National Park

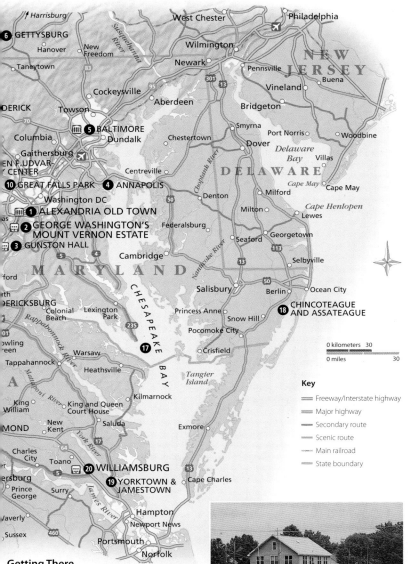

Boats moored in the Chesapeake Bay area

Getting There

Four good interstate highways lace the area: I-95 runs south and north on the eastern side of Virginia; I-81 runs south and north in western Virginia; I-66 heads west from Washington; and I-270 goes toward Frederick. Trains depart from Union Station to most of the main towns, such as Baltimore, Alexandria, Richmond, Williamsburg, and Harpers Ferry, which is also served by the MARC (see p215). Virginia Railway Express goes from Union Station to Alexandria and Fredericksburg. Greyhound buses also travel to most towns.

❶ Old Town Alexandria

Old Town Alexandria has kept a special historical flavor, dating back to its incorporation in 1749. It is still a busy seaport and offers many historic sights, as well as shops selling everything from antique hat racks to banana splits. Restaurants are abundant, art thrives here, and the socializing goes on day and night, in and around Market Square.

Exploring Alexandria

Alexandria's tree-lined streets are filled with elegant, historic buildings and make for a pleasant stroll *(see pp152–3)*. Alternatively, a boat tour offers an attractive prospect as does a leisurely lunch on the patio overlooking the waterfront. Nearby Founder's Park is the perfect place to bask on the grass by the river.

Façade of the elegant Carlyle House

🏠 Carlyle House

121 N Fairfax St. **Tel** (703) 549-2997. **Open** 10am–4pm Tue–Sat, noon–4pm Sun; Last tour at 4pm. **Closed** Jan 1, Thanksgiving, Dec 25. 🅿 🎫 ♿ (call in advance.) 📷
w nvrpa.org/park/carlyle_house

This elegant Georgian Palladian mansion was built by wealthy Scottish merchant John Carlyle in 1753. The house fell into disrepair in the 19th century but was bought in 1970 by the Northern Virginia Regional Park Authority; it has since been beautifully restored. A guided tour provides fascinating details about 18th-century daily life. One room, known as the "architecture room," has been deliberately left unfinished to show the original construction of the house. The back garden is planted with 18th-century plant species.

🏠 Stabler-Leadbeater Apothecary Museum

105 S Fairfax St. **Tel** (703) 746-3852. **Open** Apr–Oct: 10am–5pm Tue–Sat, 1–5pm Mon, Sun; Nov–Mar: 11am–4pm Wed–Sat, 1–4pm Sun. **Closed** Jan 1, Thanksgiving, Dec 25. 🅿 🎫 📷
w apothecarymuseum.org

Established in 1792, this family apothecary was in business for 141 years, until 1933. It is now a museum, and the shop's mahogany drawers still contain the potions noted on their labels. Jars containing herbal remedies line the shelves. Huge mortars and pestles and a collection of glass baby bottles are among 8,000 original objects. George Washington was a patron, as was Robert E. Lee, who bought the paint for his Arlington house here.

🏛 Gadsby's Tavern Museum

134 N Royal St. **Tel** (703) 746-4242. **Open** Apr–Oct: 10am–5pm Tue–Sat, 1–5pm Sun, Mon; Nov–Mar: 11am–4pm Wed–Sat, 1–4pm Sun. **Closed** Federal hols. 🅿 🎫 📷 🚫
w alexandriava.gov/gadsbystavern

Dating from 1770, this tavern and the adjoining hotel, owned by John Gadsby, were the Waldorf-Astoria of their day. Now completely restored, they evoke the atmosphere of a hostelry in this busy port.

You can see the dining room with buffet and gaming tables, the bedrooms where travelers reserved not the room but a space in a bed, and the private dining room for the wealthy. The hotel's ballroom, where George and Martha Washington were fêted on his last birthday in 1799, can be rented out. This is also a working restaurant.

Interior of the Old Presbyterian Meeting House

🏠 Old Presbyterian Meeting House

323 S Fairfax St. **Tel** (703) 549-6670. **Open** 8:15am–4:15pm Mon–Fri. 📷 ♿ **w** opmh.org

Memorial services for George Washington were held in this meeting house, founded in 1772. In the churchyard are buried Dr. John Craig, a close friend of Washington, merchant John Carlyle, the Reverend Muir, who officiated at Washington's funeral, and the American Revolution's unknown soldier.

🏠 Boyhood Home of Robert E. Lee

607 Oronoco St.

Unfortunately, the boyhood home of Robert E. Lee is currently a private residence and not open to the public. General Lee lived in this 1795 Federal town house from the age of 11 until he went to West Point Military Academy. The drawing room was the setting for the marriage of Mary Lee Fitzhugh to Martha Washington's grandson, George Washington Parke Custis.

Bedroom of Robert E. Lee

Lee-Fendall House Museum

614 Oronoco St. **Tel** (703) 548-1789. **Open** 10am–3pm Wed–Sat, 1–3pm Sun. **Closed** Dec 25–Jan 31 (except 3rd Sun, Lee's birthday celebration). 🅿️ 📷 once every hour, on the hour. ♿ 🌐 leefendallhouse.org

Philip Fendall built this stylish house in 1785, then married the sister of Revolutionary War hero "Light Horse" Harry Lee. Lee's descendants lived here until 1904. The house is rich with artifacts from the Revolution to the 1930s Labor Movement.

Lee-Fendall House Museum

Torpedo Factory Art Center

105 N Union St. **Tel** (703) 838-4565. **Open** 10am–6pm daily (to 9pm Thu). **Closed** Jan 1, Easter, July 4, Thanksgiving, Dec 25. 🌐 torpedofactory.org

Originally a real torpedo factory during World War II, it was converted into an arts center by a partnership between the town and a group of local artists in 1974. Today there is gallery and studio space for over 150 artists to create and exhibit their work. Visitors can watch a potter at his wheel, sculptors, printmakers, and jewelry-makers.

Christ Church

118 North Washington St. **Tel** (703) 549-1450. **Open** 9am–4pm Mon–Sat, 2–4:30pm Sun. **Closed** Jan 1, Thanksgiving, Dec 25. ♿ 🌐 historicchristchurch.org

The oldest church in continuous use in the town, this Georgian edifice was completed in 1773. George Washington's square pew is still preserved with his nameplate, as is that of Robert E. Lee.

On the other side of this Episcopalian church, a label reads "William E. Cazenove. Free pew for strangers." In the churchyard 18th-century gravestones wear away under the weather of the centuries.

Farmers Market

Market Square, King & Fairfax Sts. **Tel** (703) 746-3200. **Open** 7am–noon Sat. This market dates back to the city's incorporation in 1749. George Washington, a trustee of the market, regularly sent produce to be sold at the market from his farm at Mount Vernon (*see pp162–3*). A very pleasant aspect of the market square today is its central fountain. Shoppers can find fresh fruits and vegetables, cut flowers, herbs, baked goods, meats, and crafts.

Alexandria Old Town

Museums and Galleries
④ Gadsby's Tavern Museum
⑦ Stabler-Leadbeater Apothecary Museum

Historic Buildings
① Boyhood Home of Robert E. Lee
② Lee-Fendall House Museum
⑥ Carlyle House

Churches
③ Christ Church
⑨ Old Presbyterian Meeting House

Markets
⑤ Farmers Market

Art Centers
⑧ Torpedo Factory Art Center

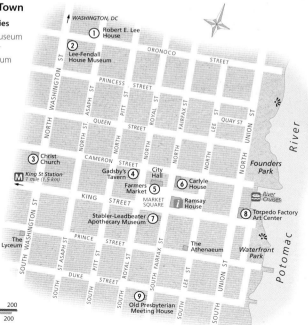

For keys to symbols *see back flap*

❷ George Washington's Mount Vernon Estate

This country estate on the Potomac River was George Washington's home for 45 years. Built as a farmhouse by his father, Augustine, Washington made many changes, including adding the cupola and curving colonnades. The house is furnished as it would have been during Washington's presidency (1789–97), and the 500-acre grounds still retain aspects of Washington's farm. The Ford Orientation Center and Donald W. Reynolds Museum offer exhibits about the life of the first US president, including his military and presidential career.

Kitchen
Set slightly apart from the main house, the kitchen has been completely restored.

★ Mansion Tour
Visitors can see the study and the large dining room, as well as Washington's bedroom and the bed in which he died.

Slave Quarters
Washington freed all his slaves in his will. Reconstructed quarters show their living conditions.

KEY

① Overseer's House

② Coach House

③ Stable

④ **The Lower Garden** was used for growing vegetables and berries. The boxwood bushes surrounding it were planted in Washington's time.

⑤ **The Bowling Green** was added to the estate by George Washington.

★ Upper Garden
The plants in this colorful flower garden are known to have grown here in Washington's time.

Wharf
Daytrip boats from central DC bring visitors to this wharf. Potomac cruise boats also stop off here.

VISITORS' CHECKLIST

Practical Information
South end of George Washington Memorial Parkway, Fairfax County, VA. **Tel** (703) 780-2000.
W **mountvernon.org**
Distillery State Route 235 South: **Open** Apr–Oct: daily.
⚓ 🅿 🔭 ♿ first floor.
🏛 🚻 📷

Transport
Ⓜ Yellow line to Huntington Station. 🚌 Fairfax Connector bus 101 to Mount Vernon: call (703) 780-2000. Boat cruises: Apr–Aug: 8am–5pm; Mar, Sep, Oct: 9am–5pm; Nov–Feb: 9am–4pm.

Pioneer Farm

④

③

②

⑤

★ Pioneer Farm
This exhibit demonstrates farming techniques that were pioneered by George Washington. There is also a replica of his unique 16-sided treading barn, which was created using authentic tools.

Washington's Tomb
In his will, Washington requested that a new brick tomb be built for his family at Mount Vernon. Washington died in 1799 but the tomb was not completed until 1831.

❸ Gunston Hall

10709 Gunston Road, Mason Neck, VA.
Tel (703) 550-9220. **Open** 9:30am–
5pm daily. **Closed** Jan 1, Thanksgiving,
Dec 25. 🏛 🅿 ♿ 📷
🆆 gunstonhall.org

This Georgian house, built in
1755, was the home of George
Mason, author of the 1776
Virginia Declaration of Rights.
Situated 20 miles (32 km) south
of Washington, DC, it is an
exquisite example of careful
historic restoration.

Of particular interest is the
finely carved woodwork in
the entrance hall, the chinoi-
serie mantel and fireplace in the
formal dining room, and the
servants' staircase which was
used by the slaves so that they
wouldn't be seen by guests.
Outside are the beautiful
boxwood gardens.

❹ Annapolis

Anne Arundel County, MD.
🚆 36,000. ℹ Annapolis and Anne
Arundel County Conference and
Visitors Bureau, 26 West St. (410)
280-0445. **Open** 9am–5pm.
🆆 visitannapolis.org

The capital of Maryland,
Annapolis is the jewel of
Chesapeake Bay. It is defined
by the nautical character that
comes with 17 miles (27 km) of
shoreline and the longtime
presence of the US
Naval Academy.

A walk down Main
Street takes you past
the 200-year-old
Maryland Inn, and the
shops and restaurants,
to the City Dock lined
with boats. It is then a
short walk to the
150-year-old **US Naval
Academy**. Inside the
visitor center is the
Freedom 7 space
capsule that
carried the first
American, Alan
Shepard, into space. The US
Naval Academy Museum in
Preble Hall is also worth
visiting, especially to see the
gallery of detailed ship
models. The **Maryland State**

The beautiful formal gardens of the William Paca House, in Annapolis

House is the oldest state
capitol in continuous use. Its
Old Senate Chamber is where
the Continental Congress
(delegates from each of the
American colonies) met when
Annapolis was briefly the capital
of the United States in 1783–4.

Annapolis teems with
Colonial-era buildings, most
still in everyday use. The
William Paca House, home of
Governor Paca, who signed
the Declaration of Independence, is a fine Georgian
house with an enchanting
garden, both of which have
been lovingly restored. The
Hammond Harwood House
has also been restored.
This masterpiece
of Georgian design
was named after
the Hammond and
Harwood families,
both prominent in
the area. Cornhill
and Duke of Gloucester
streets are beautiful
examples of the
city's historic resi-
dential streets.
Many tours
are offered
in Annapolis,
including walking,

Tiffany window in the Naval Academy, Annapolis

bus, and boat tours. It is particularly enjoyable to view
the city from the water,
be it by sightseeing boat,
chartered schooner, or even
by kayak.

🏛 **US Naval Academy**
52 King George St. **Tel** (410) 293-8687.
Open 9am–5pm daily. Photo ID
needed; visitors must be over 18.
Closed Jan 1, Thanksgiving, Dec 25.
🅿 🆆 usna.edu

🏛 **Maryland State House**
State Circle. **Tel** (410) 974-3400. **Open**
9am–5pm (call ahead). Photo ID needed. **Closed** Jan 1, Dec 25. 🕚 11am &
3pm by appt. ♿ 🆆 msa.md.gov

🏛 **William Paca House**
186 Prince George St. **Tel** (410) 990-
4543. **Open** 10am–5pm Mon–Sat,
noon–5pm Sun (weekends only in
winter). **Closed** Jan, Feb, Thanksgiving,
Dec 24 & 25. 🏛 🎦 🆆 annapolis.org

🏛 **Hammond Harwood House**
19 Maryland Ave at King George St.
Tel (410) 263-4683. **Open** Apr–Oct:
noon–5pm Tue–Sun; Nov–Dec: noon–
4pm Tue–Sun. **Closed** Jan. 🏛
🆆 hammondharwoodhouse.org

❺ Baltimore

Chesapeake Bay, MD. 🚆 785,500.
ℹ Inner Harbor West Wall (410) 837-
4636. Visitor services (877) BALTIMORE.
🚆 🚌 🆆 baltimore.org

There is much to do and see in
this pleasant city. A good place to
start is the Inner Harbor, the city's
redeveloped waterfront, with
the harborside complex of shops
and restaurants. The centerpiece
is the **National Aquarium**,
which has many exhibits,
including sharks, a seal pool, and
a dolphin show. The Harbor is
home to the **Maryland Science**

Walking along Baltimore's pleasant Inner Harbor promenade

Center, where "do touch" is the rule. The planetarium and an IMAX® theater thrill visitors with images of earth and space.

The **American Visionary Art Museum** has extraordinary works by self-taught artists whose materials range from matchsticks to faux pearls.

Uptown is the **Baltimore Museum of Art**, with its world-renowned collection of modern art, including works by Matisse, Picasso, Degas, and Van Gogh. There is also a large collection of Warhol pieces and two sculpture gardens featuring work by Rodin and Calder. Some galleries will be temporarily closed during a three-year renovation project.

The diversity of art at the **Walters Art Museum**, on Mount Vernon Square, includes pieces by Fabergé and Monet, among others; it is renowned for its ancient Egyptian art.

The Little Italy area is worth a visit for its knock-out Italian restaurants and also for the games of bocce ball (Italian lawn bowling) played around Pratt or Stiles Streets on warm evenings.

National Aquarium
501 E Pratt St, Pier 3, N side of Inner Harbor. **Tel** (410) 576-3800. **Open** Hours vary. Call ahead or check website for details. **Closed** Thanksgiving, Dec 25.
aqua.org

Maryland Science Center
601 Light St. **Tel** (410) 685-5225. **Open** Hours vary. Call ahead or check website for details. **Closed** Thanksgiving, Dec 25.
mdsci.org

American Visionary Art Museum
800 Key Highway at Inner Harbor. **Tel** (410) 244-1900. **Open** 10am–6pm Tue–Sun. **Closed** Mon, Thanksgiving, Dec 25.
avam.org

Baltimore Museum of Art
10 Art Museum Drive. **Tel** (443) 573-1700. **Open** 10am–5pm Wed–Fri, 11am–6pm Sat & Sun. **Closed** Jan 1, Jul 4, Thanksgiving, Dec 25.
artbma.org

Walters Art Museum
600 N Charles St. **Tel** (410) 547-9000. **Open** 10am–5pm Wed–Sun (8pm 1st Fri of month). **Closed** Jan 1, Memorial Day, Jul 4, Thanksgiving, Dec 24, 25.
weekends.
thewalters.org

❻ Gettysburg National Military Park

1195 Baltimore Pike, Gettysburg, Adams County, PA. **Tel** (717) 334-1124. Park: **Open** 6am–7pm daily (to 10pm Apr–Oct). Visitor Center: **Open** 8am–5pm daily (to 6pm Apr–Oct). **Closed** Jan 1, Thanksgiving, Dec 25.
nps.gov/gett

This 6,000-acre (2,500 ha) park, south of the town of Gettysburg, Pennsylvania, marks the site of the three-

The eye-catching architecture of the National Aquarium, Baltimore

The Gettysburg Address

The main speaker at the dedication of the National Cemetery in Gettysburg on November 19, 1863 was the orator Edward Everett. President Lincoln had been asked to follow with "a few appropriate remarks." His two-minute, 272-word speech paid tribute to the fallen soldiers, restated his goals for the Civil War, and rephrased the meaning of democracy: "government of the people, by the people, for the people." The speech was inaudible to many, and Lincoln declared it a failure. However, once published, his speech revitalized the North's resolve to preserve the Union. Today it is known to every schoolchild in America.

Abraham Lincoln

day Civil War battle on July 1–3, 1863. It was the bloodiest event ever to take place on American soil, with 51,000 fatalities. A two- or three-hour driving tour begins at the visitor center. The National Cemetery, where Abraham Lincoln gave his Gettysburg Address, is opposite. Other sights include the Eternal Light Peace Memorial.

❼ Frederick

Frederick County, MD. 59,000. 151 S East St (800) 999-3613, (301) 600-4047. **Open** 9am–5pm daily. **Closed** Jan 1, Easter, Thanksgiving, Dec 25. **visitfrederick.org**

Dating back to the mid-18th century, Frederick's historic center was renovated in the 1970s.

This charming town is a major antique center and home to hundreds of antique dealers. Its shops, galleries, and eateries are all in 18th- and 19th-century settings. Francis Scott Key, author of "The Star Spangled Banner," is buried in Mt. Olivet Cemetery.

❽ Antietam National Battlefield

Route 65, 10 miles (16 km) S of Hagerstown, Washington County, MD. **Tel** (301) 432-5124. **Open** Jun–Aug: 8:30am–6pm daily; Sep–May: 8:30am–5pm. **Closed** Jan 1, Thanksgiving, Dec 25. 🚗 🏠 ♿
W nps.gov/anti

One of the worst battles of the Civil War was waged here on September 17, 1862. There were 23,000 casualties but no decisive victory.

An observation tower offers a panoramic view of the battlefield. Antietam Creek runs peacefully under the costly Burnside Bridge. General Lee's defeat at Antietam inspired President Lincoln to issue the Emancipation Proclamation. The Visitors' Center movie recreating the battle is excellent.

John Brown's Fort in Harpers Ferry National Historic Park

❾ Harpers Ferry

171 Shoreline Dr, off Rte 340, Harpers Ferry, Jefferson County, WV. **Tel** (304) 535-6029. **Open** 8am–5pm daily. **Closed** Jan 1, Thanksgiving, Dec 25. 🚗 🍴 spring–fall. **W** nps.gov/hafe

Nestled at the confluence of the Shenandoah and Potomac rivers in the Blue Ridge Mountains is

Harpers Ferry National Historical Park. The town was named for Robert Harper, a builder from Philadelphia who established a ferry across the Potomac here in 1761. There are stunning views from Maryland Heights to the foot of Shenandoah Street, near abolitionist John Brown's fort. Brown's ill-fated raid in 1859 on the Federal arsenal, established by George Washington, became tinder in igniting the Civil War.

The great importance of the town led to the area being designated a national park in 1944. It has been restored by the National Park Service.

❿ Great Falls Park

Georgetown Pike, Great Falls, Fairfax County, VA. **Tel** (703) 285-2965. **Open** daily (closes at dusk). 🚗 🍴 ♿ **W** nps.gov/gwmp/grfa

The first view of the falls, near the visitor center, is breath-taking. The waters of the Potomac roar through a gorge of jagged rock over a 76 ft (23 m) drop at the point that divides Virginia's undulating Piedmont from the coastal plain. Only experienced kayakers are per-mitted to take to the turbulent whitewater below, which varies with rainfall upstream.

The park is crisscrossed by 15 miles (24 km) of hiking trails, some showing evidence of the commerce from the early 19th-century Patowmack, America's first canal. Guided nature walks are offered.

Situated just across the river, in Maryland, is the C&O Canal National Historical Park, entry to which is free for visitors to Great Falls Park.

The Red Fox Inn in Middleburg

⓫ Middleburg

Route 50, Loudoun County, VA. 🚗 600. 🛈 Visitors' Center, 12 N Madison St. **Tel** (540) 687-8888. **Open** 11am–3pm Mon–Fri, 11am–4pm Sat–Sun. **W** visitmiddleburgva.com

Horse and fox are king in this little piece of England in the Virginia countryside. Middle-burg's history began in 1728, with Joseph Chinn's fieldstone tavern on the Ashby's Gap Road, still operating today as the Red Fox Inn. Colonel John S. Mosby and General Jeb Stuart met here to plan Confederate strategy during the Civil War.

The exquisite countryside has thoroughbred horse farms, some opening during the Hunt Country Stable Tour in May.

Foxcroft Road, north of the town, winds past immaculate horse farms. East of Route 50 is **Chrysalis Vineyard and Winery**. On John Mosby Highway, between Aldie and Middleburg, is **Cana Vineyards and Winery of Middleburg**. Both have tours and tastings.

🍷 **Chrysalis Vineyard**
23876 Champe Ford Rd. **Tel** (540) 687-8222. **Open** 10am–5:30pm daily. **Closed** Jan 1, Thanksgiving, Dec 25. **W** chrysaliswine.com

🍷 **Cana Vineyards and Winery**
38600 John Mosby Hwy. **Tel** (703) 348-2458. **Open** 11am–6pm Mon, Thu–Sun. **Closed** Jan 1, Thanksgiving, Dec 25. **W** canavineyards.com

The roaring waterfalls in Great Falls Park

⓬ Steven F. Udvar-Hazy Center

14390 Air and Space Museum Parkway, Chantilly, VA. **Tel** (703) 572-4118. 🚌 Bus from Dulles International Airport. **Open** 10am–5:30pm daily (to 6:30pm May 25–Sep 3). **Closed** Dec 25. 🅿️
🆆 nasm.si.edu/udvarhazycenter

This is a must for anyone who would like to view the Space Shuttles "Enterprise" and "Discovery," or who wants to find out about rockets and satellites, or see a rare Boeing B-29 Stratoliner. Opened in 2003 to coincide with the 100th anniversary of the Wright brothers' first powered flight, and named in honor of its major donor, this museum was built to display and also preserve historic aviation and space artifacts. The vast building of over 760,000 sq ft (7,000 sq m)

houses exhibit hangars with more than 300 aircraft and spacecraft. Visitors can walk among exhibits and view hanging aircraft from elevated walkways. As well as an education center and Imax® theater, a Wall of Honor offers a permanent memorial to those men and women who contributed to America's space exploration and aviation heritage.

⓭ Skyline Drive

Skyline Drive runs along the backbone of the Shenandoah National Park's Blue Ridge Mountains. Previously farmland, the area was designated a national park in 1926. Deer, wild turkey, bears, and bobcats inhabit the park, and wildflowers, azaleas, and mountain laurel are abundant. The park's many hiking trails and its 75 viewpoints offer stunning natural scenery.

① Pinnacles Overlook
The view of Old Rag Mountain with its outcroppings of granite is spectacular.

② Whiteoak Canyon
The Whiteoak Canyon Trail passes six waterfalls on its route.

④ Camp Hoover
At the end of Mill Prong Trail, this 160 acre (64 ha) resort was President Hoover's weekend retreat until 1933, when he donated it to the Park.

0 kilometers   10
0 miles   10

North entrance station

③ Big Meadows
Close to the Visitor Center, this meadow is kept in its centuries-old state. It was probably kept clear by fire from lightning or Indians. Deer can easily be seen here.

⑤ Bearfence Mountain
Although it is a bit of a climb up this mountain, partly on rock scramble, it is not too difficult, and the reward is a breathtaking 360-degree view of the surrounding landscape.

⑥ Lewis Mountain
The views from Lewis Mountain are awe-inspiring, especially in spring, when beautiful wildflowers litter the hills and the floor of the Shenandoah Valley.

Tips for Drivers

Starting points: north at Front Royal, central at Thornton Gap, south at Rockfish Gap.
Length: 105 miles (168 km), duration of 3–8 hrs depending on how many stops are taken.
When to go: Fall leaf colors draw crowds in mid-October. Wildflowers bloom through spring and summer.
What it costs: $15 per car, valid for 7 days ($10 Nov–Feb).

Key

- - - Walk route
▬▬▬ Road

For additional map symbols *see back flap*

⓮ Charlottesville

Virginia. 🚹 41,000. 🚌 🚍 🚍 ℹ️ Visitors Bureau, 610 E Main St; Monticello Visitors Center, Route 20 South. **Tel** (434) 293-6789, (877) 386-1103 (toll free). 🅦 **visitcharlottesville.org**

Charlottesville was Thomas Jefferson's hometown. It is dominated by the University of Virginia, which he founded and designed, and also by his home, **Monticello**.

Jefferson was a Renaissance man: author of the Declaration of Independence, US president, farmer, architect, inventor, and vintner. It took him 40 years to complete Monticello, beginning in 1769. It is now one of the most celebrated houses in the country. The entrance hall doubled as a private museum, and the library held a collection of around 6,700 books.

The grounds include a large terraced vegetable garden where Jefferson grew and experimented with varieties.

The obelisk over Jefferson's grave in the family cemetery lauds him as "Father of the University of Virginia." Tours of the house are available year round.

Vineyards and wineries surround Charlottesville. Michie Tavern, joined to the Virginia Wine Museum, has been restored to its 18th-century appearance, and serves a buffet of typical Southern food.

Montpelier, on a 2,500 acre (1,000 ha) site 25 miles (40 km) to the north, was the home of former US president James Madison.

🏛 Monticello
Route 53, 3 miles (5 km) SE of Charlottesville. **Tel** (434) 984-9880. **Open** Mar–Nov: 9am–6pm; Dec–Feb: 10am–4pm. **Closed** Dec 25. 🎫 🍴 ♿ 🎁 🅦 **monticello.org**

⓯ Fredericksburg

Virginia. 🚹 22,600. 🚌 🚍 ℹ️ Fredericksburg Visitor Center, 706 Caroline St. **Tel** (540) 373-1776. **Open** 9am–5pm Mon–Sat (to 7pm May–Aug), 11am–5pm Sun. **Closed** Jan 1, Dec 25. 🅦 **visitfred.com**

Fredericksburg's attractions are its historic downtown district, and four Civil War battlefields, including The Wilderness. The Rising Sun Tavern and Hugh

The elegant dining room at Kenmore House

Mercer Apothecary Shop offer living history accounts of life in a town that began as a port on the Rappahannock River. **Kenmore Plantation**, home of George Washington's sister, is famous for its beautiful rooms.

The visitor center offers useful maps as well as horse-and-carriage or trolley tours.

🏛 Kenmore Plantation
1201 Washington Ave. **Tel** (540) 373-3381. **Open** Mar–Oct: 10am–5pm daily; Nov, Dec: 10am–4pm daily. **Closed** Jan, Feb, Thanksgiving, Dec 24, 25, 31. 🅦 **kenmore.org**

George Washington's Ferry Farm
268 Kings Hwy. **Tel** (540) 370-0732. **Open** as above.

Monticello, Charlottesville

Situated in the leafy foothills of the Blue Ridge Mountains, this Palladian masterpiece was built between 1769 and 1809 by Thomas Jefferson.

East portico

The greenhouse was used by Jefferson to cultivate a variety of plants.

North piazza

Jefferson's bed straddles his cabinet (office) and bed chamber.

The entrance hall, where guests and visitors were greeted, is also a museum.

⓰ Richmond

Virginia. 🚉 202,000. 🚌 🚐
ℹ️ Richmond Metropolitan
Convention and Visitors Bureau,
401 N Third St. **Tel** (804) 783-7450.
Toll free 888-RICHMOND.
Open 9am–5pm Mon–Fri.
Ⓦ visitrichmondva.com

Richmond, the old capital of
the Confederacy (see p20), still
retains an Old South aura.
Bronze images of Civil War
generals punctuate Monument
Avenue. Brownstones and
Victorian houses testify to
this area's postwar prosperity.

The **Museum of the
Confederacy** contains Civil War
artifacts, including Robert E.
Lee's coat and sword. Another
popular museum is the
fascinating **Science Museum
of Virginia**.

The Neo-Classical State
Capitol, inside which is
the life-sized Houdon
sculpture of George
Washington, was
designed by Charles
Louis Clérisseau.

The **Virginia
Museum of Fine
Arts** has a fine
collection of world
art and hosts acclaimed
special exhibitions.

Statue of Robert E. Lee
in Richmond

🏛️ **Museum of the Confederacy**
1201 E Clay St. **Tel** (804) 649-1861.
Open 10am–5pm daily.
Closed Jan 1, Thanksgiving,
Dec 25. 🅿️ 🎁 Ⓦ moc.org

🏛️ **Science Museum of Virginia**
2500 W Broad St. **Tel** (804) 864-1400.
Open 9:30am–5pm Tue–Sat,
11:30am–5pm Sun.
Closed Thanksgiving, Dec 24 & 25.
🅿️ ♿ 🖥️ 🎁 Ⓦ smv.org

🏛️ **Virginia Museum of Fine Arts**
200 N Boulevard. **Tel** (804) 340-1400.
Open 10am–5pm Sat–Wed, 10am–
9pm Thu & Fri. Ⓦ vmfa.state.va.us

⓱ Chesapeake Bay

Ⓦ baydreaming.com
ℹ️ Tilghman Island: Ⓦ tilghman
island.com

Known as "the land of pleasant
living," Chesapeake Bay offers
historic towns, fishing villages,
bed-and-breakfasts, seafood

restaurants, beaches, wildlife,
and farmland. The Chesapeake
Bay Maritime Museum, in the
town of St. Michael's, depicts
life on the bay, both past and
present. **Tilghman Island**, in
mid Chesapeake, has the last
commercial sailing fleet in
North America and hosts a
seafood festival every June.

⓲ Chincoteague and Assateague

Chincoteague, Accomack County, VA.
🚉 4,000. Assateague, Accomack
County, VA and MD (unpopulated).
Ⓦ nps.gov/asis ℹ️ Chincoteague
Chamber of Commerce, 6733 Maddox
Blvd. (757) 336-6161.
Ⓦ chincoteaguechamber.com

These sister islands offer a wealth
of natural beauty. Chincoteague
is a town situated on the
Delmarva (Delaware,
Maryland and
Virginia) Peninsula.
Assateague is an
unspoiled strip of
nature with an ocean
beach and hiking trails
that wind through
woods and marshes.
It is famously popu-
lated by wild ponies, thought
to be descended from animals
grazed on the island by 17th-
century farmers. The woodlands
and salt marshes of Assateague
attract over 300 species of birds,
and in fall peregrine falcons and
snow geese fly in. Monarch
butterflies migrate here in
October. There are several camp-
grounds in the area, and the
ocean beach is ideal for swimming and surf fishing. **Toms Cove
Visitor Center** and **Chincoteague**

Wildlife Refuge Center can
provide extra information.

ℹ️ **Toms Cove Visitor Center**
8128 Beebe Rd. **Tel** (757) 336-6577.
Ⓦ tomscovepark.com

ℹ️ **Chincoteague
Wildlife Refuge Center**
8231 Beech Rd. **Tel** (757) 336-6122.
Ⓦ fws.gov/refuge/chincoteague

⓳ Yorktown and Jamestown

York County, VA, and James City
County, VA. ℹ️ York County Public
Information Office (757) 890-3300.

Established in 1607, James-town
was the first permanent English
settlement in America. It has
1,500 acres (600 ha) of marsh-
land and forest, threaded
with tour routes. There are
ruins of the original English
settlement and a museum at
Historic Jamestowne. There
is a recreation of James Fort,
full-scale reproductions of the
ships that brought the first
colonists to America and a
traditional Indian village.

Yorktown was the site of the
decisive battle of the American
Revolution in 1781. **Colonial
National Historical Park**'s
battlefield tours and exhibits
explain the siege at Yorktown.

🏛️ **Historic Jamestowne**
Tel (757) 220-4997.
Open 8:30am–4:30pm daily.
Closed Jan 1, Dec 25. 🅿️ ♿ 🎁
Ⓦ historicjamestowne.org

🌼 **Colonial National
Historical Park**
Tel (757) 909-3400. **Open** 9am–5pm
daily. **Closed** Jan 1, Thanksgiving,
Dec 25. 🅿️ ♿ Ⓦ nps.gov/colo

Historic Jamestowne, a re-creation of Colonial James Fort

⓴ Colonial Williamsburg

As Virginia's capital from 1699 to 1780, Williamsburg was the hub of the loyal British colony. After 1780 the town went into decline. Then in 1926, John D. Rockefeller embarked on a massive restoration project. Today, in the midst of the modern-day city, the 18th-century city has been re-created. People in colonial dress reenact the lifestyle of the original townspeople; blacksmiths, silversmiths, and cabinet makers show off their skills while horsedrawn carriages pass through the streets, providing visitors with a fascinating insight into America's past.

★ **Governor's Palace**
Originally built in 1720 by Governor Alexander Spotswood, the palace has been reconstructed in its full pre-Revolution glory.

0 meters — 200
0 yards — 200

Courthouse
Built in 1770–71, this was the home of the county court for more than 150 years.

Key

— Suggested route

Nursery
Costumed living-history interpreters work the land in Colonial Williamsburg using replica tools and the same techniques as the original settlers.

Fifes and Drums Display
Revolutionary field music is recreated in these colorful parades. Local school children begin learning these instruments aged ten.

Print Office
This store stocks authentic 18th-century foods, including wine, Virginia ham, and peanuts.

VISITORS' CHECKLIST

Practical Information
101a Visitor Center Drive, Virginia
🅦 colonialwilliamsburg.com
ℹ️ Colonial Williamsburg:
(888) 965-7254. ♿ 🖼

Transport
🚇 🚌

Milliner
Owned by Margaret Hunter, the milliner shop stocked a wide range of items. Imported clothes for women and children, jewelry, and toys could all be bought here.

Raleigh Tavern
The Raleigh was once an important center for social, political and commercial gatherings. The original burned in 1859, but this reproduction has its genuine flavor.

NICHOLSON STREET

BOTETOURT ST

NIAL ST

DUKE OF GLOUCESTER STREET

★ Capitol
The capitol is a 1945 reconstruction of the original 1705 building. The government resided in the West Wing, while the General Court was in the East Wing.

TRAVELERS' NEEDS

TEXAS BAR·B·Q FACTORY

WHERE TO STAY

If you plan to be visiting the sights in Washington from dawn until midnight, you may simply need a roof over your head and a bed for your weary body. If you intend to take your time and relax, you may want to stay in a hotel with all the amenities: pool, health club, deluxe restaurant, and room service. Whatever your needs, Washington has a range of accommodations to choose from. Generally, hotels that are closer to downtown and the Mall are more expensive, and those in the suburbs are more affordable. As the city is a tourist destination as well as a business center, room rates are the second highest in the United States next to New York City. However, there are bargains to be had, especially during the off season and on weekends. A number of websites (see directory on p175) also offer special deals.

Lobby of the plush Capital Hilton *(see p178)*

How to Reserve

Many hotels have toll-free numbers for making reservations. It is also often possible to preview the accommodation options on the hotel's website. Weekend rates are often much cheaper than week-day rates.

Hotel Grading and Facilities

A five-star hotel will offer everything the visitor could wish for. Room service, health facilities, bathrooms with a Jacuzzi, valet parking, and 24-hour maid and butler service are just some of the luxury amenities provided, but at a price. In contrast, a one-star hotel will have a tele-vision and a telephone in the bedroom but may have shared bathrooms. Hotels of all price ranges are available in the city.

Discounts

Washington has different "seasons" from other cities. When the cherry blossoms around the Tidal Basin bloom in April, it is impossible to find a reasonably priced room in the city. Then in June the city is full of school groups taking end-of-the-year trips. Despite often broiling temperatures, families are lured to the capital in the summer. Labor Day in September is very big for tourists as is, of course, the Fourth of July.

However, you can find bargains during the winter months from November through March. Washington is a Monday-through-Friday convention town, so the best prices are on weekends, often at a fraction of the vacation season, midweek rate.

Hidden Extras

Beware the hefty 14.5 percent tax levied on hotels in Washington. Also note that most establishments will charge you extra for parking in the hotel's parking lot. There is no way to escape the tax, but you can shop around for a hotel with free parking. If you have to park your car in a garage, you may have to pay close to $40 per day.

Chains and Boutique Hotels

Staying at a **Hilton**, **Holiday Inn**, **Hyatt**, or **Marriott** hotel will guarantee a level of service and cleanliness mandated by the chain. An alternative to the large chain hotels are the increasingly popular boutique hotels. **Kimpton Hotels**, a national chain many of whose boutique hotels are housed in historic buildings, has several properties in Washington. These small, unique places all have their own character. The George Hotel on Capitol Hill *(see p176)*, for instance, is sleek and modern. It also houses Bistro Bis *(see p183)*, one of the city's most talked-about restaurants.

Other boutique hotels include the Henley Park *(see p177)*, which has the decor of a British aristocratic home and serves afternoon tea. The Morrison-Clark Inn *(see p177)* in Penn Quarter is a restored mansion filled with Victorian antiques. The Phoenix Park Hotel *(see p176)* on Capitol Hill has an Irish theme and staff – and a pub popular with Irish nationals and Irish-American politicians.

Stylish decor at Hotel George *(see p176)*

Business Travelers

Washington hotels take into account the sophisticated communications needs of the business traveler. Wi-Fi is almost universally available in all rooms.

Bed-and-Breakfasts

Although bed-and-breakfast accommodations are not as popular in the United States as they are in Europe, both American and foreign travelers are increasingly seeking them out as an alternative to the more sterile and expensive hotels.

Bed-and-Breakfast Accommodations Ltd. matches visitors with the perfect room in a bed-and-breakfast, an apartment or small hotel, or even a private home. They have 85 properties in the city and suburbs, and charge a one-time booking fee of $10. The online booking services **airbnb.com** and **vrbo.com** offer a wide selection of unfurnished apart-ments and rooms in private homes at reasonable rates.

Entrance to the Hay-Adams *(see p179)*

Budget Options

The best value accommodation option for young travelers in Washington is the welcoming **Hosteling International-Washington, DC**. It is located in the center of the city, in an area that is close to all major amenities and sights. Young travelers are advised to be cautious when returning after dark. The rate is around $40 per night for a bunk bed in a single-sex dormitory room.

Disabled Travelers

Nearly all the large, modern hotels are wheelchair accessible, but the independent hotels and bed-and-breakfasts may not be. Call in advance to ask about stairs, elevators, and door widths if you have special needs.

Children

Traveling with children may dictate your hotel reservations. There are many hotels, such as Sheraton Suites *(see p179)* and Georgetown Suites *(see p179)*, that have kitchenettes and living rooms with sofabeds that provide privacy to parents. Look out for hotels with a pool or a games room. Consider a more expensive room in town rather than a less expensive room in the suburbs. The suburban rates may look appealing until you face a long drive to your hotel during the rush hour.

Some bed-and-breakfasts furnished with antiques may not allow children. More often than not, however, hotels will be very accommodating toward young guests.

Recommended Hotels

The hotels listed on pages 176–9 are grouped under five categories: Bed-and-Breakfast, Boutique, Business, Family, and Luxury. For those with limited funds, bed-and-breakfast hotels might be a good choice. While there are relatively few within the city, many can be found farther from the Mall and the city center. Accommodations for families may have special child-ren's programs, games rooms, a pool, or suite arrange-ments that include a kitchen. Business hotels have a full range of amenities, although they are not in the luxury category. Luxury hotels have spas, concierge services, and large restaurants – at a price of more than $400 a night. Finally, boutique hotels are smaller and often have a theme, but perhaps without the splendor of the luxury options. Throughout the listings,

The historic Jefferson hotel *(see p178)*

notable accommodations from each category are highlighted as DK Choice. These hotels offer a special experience, because of their superb amenities, beautiful interiors, excellent restaurant, or a combination of these.

DIRECTORY

Special Deals

w hotels.com
w kayak.com
w priceline.com
w tripadvisor.com

Chain Hotels

Hilton
Tel (800).HILTONS.
w hilton.com

Holiday Inn
Tel (800) HOLIDAY.
w holidayinn.com

Hyatt
Tel (800) 233-1234.
w hyatt.com

Kimpton Hotels
Tel (800) 546-7866.
w kimptonhotels.com

Marriott
Tel (888) 236-2427.
w marriott.com

Bed-and-Breakfast

Bed-and-Breakfast Accommodations Ltd.
Tel (877) 893-3233 (toll free).
w bedandbreakfastdc.com

Budget Options

Hosteling International
1009 11th St, NW.
Tel (202) 737-2333.
w hiwashingtondc.org

Where to Stay

Bed-and-Breakfast

Penn Quarter

Hosteling International $
1009 11th St NW, 20001
Tel *737-2333*   **Map** 3 C2
w hiwashingtondc.org
Over 200 dorm-style beds are
on offer at this lodging in a
gentrified neighborhood. Most
rooms have shared bathrooms.

Farther Afield

Adams Inn $
*1746 Lanier Place NW, Adams
Morgan, 20009*
Tel *745-3600*
w adamsinn.com
Good budget choice in an
upmarket neighborhood. Not all
rooms have their own bathroom.

DK Choice

Kalorama Guest House $
*2700 Cathedral Ave NW,
Woodley Park, 20008*
Tel *297-4999*
w kaloramaguesthouse.com
One of the best deals in the
city, this homey, comfortable
B&B has a choice of rooms with
or without a private bathroom.
A delicious breakfast is served,
and home-made chocolate
chip cookies are on offer later in
the day. The beds are very
comfortable, but there are no
TVs in the guest rooms.

**Embassy Circle
Guest House** $$
2224 R St NW, 20008
Tel *232-7744*
w dcinns.com
Situated close to Dupont Circle,
with a private bath and free Wi-Fi
in each room, but no TVs. Parking
is restricted and the elevator is
only for luggage.

The Swann House $$
*1808 New Hampshire Ave NW,
Dupont Circle, 20009*
Tel *265-4414*   **Map** 2 F1
w swannhouse.com
The rooms in this stunning
19th-century mansion all have
private bathrooms, some with
a Jacuzzi, and there is a
swimming pool.

Beyond Washington

DK Choice

Colonial Houses $$
*136 East Francis St,
Williamsburg, VA 23187*
Tel *(800) 447-8679*
w colonialwilliamsburg.com
Set in the grounds of the
reconstructed colonial town of
Williamsburg, these 18th-century
houses are furnished with period
reproductions. Do not expect
the spacious accommodations
of a modern hotel. Step out of
the front door to see people in
18th-century costume re-
enacting the former colonial
lifestyle on the unpaved streets.

Kenmore Inn $$
*1200 Princess Anne St,
Fredericksburg, VA 22401*
Tel *(540) 371-7622*
w kenmoreinn.com
This nine-room establishment has
a gourmet restaurant that serves
an excellent Southern breakfast.

The Red Fox Inn & Tavern $$$
*2 East Washington St,
Middleburg, VA 20117*
Tel *(540) 687-6301*
w redfox.com
Antique furnishings, a hearty
breakfast, and a great restaurant
are on offer at this inn set in
Virginia hunt and wine country.
The staff is very hospitable.

Price Guide

Prices are based on one night's stay in
high season for a standard double room,
inclusive of service charges and taxes.

$	up to $200
$$	$200–$400
$$$	over $400

Boutique

Capitol Hill

The Liaison $$
415 New Jersey Ave NW, 20001
Tel *638-1616*   **Map** 4 E3
w affinia.com/liaison
Part of the Affinia chain,
The Liaison has an acclaimed
restaurant, rooftop pool, and
attentive staff. At a convenient
distance from the Capitol and
Union Station.

Phoenix Park Hotel $$
520 North Capitol St NW, 20001
Tel *(800) 824-5419*   **Map** 4 E3
w phoenixparkhotel.com
A comfortable, historic hotel
with an Irish theme, above the
Dubliner restaurant *(see p183)*.

DK Choice

Hotel George $$$
15 E St NW, 20001
Tel *347-4200*   **Map** 4 E3
w hotelgeorge.com
All 139 rooms at the Hotel
George have had an exten-
sive makeover and feature
contemporary references to
American history; the pillows
echo George Washington's
military uniform while the
wallpaper depicts Washington's
inaugural address.

Penn Quarter

Henley Park Hotel $$
926 Massachusetts Ave NW, 20001
Tel *638-5200*   **Map** 3 C2
w henleypark.com
This English-style hotel serves an
elegant high tea in front of the
lobby fireplace. However, a year-
long construction project nearby
may result in a lot of street noise.

Hotel Monaco $$$
700 F St NW, 20004
Tel *628-7177*   **Map** 3 C3
w monaco-dc.com
A National Historic Landmark
retrofitted into a colorful hotel
with a chic bar and restaurant.
Close to the Spy Museum,
National Portrait Gallery, and
National Museum of American Art.

Luxurious bedroom in The Swann House, near Dupont Circle

DK Choice

Morrison-Clark Inn $$$
1015 L St NW, 20001
Tel 898-1200 **Map** 3 C2
W morrisonclark.com
A well-appointed hotel, built in 1864 and filled with Victorian antiques. Rooms vary from standard doubles to two-room parlor suites with marble fireplaces and private balconies. It has a lovely, wide veranda, an excellent restaurant serving Southern cuisine, and a two-story carriage house with a luxurious living area.

The White House and Foggy Bottom

Hotel Lombardy $$
2019 Pennsylvania Ave NW, 20002
Tel 828-2600 **Map** 2 E3
W hotellombardy.com
A historic hotel with 1920s decor, but modern amenities. Spacious rooms and attentive service. Next to George Washington University.

Georgetown

The Georgetown Inn $$
1310 Wisconsin Ave NW, 20007
Tel 333-8900 **Map** 1 C2
W georgetowninn.com
An elegant hotel, but the rooms overlooking the street can be noisy. Good restaurant.

Farther Afield

The Churchill $$
1914 Connecticut Ave NW, Dupont Circle, 20009
Tel 797-2000 **Map** 2 E1
W thechurchillhotel.com
In a Beaux-Arts building, this cozy hotel has full amenities, including 24-hour room service and a spa.

Palomar $$
2121 P St NW, Dupont Circle, 20037
Tel 448-1800 **Map** 2 E2
W hotelpalomar.com
Large rooms and modern decor feature here. Enjoy outstanding dining at Urbana restaurant.

Tabard Inn $$
1739 N St NW, Dupont Circle, 20036
Tel 758-1277 **Map** 2 F2
W tabardinn.com
A quaint, romantic inn tucked into a side street. Meals are served by a fire. A favorite for brunch. No TVs in the rooms and not all rooms are en suite.

Topaz $$
1733 N St NW, Dupont Circle, 20036
Tel 393-3000 **Map** 2 F2
W topazhotel.com
A Kimpton hotel with a wellness theme, in-room spa treatments, and a nightly wine reception. Bicycles available to rent.

Dupont Circle Hotel $$$
1500 New Hampshire Ave, Dupont Circle, 20009
Tel 483-6000 **Map** 2 F2
W doylecollection.com
This cosmopolitan hotel, part of the Irish-owned Doyle Collection, has a fitness center, attentive service, and free Wi-Fi.

Hotel Rouge $$$
1315 16th St NW, Dupont Circle, 20036
Tel 232-8000 **Map** 3 B1
W rougehotel.com
A hip, Kimpton retreat, decorated in red. The Bar Rouge hosts the Red Hot Happy Hour. Yoga mats in every room and bicycles available for exploring the city.

Beyond Washington

The Bavarian Inn $$
164 Shepherd Grade Rd, Shepherdstown, WV 25443
Tel (304) 841-0761
W bavarianinnwv.com
This romantic country chalet overlooking the Potomac River has gas fireplaces and whirlpool baths. Ask for a room with a balcony.

Boar's Head Inn $$
200 Ednam Drive, Charlottesville, VA 22903
Tel 855-580-3847
W boarsheadinn.com
Owned by the University of Virginia, this lovely inn in a historic college town has a golf course and a spa.

The Ashby Inn $$$
692 Federal St, Paris, VA 20130
Tel 540-592-3900
W ashbyinn.com
Every room is different at this 18th-century inn. It has a Michelin-rated restaurant.

Lorien Hotel and Spa $$$
1600 King St, Alexandria, VA 22314
Tel 866-813-9643
W lorienhotelandspa.com
This luxury, eco-friendly hotel, part of the Kimpton chain, in Old Town Alexandria has an excellent spa.

Maryland Inn $$$
58 State Circle, Annapolis, MD 21401
Tel 410-263-2641
W historicinnsofannapolis.com
Three historic houses, full of antiques, make up this hotel,

Front entrance of the Hotel Monaco in Alexandria

which offers 18th-century charm amid 21st-century comfort.

Wyndham Baltimore Peabody Court Hotel $$$
612 Cathedral St, Baltimore, MD 21201
Tel 888-595-9874
W wyndham.com/baltimore
Expect attentive service in this old-world hotel. Good promotional packages.

Business

Capitol Hill

Washington Court Hotel $$
525 New Jersey Ave NW, 20001
Tel 628-2100 **Map** 4 E3
W washingtoncourthotel.com
This good-value hotel has in-room Wi-Fi, flatscreen TVs, a restaurant, and offers special deals.

Hyatt Regency Washington on Capitol Hill $$$
400 New Jersey Ave NW, 20001
Tel 737-1234 **Map** 4 E3
W washingtonregency.hyatt.com
This 800-room hotel has full amenities, including valet parking, a large restaurant, an indoor pool, and a gym.

The Mall

L'Enfant Plaza Hotel $$$
480 L'Enfant Plaza SW, 20024
Tel 484-1000 **Map** 3 C4
W lenfantplazahotel.com
This pet-friendly hotel has several dining venues and a pool. Perfect for visiting the Smithsonian.

Mandarin Oriental $$$
1330 Maryland Ave SW, 20024
Tel 554-8588 **Map** 3 C5
W mandarinoriental.com
Luxury and convenience at a price. An easy walk from all the museums and monuments, with an indoor pool for tired tourists.

For more information on types of hotels *see p175*

The comfortable, modern Four Seasons hotel in Georgetown

Penn Quarter

Grand Hyatt $$$
1000 H St NW, 20001
Tel 582-1234 **Map** 3 C3
W grandwashington.hyatt.com
A huge convention hotel with an indoor pool, 32 meeting rooms, and a business center.

Loews Madison Hotel $$$
1177 15th St NW, 20005
Tel 862-1600 **Map** 3 B2
W madisonhoteldc.com
This relatively small hotel offers a personal service. Each room has individual decor.

Renaissance Marriott $$$
999 9th St NW, 20001
Tel 898-9000 **Map** 3 C2
W marriott.com
Popular for conferences, this hotel's amenities include a fitness center and several dining venues.

The Westin $$$
1400 M St NW, 20005
Tel 429-1700 **Map** 3 B2
W westinwashingtondccitycenter.com
A large hotel with great weekend special deals, two full-service restaurants, plus a Starbucks.

The White House and Foggy Bottom

Capital Hilton $$$
1001 16th St NW, 20036
Tel 393-1000 **Map** 2 F2
W hilton.com
A stylish hotel with a health club. Separate living rooms in junior suites and complimentary break-fast for guests in executive rooms.

The Fairmont $$$
2401 M St NW, 20037
Tel 429-2400 **Map** 2 E2
W fairmont.com
The Fairmount boasts a state-of-the-art fitness center with an indoor pool, and two restaurants.

Renaissance Mayflower $$$
1127 Connecticut Ave NW, 20036
Tel 347-3000 **Map** 2 F3
W marriotthotels.com
Oozing historic charm, this hotel is a Washington landmark. Formal afternoon tea is served.

The Westin $$$
2350 M St NW, 20037
Tel 429-0100 **Map** 2 E2
W westingeorgetown.com
This hotel in historic Georgetown features modern decor and a full-service restaurant. Luxurious rooms and great hospitality.

Georgetown

DK Choice

Four Seasons $$$
2800 Pennsylvania Ave NW, 20007
Tel 342-0444 **Map** 2 D3
W fourseasons.com
A highly acclaimed hotel overlooking parkland and the Potomac River, the Four Seasons offers large rooms, a great bar, three fitness centers and world-class restaurants, and impeccable service. The modern decor includes over 1,500 artworks scattered across the hotel.

Farther Afield

Marriott Wardman Park $$
2660 Woodley Rd NW, Woodley Park, 20008
Tel 328-2000
W marriott.com
A grand hotel with four dining venues, a pool, and a fitness center. Special packages on offer.

Omni Shoreham $$
2500 Calvert St NW, Woodley Park, 20008
Tel 234-0700
W omnihotels.com
A luxurious hotel with 836 rooms, three dining venues, and a pool and Jacuzzi. Internet is chargeable. Located close to the National Zoo.

Beyond Washington

Hyatt Arlington $$
1325 Wilson Blvd, Arlington, VA 22209
Tel 703-525-1234
W arlington.hyatt.com
This comfortable hotel, close to the Rosslyn Metro, offers hypo-allergenic rooms on request. Fitness center is open 24 hours.

The Jefferson $$
101 West Franklin St, Richmond, VA 23220
Tel 804-597-0919
W jeffersonhotel.com
This elegant historic hotel offers excellent Southern hospitality and modern amenities.

Renaissance Harborplace $$$
202 East Pratt St, Baltimore, MD 21202
Tel 410-547-1200
W marriott.com
A luxurious hotel offering large rooms and great views of Baltimore harbor. There is an extra fee for parking and Wi-Fi.

Ritz Carlton $$$
1250 South Hayes St, Pentagon City, VA 22202
Tel 703-415-5000
W ritzcarlton.com
Plush and convenient, this hotel is minutes from downtown DC and the National Airport, with covered access to the Fashion City mall.

Family
Capitol Hill

Capitol Hill Hotel $$
200 C St SE, 20003
Tel 543-6000 **Map** 4 F5
W capitolhill-dc.com
This all-suite hotel is pet-friendly and has kitchenettes. Good for long stays.

Courtyard Marriott $$
140 L St NW, 20002
Tel 479-0027 **Map** 4 D2
W marriott.com
A stylish hotel, housed in a former bank, with comfortable rooms, indoor pool, and a fitness center.

The Mall

Holiday Inn $$
550 C St SW, 20024
Tel 479-4000 **Map** 4 D5
W holidayinn.com
Although a little worn, the Holiday Inn is in a good location and has a full restaurant service. All major attractions can be reached on foot.

Penn Quarter

Hotel Harrington $
436 11th St NW, 20004
Tel 628-8140 **Map** 3 C3
W hotel-harrington.com
This funky hotel offers simple, family rooms at a reasonable price. It has both a full-service and a fast-food restaurant.

The White House and Foggy Bottom

One Washington Circle $$
1 Washington Circle NW, 20037
Tel *872-1680*   **Map** 2 E3
🅦 thecirclehotel.com
A modern, pet-friendly hotel offering a variety of good-sized rooms with kitchenettes.

Georgetown

Holiday Inn $$
2101 Wisconsin Ave NW, 20007
Tel *338-4600*   **Map** 1 C1
🅦 holidayinn.com
This standard Holiday Inn has a complimentary shuttle service to the Metro and an outdoor pool.

Georgetown Suites $$$
1111 30th St NW, 20007
Tel *298-7800*   **Map** 2 D2
🅦 georgetownsuites.com
A hotel with spacious, modern suites and fully equipped kitchens. Close to C&O Canal.

Farther Afield

Days Inn $
4400 Connecticut Ave NW, Van Ness, 20008
Tel *244-5600*
🅦 daysinn.com
A basic motel with few amenities, but offering a good price. Near to the Red Line Metro.

Beyond Washington

Cacapon Resort State Park $
818 Cacapon Lodge Dr, Berkeley Springs, WV 25411
Tel *304-258-1022*
🅦 cacaponresort.com
Cabins, cottages, and bungalows in a state park with nature trails, horseback riding, and swimming.

Refuge Inn $
7058 Maddox Blvd, Chincoteague, VA 23336
Tel *757-336-5511*
🅦 refugeinn.com
A resort near the Chincoteague Wildlife Refuge, with a pool, fitness center, plus rental bikes.

Hyatt Regency Bethesda $$
7400 Wisconsin Ave, Bethesda, MD 20814
Tel *301-657-1234*
🅦 bethesda.hyatt.com
This hotel has a restaurant, a pool, and hypoallergenic rooms.

Sheraton Suites $$
801 North Saint Asaph St, Alexandria, VA 22314
Tel *1-703-836-4700*
🅦 sheratonsuitesalexandria.com

An all-suite hotel with sofa beds, refrigerators, and microwaves. Rooms can accommodate a family of four.

Williamsburg Inn $$
136 East Francis St, Wiliamsburg, VA 23187
Tel *757-229-1000*
🅦 colonialwilliamsburg.com
Comfortable, spacious rooms with Regency-style furnishings are on offer at this country inn.

Luxury

Penn Quarter

Willard InterContinental $$$
1401 Pennsylvania Ave NW, 20004
Tel *628-9100*   **Map** 3 B3
🅦 washington.intercontinental.com
This historic hotel, a block away from the White House, has hosted almost every US president. Adjacent to the National Theater.

The White House and Foggy Bottom

DK Choice

Hay-Adams $$$
800 16th St NW, 20006
Tel *638-6600*   **Map** 3 B2
🅦 hayadams.com
A neighbor of the White House, this historic 1920s hotel is elegant and well appointed. The 145 rooms include 21 luxury suites, some with a view of the Washington Monument.

The Jefferson $$$
1200 16th St NW, 20036
Tel *448-2300*   **Map** 2 F2
🅦 jeffersondc.com
This historic hotel has a quiet, refined ambience and 96 elegantly appointed rooms. Exceptional service and facilities.

St. Regis $$$
923 16th St and K St NW, 20006
Tel *638-2626*   **Map** 3 B2
🅦 stregiswashingtondc.com
Founded in 1926, this supremely elegant hotel has a sophisticated bar and restaurant.

W Hotel $$$
515 15th St NW, 20004
Tel *661-2400*   **Map** 3 B3
🅦 wwashingtondc.com
A hip hotel that attracts dance crowds on the weekends. The rooftop bar has stunning views.

Georgetown

The Graham Hotel $$$
1075 Thomas Jefferson St NW, 20007
Tel *202-337-0900*   **Map** 2 D3
🅦 thegrahamgeorgetown.com
Luxury hotel with spacious, tranquil suites, a roof deck bar, and a restaurant called the Alex.

Farther Afield

The Fairfax at Embassy Row $$$
2100 Massachusetts Ave NW, Embassy Row, 20008
Tel *293-2100*   **Map** 2 E2
🅦 fairfaxhoteldc.come
This splendid hotel is a favorite among the city's political elite. Situated close to Dupont Circle.

Mansion on O Street $$$
2020 O St NW, Dupont Circle, 20036
Tel *496-2020*   **Map** 2 E2
🅦 omansion.com
A 19th-century mansion with quirky decor. Features hidden rooms and secret passages.

Beyond Washington

Inn at Little Washington $$
Middle St and Main St, Little Washington, VA 22747
Tel *540-675-3800*
🅦 theinnatlittlewashington.com
A sumptuous inn with extravagant decor, impeccable service, and a Michelin-starred restaurant.

The elegant dining room in The Jefferson hotel on 1200 16th St NW

WHERE TO EAT AND DRINK

Joseph Alsop, a renowned Washington host of the early 1960s, routinely gave lavish dinner parties in his Georgetown home. When asked why he gave so many parties, Alsop replied that it was because Washington had no good restaurants. Today the capital rivals New York, offering restaurants of every cuisine and price range.

Washington's cosmopolitan population enjoys a wide array of cuisines, from Ethiopian to Vietnamese, with many new styles of "fusion food" in between. The seafood is also superb, freshly caught from the nearby waters of Chesapeake Bay. Crab and shellfish feature regularly on menus, especially in coastal areas outside the city.

Graffiato restaurant *(see p185)*

Places to Eat

Washington's restaurants are a reflection of its neighborhoods. Adams-Morgan has a mix of ethnic establishments, especially Salvadoran and Ethiopian, and cutting-edge cuisine. Perry's and Cashion's Eat Place *(see p190)* offer inventive fusion food with Asian and French influences, and the crowd is young and hip. An easy walk from the Mall, Washington's compact Chinatown in the Penn Quarter district has both expensive and moderately priced restaurants, such as the Spanish Jaleo *(see p184)*, Italian Graffiato, and Mexican Rosa Mexicana *(see p185)*. Few Asian restaurants have survived the gentrification of this area. Closer to the White House, a few of the old-guard stalwarts remain, including the historic Old Ebbitt Grill *(see p185)*, which specializes in regional seafood, and Georgia Brown's *(see p186)*, whose menu features Southern cuisine. Georgetown has a mix of expensive and inexpensive establishments. Good value can be found at Indian and Vietnamese restaurants. More reasonable places, again mostly ethnic restaurants, are found closer to the Circle. The vortex of 14th Street and U Street has restaurants for a young crowd, including Eatonville, Busboys and Poets, and Marvin *(see p189)*.

All restaurants in Washington are air conditioned and most (except for a few located in historic buildings) are wheelchair accessible.

Reservations

Reservations may be necessary for popular restaurants; the most fashionable can get booked up weeks in advance. Call ahead if there is somewhere you really want to go. However, walk-in diners are expected in most places. You may be placed on a waiting list and expected to return at the appointed time or wait in the adjacent bar.

Prices and Paying

Restaurant prices range from the very cheap to the very expensive in Washington. Prices vary according to location, cuisine, and decor. All restaurants take major credit cards, although street vendors and fast food places may only accept cash. Waiters rely on earnings from tips and a 15–20 percent tip is expected for good service in restaurants. The tip is not automatically added to the bill except in the case of large parties, which may incur an automatic 15 percent gratuity.

Unlike in many European cities, the fixed-price meal is uncommon in Washington. Items are usually listed à la carte unless specified in the menu. Diners should expect to spend between $20 and $40 for dinner and a drink, including a tip, at a moderate restaurant. However, Indian, Ethiopian, Chinese, and Vietnamese restaurants are often considerably less expensive. You will generally be charged about 25 percent less for the same meal if you eat at lunchtime rather than in the evening, so visitors on a budget may choose to eat their main meal at lunchtime. Breakfasts are usually under $10 for bacon and eggs with coffee and juice, but some hotels include a free continental breakfast (rolls, coffee, and juice) in the cost of the room.

Chic interiors of Cashion's Eat Place in the Adams-Morgan neighborhood *(see p190)*

Mural on the side of Madam's Organ bar in Adams-Morgan *(see p189)*

Opening Hours

Most restaurants are open all year (except Thanksgiving and Christmas Day) but a few may be closed on Sunday or Monday. It is best to call in advance. It is unusual for a restaurant to be open 24 hours, except for those in very large hotels. Restaurants also rarely serve food continuously throughout the day; they usually have a break of a few hours after lunch. Restaurants often open for dinner between 5pm and 6pm, with the busiest period usually between 7pm and 8pm. The last seating is often at 9pm, and the last customers usually leave by 11pm. Bars are open until 2am. Remember that Metrorail trains stop running at 3am on Friday and Saturday, and at midnight the rest of the week.

Alcohol

Restaurants are required by law to have a liquor license in order to sell alcohol, so some do not offer it. Others may serve beer and wine only but not hard liquor or mixed drinks.

Bars rarely serve food other than perhaps some appetizers. Other restaurants may have a separate bar as well as a dining section. Patrons are not permitted to bring their own drinks to a restaurant.

The drinking age in DC, in Maryland, and in Virginia is 21. Restaurateurs can and will ask for proof of age in the form of a driver's license or passport since the penalty for serving alcohol to underage drinkers is severe.

Smoking

In the Districts of Columbia and Maryland smoking is not allowed in restaurants or any public buildings. The Smoke-free Workplace law came into effect in 2006 and extended to restaurants in 2007. If caught smoking, you could be fined several hundred dollars.

In the District of Virginia smoking is prohibited in many public buildings. Some restaurants allow smoking but must have a no-smoking area.

Dress Code

Dress varies from the very casual (shorts, t-shirt, and sneakers) to the very formal. In some restaurants men will not be admitted without a jacket and tie (the maître d' may have spares). But as a general guide, the more expensive the restaurant, the more formal the dress code will be. Some bars also have a very strict dress code. Respectable but casual attire is acceptable in the majority of establishments.

What to Eat

Washington's cuisine is immensely multicultural, and you will find French, Chinese, Ethiopian, and Vietnamese restaurants, among others. The hot dog vendors along the Mall offer an alternative to a sit-down meal. Like many cities in the US, Washington has a proliferation of reasonably priced food trucks that assemble at various places throughout the day, including tourist areas (track them on foodtruckfiesta.com).

Children

The best indication as to whether children are welcome in a restaurant is the presence of a children's menu or the availability of high chairs. When dining in more formal places with children, it is best to reserve the earliest seating when the restaurant will not be too busy.

Wheelchair Access

Restaurants are not required to be wheelchair accessible. In general, restaurants in older neighborhoods like Dupont Circle and Adams-Morgan are less likely to accommodate wheelchairs than modern establishments on K Street. The Smithsonian Museum restaurants are all accessible for the disabled.

Recommended Restaurants

Washington has a broad spectrum of dining choices, ranging from food trucks to haute cuisine establishments. The restaurants listed on pages 183–91 include reasonably priced ethnic options, regional American cuisine, fine dining, and fast food establishments for busy families. From burgers and pizza to Ethiopian *wat* (stew), served on top of *injera* (flatbread), and Chesapeake Bay crab cakes, Washington has a plate for every palate.

Throughout the listings, DK Choice recommendations are highlighted in each area of the city. These offer the traveler a special experience and an insight into Washington, such as excellent local cuisine, dining in a historic building, superb ethnic food, a venue particularly popular with locals, or a fun and unusual setting such as a combination of restaurant, bookstore, and performance space.

Tony and Joe's Seafood Place on the side of Washington harbor *(see p188)*

The Flavours of Washington, DC

Washington is a place where everyone has an opinion, and culinary preferences are no exception. For some it's a power dining town, where châteaubriand is the dish of choice and "two-martini lunches" are common. Others would point to nearby Chesapeake Bay, and its delectable seafood dishes that appear on many menus. Still others would see the city's vibrant ethnic communities as the key to current food trends. There's no disagreement, however, that DC's dining scene reflects the diversity of the city. As well as drawing on the bountiful harvest of the Atlantic, the city's chefs also make good use of seasonal, local produce from the farms of Maryland and Virginia.

Chef adding finishing touches to a dish at Founding Farmers (see p186)

Global Flavours

As the capital of the United States, Washington has long served as a gathering place for leaders and dignitaries from across the country and around the world, who have brought their own recipes and culinary traditions to the city. Refugees from places such as El Salvador, Ethiopia, and Cambodia have settled in Washington, introducing its well-traveled, globally-minded citizens to unusual flavors and dishes. In such ethnically diverse neighborhoods as Adams-Morgan or Mount Pleasant, it's not unusual to find African, Asian, and South American restaurants standing side by side.

Power Dining

True to its reputation, the city boasts an impressive collection of "power dining" restaurants, where lobbyists, pundits, and lawyers gather for steaks and cocktails. Slip into a cozy booth at one of these reputed steakhouses and you're likely to spot at least a few members of the United States Congress.

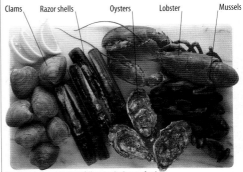

Clams   Razor shells   Oysters   Lobster   Mussels

Mouthwatering selection of Chesapeake Bay seafood

Washington's Signature Dishes

Maryland crab cakes

The unique nature of the capital makes it difficult to pin down its specialty dishes. The *Washington Post* has made a case for the "half-smoke," a mildly spicy hybrid of hot dog and smoked sausage, smothered in chili and cheese and often sold in sidewalk kiosks. Ben's Chili Bowl (see p189), is the best known purveyor, and a favorite of comedian Bill Cosby. Maryland Blue Crabs are also popular, often appearing as succulent crab cakes or tangy She-Crab Soup. The federal side of the city could be summed up with Senate Navy Bean Soup which has been served every day in the Senate Dining Room for more than 100 years. It's a humble, unassuming dish, and yet it is eaten on a regular basis by some of Washington's most influential residents.

Senate Navy Bean Soup uses navy (haricot) beans and ham hock to make a delicious, simple yet hearty soup fit for senators.

Where to Eat and Drink

Capitol Hill

Banana Café
Cuban $ Map 4 F5
500 8th St SE, 20003
Tel 543-5906
Enjoy a taste of the Carribean at reasonable prices. Occasional live music.

Five Guys
American $ Map 4 E5
1100 New Jersey Ave SE, 20003
Tel 863-0570
This national chain started in Virginia. The burgers are often voted as the best in the country.

Market Lunch
American $ Map 4 F5
Eastern Market, 225 7th St SE (at C St), 20003
Tel 547-8444
Crab cakes, local seafood, and excellent pancakes are served in a no-nonsense setting. Expect lines on weekends.

Bullfeathers
American $$ Map F E5
410 1st St SE, 20003
Tel 484-0228
This restaurant-bar popular with local workers is known for its burgers and Trivia Night.

Cava Mezze
Mediterranean $$ Map 4 F5
527 8th St SE, 20003
Tel 543-9090   **Closed** *Mon*
Incredible small plates and outstanding gyros are on offer here. The place is always packed.

Dubliner
Irish $$ Map 4 E3
520 North Capitol St NW, 20001
Tel 737-3773
A favorite of Washington's Irish community, Dubliner serves generous helpings of pub food.

Ethiopic
Ethiopian $$ Map 4 F3
401 H St NE, 20002
Tel 675-2066
A fresh, friendly addition to the city's Ethiopian culinary scene, with a pleasant dining room that overlooks the buzzing H Street.

Good Stuff Eatery
American $$ Map 4 F4
303 Pennsylvania Ave SE, 20003
Tel 543-8222   **Closed** *Sun*
Great burgers and fries, including the Obama Burger. First Lady Michelle Obama is a patron.

Sonoma
Italian $$ Map 4 F4
223 Pennsylvania Ave SE, 20003
Tel 544-8088
Great for sharing a big meal of locally sourced products. Elegant seating downstairs and casual dining upstairs.

Tortilla Coast
Mexican $$ Map 4 F5
329 Pennsylvania Ave SE, 20003
Tel 546-6768
A friendly atmosphere and Tex-Mex food are the draw here. Kids will enjoy the burritos, and adults, the frozen margaritas.

Price Guide
Prices are based on a three-course meal per person, including tax, service, and half a bottle of house wine.

$	up to $20
$$	$20–$40
$$$	over $40

We, the Pizza
Italian $$ Map 4 F4
305 Pennsylvania Ave SE, 20003
Tel 544-4008   **Closed** *Sun*
Known for their pizzas cooked in cast-iron pans, which some say are the best in the city. Also serves pasta, salads, and icecream.

Acqua Al 2
Italian $$$ Map 4 F5
212 7th St SE, 20003
Tel 525-4375   **Closed** *Mon*
A duplicate of the flagship Acqua Al 2 in Florence, Italy. Pricey and crowded, but offers authentic fare.

Belga Café
Belgian $$$ Map 4 F5
514 8th St SE, 20003
Tel 544-0100
A rare Belgian restaurant with a great selection of beer and, of course, mussels.

Bistro Bis
French $$$ Map 4 E3
15 E St NW, 20001
Tel 661-2700
Upscale dining in the classy Hotel George Bistro Bis. Excellent duck and lamb dishes, and cream puffs.

The Monocle
American $$$ Map 4 E3
107 D St NE, 20002
Tel 546-4488
A solid seafood and steak establishment near the Capitol. It gets crowded when Congress is in session.

Montmartre
French $$$ Map 4 F5
327 7 St, SE 20003
Tel 544-1244   **Closed** *Mon*
A casual neighborhood restaurant right across from Eastern Market, Montmartre is a favorite for brunch.

Toscana Café
Italian $$$ Map 4 F3
601 2nd St NE, 20002
Tel 525-2693
This is a small, hole-in-the wall eatery behind Union Station, but it serves authentic Tuscan cuisine. Reservations are needed as seating is limited in the tiny dining room.

Outdoor dining at the Bullfeathers restaurant-bar

For more information on types of restaurants *see p181*

The Mall

Atrium Cafe $
American   **Map** 3 D5
400 Virginia Ave SW, 20560
Tel 863-7590
Tucked away in L'Enfant Plaza, this tiny deli offers big, inexpensive sandwiches.

Atrium Café $$
American   **Map** 3 C4
10th St & Constitution Ave NW, 20560
Tel 633-1000
Dig into pizzas, burgers, chicken tenders, and mac 'n' cheese at this café, situated in the National Museum of Natural History.

Cascade Café $$
American   **Map** 4 D4
4th St & Constitution Ave NW, 20565
Tel 712-7458
High-class cafeteria food in a stunning setting within the National Gallery of Art.

DK Choice

Mitsitam Café $$
American   **Map** 4 D4
4th St & Independence Ave SW, 20565
Tel 866-868-7774
Probably the most unusual, and one of the best, restaurants in DC. Located in the National Museum of the American Indian, this café serves Native American cuisine from many tribes. The menu changes seasonally, but always includes bison and salmon. The Value Meal is a five-tribe sampler that is enough for two to share.

Pavilion Café $$
American   **Map** 4 D4
4th St & Constitution Ave NW, 20565
Tel 289-3360
Enjoy sandwiches and salads in the National Gallery's Sculpture Garden. Wine is available too.

Penn Quarter

Chipotle $
Mexican   **Map** 3 C3
601 F St NW, 20005
Tel 347-4701
One of the few Mexican chains in the city. Stop here for fresh and cheap giant burritos.

District of Pi $
Italian   **Map** 3 C3
901 F St NW, 20004
Tel 393-5484
Choose between the thick-crust "Chicago" or the thin-crust

Entrance of the popular Carmines on 7th Street NW

St. Louis pizza. District of Pi is big, noisy, and popular with families.

Full Kee $
Chinese   **Map** 4 D3
509 H St NW, 20001
Tel 371-2233
Inexpensive, authentic Hong Kong-style food at one of the last Chinese restaurants in the area.

Luke's Lobster $
Seafood   **Map** 3 C3
624 E St NW, 20004
Tel 347-3355
A tiny, shack-like restaurant serving unmatched Maine-style lobster rolls (cold lobster with melted butter in a split-top bun).

Merzi $
Indian   **Map** 3 C3
415 7th St NW, 20004
Tel 656-3794
Healthy Indian food that is ideal for a fast lunch or a reasonably priced dinner.

Paul Bakery $
French   **Map** 3 C3
801 Pennsylvania Ave NW, 20004
Tel 524-4500
The DC branch of a famous French bakery offers takeouts as

well as sit-down brunches. Try the ham and cheese crepe.

Austin Grill $$
Mexican   **Map** 3 C3
750 E St NW, 20004
Tel 393-3776
Ideal for families, this no-frills chain serves all the Tex-Mex classics, including taquitos, tacos and enchiladas.

Carmines $$
Italian   **Map** 3 C3
425 7th St NW, 20004
Tel 737-7770
The DC branch of the Manhattan classic. Huge, family-style place serving large portions.

District Chophouse & Brewery $$
American   **Map** 3 C3
509 7th St, 20002
Tel 347-3434
Burgers, giant salads, and huge plates of seafood and beef are served here with handcrafted ales.

DK Choice

Jaleo $$
Spanish   **Map** 3 C3
480 7th St NW, 20004
Tel 628-7949
Owned by chef José Andrés, this restaurant offers some of the best tapas and sangria in the city. The menu changes often, keeping Jaleo fresh and witty, while retaining the old favorites such as spinach with pine nuts and chorizo.

Oyamel $$
Mexican   **Map** 3 C3
401 7th St NW, 20004
Tel 628-1005
Enjoy a creative and modern menu at this popular Mexican joint. The guacamole is made fresh to your taste. Great margaritas.

Eye-catching exterior of the Pavilion Café at the National Gallery

Key to prices *see p183*

Proof
American $$
Map 3 C3
775 G St NW, 20001
Tel *737-7663*
Chic, contemporary cuisine and an impressive wine list. The entrées are excellent.

Rasika
Indian $$
Map 4 D3
633 D St NW, 20004
Tel *637-1222*   **Closed** *Sun*
High-end Indian cuisine served in a modern setting. Regional dishes plus traditional *tandoori* (cooked in a clay oven) and *sigri* (open barbecue).

Rosa Mexicana
Mexican $$
Map 3 C3
575 7th St NW, 20004
Tel *783-5522*
Fresh Mexican food served outdoors. Very popular, so expect a wait without a reservation.

Teaism
Japanese $$
Map 3 C3
400 8th St NW, 20004
Tel *638-6010*
Choose one of the many varieties of tea as an accompaniment to your delicate Japanese Bento meal are a winner. The salty oat cookies are a winner.

Zaytinya
Mediterranean $$
Map 3 C3
701 9th St NW, 20001
Tel *638-0800*
Another restaurant by renowned chef José Andrés. Stop here for Mediterranean tapas in a glamorous setting.

Acadiana
American $$$
Map 3 C2
901 New York Ave NW, 20004
Tel *408-8848*
A classy evocation of New Orleans serving amazing gumbo, turtle soup, and oysters. The brunch is excellent.

Brasserie Beck
Belgian $$$
Map 3 C2
1101 K St NW, 20005
Tel *408-1717*
Owned by local star chef, Robert Wiedmaier, Brasserie Beck serves *moules frites* and around 100 types of Belgian beer.

Fogo de Chao
Brazilian $$$
Map 3 C3
1101 Pennsylvania Ave NW, 20004
Tel *347-4668*
This all-you-can-eat Brazilian eatery is a meat lover's dream. Just signal the attending waiter to receive an unlimited supply of pork or beef.

Elegant dining room at Acadiana

Graffiato
Italian $$$
Map 4 D3
707 6th St NW, 20004
Tel *289-3600*
Top chef Mike Isabella serves his Italian-American grandmother's recipes. Great pizza and pasta. Patrons rave about the pepperoni sauce.

Oceanaire
Seafood $$$
Map 3 C3
1201 F St NW, 20004
Tel *347-2277*
This is a branch of the upscale national chain that specializes in excellent seafood including lobster and crab cakes.

Old Ebbitt Grill
American $$$
Map 3 B3
675 15th St NW, 20005
Tel *347-4800*
Stop at Washington DC's oldest saloon for traditional American fare. Old Ebbitt Grill specializes in seafood, including outstanding crab cakes, and steak.

Diners in the Mediterranean-style Zaytinya restaurant

Poste
French $$$
Map 3 C3
555 8th St NW, 20004
Tel *783-6060*
Enjoy great cocktails complemented by small plates such as sliders and fries at this bar in the stylish Hotel Monaco.

The Source
Asian $$$
Map 4 D4
575 Pennsylvania Ave NW, 20001
Tel *637-6100*
Wolfgang Puck's pricey Asian fusion restaurant is located on the first floor of the Newseum.

The White House and Foggy Bottom

The 51st State Tavern
American $
Map 2 D3
2512 L St NW, 20037
Tel *625-2444*
A bi-level sports bar offering typical bar fare; frequented by New York state team loyalists.

City Bites
American $
Map 2 F3
1800 G St NW, 20006
Tel *289-1820*
This tiny deli whips up delicious sandwiches and salads. Open for breakfast and lunch only.

Johnny Rockets
American $
Map 2 E3
2000 Pennsylvania Ave NW, 2006
Tel *822-1260*
A franchise of great burger, fries, and shake joints that echo the 1950s.

Potbelly Sandwich Shop
American $
Map 2 F3
1701 Pennsylvania Ave, 20004
Tel *775-1450*
Huge sandwiches, and a "skinny" menu with 30 percent fewer calories for the diet-conscious.

For more information on types of restaurants *see p181*

Façade of the sprawling Founding Farmers restaurant on Pennsylvania Avenue

Aroma $$
Indian   **Map** 3 A2
1919 I St NW, 20037
Tel *833-4700*   **Closed** *Sun*
Tandoori, *biryani* (a rice-based dish), and *vindaloo* (a spicy curried dish) feature on the traditional menu.

Bayou $$
American   **Map** 2 D3
2519 Pennsylvania Ave NW, 20037
Tel *223-6941*
A casual New Orleans restaurant with an easy vibe, live music, and Southern fare.

Café Lombardy $$
Mediterranean   **Map** D5
2019 Pennsylvania Ave NW, 20006
Tel *828-2600*
The French and Italian influenced menu here provides a rare grace note in the University district.

Firefly $$
American   **Map** 3 A1
1310 New Hampshire Ave NW, 20036
Tel *861-1310*
Comfort food such as *matzoh* (dumplings) soup and pot roast can be enjoyed here. Great brunch.

One Fish, Two Fish $$
Asian   **Map** 2 D3
2423 Pennsylvania Ave NW, 20037
Tel *882-0977*
Reliably good sushi and other Asian standards such as curries and pan-fried noodles.

The Public Bar $$
American   **Map** 2 F2
1214 18th St, 20036
Tel *223-2200*
A popular sports bar serving wings, chips, and burgers. Large crowds come to watch games.

Ancora $$$
Italian   **Map** 2 D3
600 New Hampshire Ave NW, 20037
Tel *333-1600*
Tucked into the Watergate, Ancora is chef Robert Kinkead's

take on contemporary Italian cuisine. Pair it with a night at the nearby Kennedy Center.

Blue Duck Tavern $$$
American   **Map** 2 E3
1201 24th St NW, 20037
Tel *419-6755*
Consistently rated as one of the best restaurants in DC, this trendy spot has a wood-burning oven. The duck, of course, is a specialty.

The Bombay Club $$$
Indian   **Map** 2 F3
815 Connecticut Ave NW, 20006
Tel *659-3727*
Refined Indian cuisine by the Rasika group. Fancy setting; one of Bill Clinton's favorite eateries.

DK Choice

Founding Farmers $$$
American   **Map** 2 E3
1924 Pennsylvania Ave NW, 20006
Tel *822-8783*
Everything at Founding Farmers is organic, sustainable, and made from scratch. The ingredients are high quality, seasonal, and locally sourced. The resolutely American menu includes Yankee pot roast, shrimp and grits, and chicken pot pie. Vegetarians are well-catered for as well. The delicious apple pie and red velvet cake are universal favorites.

Georgia Brown's $$$
American   **Map** 3 B2
950 15th St NW, 20005
Tel *393-4499*
This restaurant serves Lowcountry cuisine to a clientele that includes high-powered politicians.

Marcel's $$$
Belgian   **Map** 2 D3
2401 Pennsylvania Ave NW, 20037
Tel *296-1166*
This restaurant has impeccable service and a great menu. It

offers a free shuttle service to the Kennedy Center for the pre-theater crowd.

Rasika West End $$$
Indian   **Map** 2 E3
1190 New Hampshire Ave NW, 20037
Tel *466-2500*
Modern Indian cuisine. The highly rated menu is rivaled by the dining room's elegant decor.

Roof Terrace Restaurant $$$
American   **Map** 2 D4
2700 F St NW, 20037
Tel *416-8555*   **Closed** *Mon*
A casual eatery on the roof of the Kennedy Center with skyline views. Popular with theatergoers.

Vidalia $$$
American   **Map** 3 A2
1990 M St NW, 20036
Tel *659-1990*
A high-end restaurant with Southern roots. Sweetbreads, shrimp and grits, duck, and the Pie Plate are specialties.

Westend Bistro $$$
American   **Map** 2 E3
1150 22nd St NW, 20037
Tel *974-4900*
A popular restaurant located in the chic Ritz-Carlton hotel. The

Helpful waiting staff at Firefly, a restaurant serving American comfort food

deceptively simple but sophisticated menu includes *tuna carpaccio* and flat iron steaks.

Georgetown

Booeymonger $
American   **Map** 1 C2
3265 Prospect St NW, 20007
Tel *333-4810*
Consistently rated as the best in "cheap eats." Offers great sandwiches, sides, and soups.

Café Divan $
Turkish   **Map** 1 C2
1834 Wisconsin Ave NW, 20007
Tel *338-1747*
Well-priced Turkish food served in a stylish dining room, or as a takeout. Excellent doner kebabs and meze platter.

Five Guys $
American   **Map** 1 C2
1335 Wisconsin Ave, 20007
Tel *337-0400*
A franchise of the family-favorite burger chain. Unlimited peanuts, and excellent burgers and fries.

Georgetown Cupcake $
American   **Map** 1 C2
3302 M St NW, 20007
Tel *333-8448*
Popular for its delicious designer cakes, this shop has been featured on a reality series. Limited seating.

Johnny Rockets $
American   **Map** 2 D2
3131 M St NW, 20007
Tel *333-7994*
Part of a kitschy 1950s-themed chain that whips up great burgers, fries, and milkshakes.

ShopHouse Southeast Asian Kitchen
Pan-Asian $ **Map** 2 D2
2805 M St NW, 20007
Tel *627-1958*
Build yourself a satisfying budget meal from rice or noodles, meat or tofu, vegetables, and toppings.

Sweetgreen $
American   **Map** 1 C2
3333 M St, 20007
Tel *337-9339*
One of a small local chain that serves custom-made salads and superb frozen yogurt.

Café Bonaparte $$
French   **Map** 1 C2
1522 Wisconsin Ave NW, 20007
Tel *333-8830*
A tiny bistro-bar serving crepes, *croques monsieur* (grilled ham and cheese sandwiches), and

classic coffees. Ample choice for brunch or dessert.

Das Ethiopian Cuisine $$
Ethiopian   **Map** 2 D2
1201 28th St NW, 20007
Tel *333-4710*
A range of meat, seafood, and vegetable entrées are on the menu here. Samplers are available for the uninitiated.

El Centro D.F. $$
Mexican   **Map** 2 C2
1218 Wisconsin Ave NW, 20007
Tel *333-4100*
Outstanding tacos, *carnitas*, and margaritas at the Georgetown branch of this Mexican favorite.

Kafe Leopold $$
Austrian   **Map** 1 C3
3315 M St NW, 20007
Tel *965-6005*
A beautiful café in a lovely setting near the canal. Well-prepared small entrées, stellar desserts, and coffee.

DK Choice

Martin's Tavern $$
American   **Map** 1 C2
1264 Wisconsin Ave NW, 20007
Tel *333-7370*
This Washington institution has been in the Martin family for four generations. Stop here for comfort food, including oyster stew, welsh rarebit, and burgers. For an intimate dinner sit in the "dugout" – a cozy space at the rear of the bar. This is where famous politicians have been known to eat and drink, and where JFK proposed to Jackie. Great atmosphere.

Le Pain Quotidien $$
French   **Map** 2 D2
2815 M St NW, 20007
Tel *315-5420*
A *boulangerie* (bakery) chain that has both takeout and dine-in at communal tables. Great brunch.

Colorful interior of the Italian restaurant Paolo's

Paolo's $$
Italian   **Map** 1 C2
1303 Wisconsin Ave NW, 20007
Tel *333-7353*
Italian fare made California style. Great for people-watching, especially in the outdoor café.

Patisserie Poupon $$
French   **Map** 1 C2
1645 Wisconsin Ave NW, 20007
Tel *342-3248*   **Closed** *Mon*
A classic bistro-bakery with light fare including sandwiches, salads, and irresistible desserts. Possibly the best croissants outside of Paris.

Paul $$
French   **Map** 1 C2
1078 Wisconsin Ave NW, 20007
Tel *524-4630*
An outstanding bakery with a small café serving croissants, sandwiches, and quiches.

Pizzeria Paradiso $$
Italian   **Map** 1 C2
3282 M St NW, 20007
Tel *337-1245*
Known for its artful thin-crust pizza and plethora of toppings, this pizzeria also has a large beer menu. Always crowded.

Alfresco dining at Kafe Leopold, Georgetown

For more information on types of restaurants *see p181*

Patrons enjoying a meal on the patio of Café Milano, Georgetown

The Tombs $$
American   Map 1 B2
1226 36th St NW, 20007
Tel *337-6668*
A hang-out for Georgetown University students, with a menu of sandwiches and salads.

1789 $$$
American   Map 1 B2
1226 36th St NW, 20007
Tel *965-1789*
Traditional fine American food and impeccable service. A special-occasion restaurant with prices to match.

Bandolero $$$
Mexican   Map 1 C2
3241 M St NW, 20007
Tel *625-4488*
Chef Mike Isabella whips up modern Mexican cuisine and artisanal cocktails at this big, casual, and fun restaurant.

Café Milano $$$
Italian   Map 1 C2
3251 Prospect St NW, 20007
Tel *333-6183*
One of the best places for celebrity-watching. Fine Italian food as well as lighter fare, such as pizza.

The elegant Middleburg Room at 1789, roofed with New England barn siding

La Chaumiere $$$
French   Map 2 D2
2813 M St NW, 20007
Tel *338-1784*
A charming eatery with a quaint atmosphere; great for a date. Duck, mussels, *escargot*, and rabbit are the specialties.

Chez Billy Sud $$$
French   Map 2 D3
1039 31st St NW, 20007
Tel *965-2606*   **Closed** *Mon*
Located on a charming side street, this restaurant recreates the flavors of southern France. Lovely outdoor patio; perfect for a weekend brunch.

Clyde's $$$
American   Map 1 C2
3236 M St NW, 20007
Tel *333-9180*
A big, raucous pub with an excellent bar menu including ribs and crab cakes. Brunch lovers rave about the *challah* (yeast-leavened) French toast.

Farmers Fishers Bakers $$$
American   Map 2 D3
3000 K St NW, 20007
Tel *298-8783*
Waterfront restaurant with an eclectic, farm-to-table menu featuring fresh regional produce. Try the all-you-can-eat brunch menu.

Filomena $$$
Italian   Map 1 C3
1063 Wisconsin Ave NW, 20007
Tel *338-8800*
This family-run restaurant serves food from Abruzzi, central Italy. Its dining room is decorated like a holiday fantasy during Christmas.

Fiola Mare $$$
Italian   Map 2 D3
3050 K St NW, 20007
Tel *628-0065*
A seafood haven, with outdoor seating overlooking the Potomac.

The desserts, lobster ravioli, and bucatini with prawns are highly recommended. Book in advance.

Sea Catch $$$
American   Map 2 C3
1054 31st St NW, 20007
Tel *337-8855*   **Closed** *Sun*
Stop here for simple and tasty dishes of fresh, locally caught seafood, including huge lobsters and oysters.

Sequoia $$$
American   Map 2 D3
3000 K St NW, 20007
Tel *944-4200*   **Closed** *Mon*
The best restaurant on the riverfront and a favorite for brunch ($35 fixed price). It boasts a huge patio.

Tony and Joe's Seafood Place $$$
American   Map 2 D3
3000 K St NW, 20007
Tel *944-4545*
Enjoy seafood and salads on the riverfront patio here. Live jazz during the Sunday brunch.

Unum $$$
American   Map 2 D2
2917 M St NW, 20007
Tel *621-6959*
This highly rated restaurant has been dubbed a "small wonder" for its craft beers and seasonal menu of American fare with international influences.

Farther Afield

Ben's Chili Bowl $
American
1213 U St NW, 20009
Tel *667-0909*
Everyone, including Larry King and President Obama, eats at Ben's. Famous for its chili dog and half-smoke.

BGR The Burger Joint $
American   **Map** 2 E1
*1514 Connecticut Ave NW,
Dupont Circle, 20036*
Tel 387-9338
Sample fresh, seasonal burgers; the Greek burger with lamb is a favorite. The sweet potato fries are a must.

Cactus Cantina $
Mexican
*3300 Wisconsin Ave NW,
Cleveland Park, 20016*
Tel 686-7222
Huge plates of Tex-Mex food make Cactus Cantina ideal for families. It has a big dining room and a large patio for eating alfresco.

Dolcezza $
Mediterranean   **Map** 1 C2
1560 Wisconsin Ave NW, 20007
Tel 333-4646
Part of a local chain, Dolcezza serves artisan gelato and a variety of coffee.

Fat Pete's BBQ $
American
3407 Connecticut Ave NW, 20008
Tel 362-7777
Smoked meat afficionados will enjoy the ten different kinds of barbecue on offer. Sides include mac 'n' cheese and hush puppies.

Firehook Bakery $
American
3411 Connecticut Ave NW, 20008
Tel 362-2253
Renowned for its artisanal bread and desserts, this bakery also serves salads and sandwiches. Enjoy a meal in the beautiful vine garden.

Tony and Joe's Seafood Place, on the bank of the Potomac

The iconic Ben's Chili Bowl, a Washington institution

Madam's Organ $
American
*2461 18th St NW,
Adams Morgan, 20009*
Tel 667-5370
Live music every night, beer, and pub food. This mother-of-all dive bars is in Adams-Morgan – hence the pun.

Nam-Viet Pho 79 $
Asian
3419 Connecticut Ave NW, 20008
Tel 237-1015
Drop in here for good, inexpensive Vietnamese fare. Savor the seafood salad during summer and try the comforting soups in winter.

Pizza Mart $
Italian
*2445 18th St NW,
Adams Morgan, 20009*
Tel 234-9700
Known locally as "the big slice" for its mammoth, inexpensive pizza slices. Not the best pizza in town, but reasonable and quick.

Sweetgreen $
American   **Map** 2 E1
*1512 Connecticut Ave NW,
Dupont Circle, 20036*
Tel 387-9338
The Dupont Circle branch of a local chain that makes healthy salads. It has both standard and custom dishes for less than $10.

2Amys $$
Italian
*3715 Macomb St NW,
Cleveland Park, 20016*
Tel 885-5700
Stop here for genuine Italian pizza or unmatched small plates, including deviled eggs, *burrata* (Italian cheese), eggplant confit, and olives.

Barcelona Wine Bar $$
Mediterranean
3310 Wisconsin Ave NW, 20016
Tel 800-4100
An innovative take on tapas, using locally sourced ingredients such as seafood from the Chesapeake. Try the excellent drinks, which include varieties of sangria.

Bistro La Bonne $$
French   **Map** 3 B1
1340 U St NW, 20009
Tel 758-3413
French staples include *steak-frites, escargot*, and lots of mussel choices. The bar on the third floor often has happy hour specials.

> ## DK Choice
>
> ### Busboys and Poets $$
> American
> *2021 14th St, 20009*
> **Tel** 387-6138
> A restaurant, bookstore, and performance space that hosts poetry readings, author talks, and improv theater, frequented by a cross-section of locals. The food is excellent too. Popular for brunch, but get here before noon to avoid a packed house.

Café Deluxe $$
American
*3228 Wisconsin Ave NW,
Cleveland Park, 20008*
Tel 686-2233
A bustling tavern and bistro serving comfort food. The service is attentive.

Café Saint Ex $$
American   **Map** 3 B1
1847 14th St NW, 20009
Tel 265-7839
Named for the author of *The Little Prince*, this cozy aviation-themed bar/restaurant has impressive bar food and a good brunch menu.

Le Diplomate $$
French   **Map** 3 B1
1601 14th St NW, 20009
Tel 332-3333
A hotspot for the hip, with a retro Parisian decor and feel. Book ahead for dinner.

Eatonville $$
American
2121 14th St NW, 20009
Tel 332-9672
Southern food served with style and wit. The menu features catfish, fried green tomatoes, and po'boys (traditional Louisiana sandwiches). Ice tea is served out of a jar.

For more information on types of restaurants *see p181*

Outdoor seating at Cashion's Eat Place in Adams Morgan

Marvin $$
American
2007 14th St NW, 20009
Tel *797-7171*
Named after singer and
songwriter Marvin Gaye, a DC
native, this bistro has a rooftop
beer garden and a casual vibe.

Medium Rare $$
American
*3500 Connecticut Ave NW,
Cleveland Park, 20008*
Tel *237-1432*
A great place for steak lovers,
with a good-value fixed-price
menu of steak, fries, salad, and
bread. Amazing desserts.

Mission $$
Mexican   **Map** 3 A1
1606 20th St NW, 20009
Tel *525-2010*
A cocktail bar and restaurant
featuring bottomless drinks,
chicken enchiladas, and salsa on
the menu. Dine alfresco on the
charming patio.

Perry's Restaurant $$
American
*1811 Columbia Rd NW, Adams
Morgan, 20009*
Tel *234-6218*
The top-floor roof garden at this
restaurant offers a fantastic view

of Washington. It offers an
eclectic menu, but is best known
for its Sunday brunch.

St. Arnold's Mussel Bar $$
Belgian
*3433 Connecticut Ave NW,
Cleveland Park, 20008*
Tel *621-6434*
Mussels of every description, as
well as a great choice of Belgian
beer, can be found at this bar.
Reasonably priced happy hour.

Ardeo + Bardeo $$$
American
*3311 Connecticut Ave NW,
Cleveland Park, 20008*
Tel *244-6750*
Two side-by-side eateries
knocked into one, serving
delicious modern American
cuisine with Asian and
Mediterranean influences.
Dine on the romantic rooftop
terrace in warm weather.

BlackSalt $$$
American
*4883 MacArthur Blvd NW,
Palisades, 20007*
Tel *342-9101*
A restaurant specializing in
inventive seafood; the corn-
encrusted oysters and mussels
are particular highlights.

Cashion's Eat Place $$$
American
*1819 Columbia Rd NW,
Adams Morgan, 20009*
Tel *797-1819*
Seasonal American cuisine with
Mediterranean influences. The
menu changes daily and always
includes a vegetarian entrée.

Makoto $$$
Japanese
*4822 MacArthur Blvd NW, Palisades,
20016*
Tel *298-6866*   **Closed** Mon
The best Japanese restaurant
in DC, with a delicious fixed-
price chef's menu. Take off
your shoes at the threshold
and enter Japan.

Obelisk $$$
Italian   **Map** 3 A1
2029 P St NW, 20036
Tel *872-1180*   **Closed** Sun &
Mon
The fixed-price menu includes
10 courses served in a tiny dining
room. High-end Italian cuisine.

**Pearl Dive
Oyster Palace** $$$
Seafood   **Map** 3 B1
1612 14th St NW, 20009
Tel *986-8778*
The waiters here explain the
provenance of the oysters, most
of which are served raw. Be sure
to try the bourbon pecan pie.
Trendy and expensive.

Restaurant Nora $$$
American   **Map** 2 E1
*2132 Florida Ave NW, Dupont
Circle, 20008*
Tel *462-5143*
America's first certified organic
restaurant, supervised by organic
food pioneer Nora Poullion.
Seasonal dining at its best.

Ripple $$$
American
*3417 Connecticut Ave NW,
Cleveland Park, 20008*
Tel *244-7995*
The intriguing menu here
includes a charcuterie and grilled
cheese bar, mushroom *agnolotti*
(ravioli), and okra with ricotta.

Beyond Washington

Bittersweet Café $
American
823 King St, Alexandria, VA 22314
Tel *(703) 549-1028*
Known for its giant sandwiches
and homemade soups, this café
has a salad bar and offers outdoor
seating. Takeout available.

The cozy and inviting Restaurant Nora, America's original organic restaurant

Michie Tavern, set amid sprawling gardens

The Crab Claw $
American
304 Burns St, St. Michaels, MD 21663
Tel *(410) 745-2900*
A popular crab eatery since 1965. The decor is simple, but the fresh seafood and cold beer are superb.

Michie Tavern $
American
683 Thomas Jefferson Pkwy, Charlottesville, VA 22902
Tel *(434) 977-1234*
The Michie Tavern has been serving traditional American fare for over 200 years. Delicious fried chicken is the speciality.

Yellow Brick Bank $
American
201 East German St, Shepherdstown, WV 25443
Tel *(304) 876-2208*   **Closed** *Sun & Mon*
Set in a former bank building, Yellow Brick Bank serves locally sourced food and rich desserts.

Christiana Campbell's $$
American
101 South Waller St, Williamsburg, VA 23187
Tel *(757) 229-2141*   **Closed** *Sun & Mon*
A colonial tavern that has been serving traditional cuisine since George Washington's time.

Gadsby's $$
American
134 North Royal St, Alexandria, VA 22314
Tel *(703) 746-4242*
Food from the Revolution era served in a genuine 18th-century tavern. Martha Washington's apple pie is a winner.

Mama's on the Half Shell $$
Seafood
2901 O'Donnell St, Baltimore, MD 21224
Tel *(410) 276-3160*
A neighborhood restaurant with excellent regional seafood.

Oysters, crabs, and crab cakes are served in huge portions.

Mon Ami Gabi $$
French
7239 Woodmont Ave, Bethesda, MD 20814
Tel *(301) 654-1234*
A French bistro in suburban Maryland with traditional specialties: *steak-frites*, *bouillabaisse*, and crepes.

Le Refuge $$
French
127 North Washington St, Alexandria, VA 22314
Tel *(703) 548-4661*   **Closed** *Sun*
Sample the superb Dover sole, frog legs, beef Wellington, and crème brulée at this family-run French restaurant.

Vermilion $$
American
1120 King St, Alexandria, VA 22314
Tel *(703) 684-9669*
This restaurant is committed to supporting local farmers and regionally grown produce. Fixed-price "farm table" nights offer a chance to dine with chef Tony Chittum.

DK Choice
Inn at Little Washington $$$
American
309 Middle St, Little Washington, VA 22747
Tel *(540) 675-3800*
One of America's most famous restaurants. Chef Patrick O'Connell's culinary jewel offers flawless service, and has a refined, seasonal menu. The herbs come from O'Connell's kitchen garden. Do not miss the decadent chocolate Seven Deadly Sins dessert. Dining at this Michelin-starred organic restaurant is a once-in-a-lifetime experience.

Old Angler's Inn $$$
American
10801 MacArthur Blvd, Potomac, MD 20854
Tel *(301) 365-2425*
This inn, dating from 1860, is next to the C&O Canal. Dine by the fire in winter and on the patio in summer. There's a formal menu for dinner and a choice of mussels or burgers for lunch.

Ray's the Steaks $$$
American
2300 Wilson Blvd, Arlington, VA 22209
Tel *(703) 841-7297*
Enjoy giant, perfectly cooked steaks in a no-frills setting. Fans also recommend the crab bisque.

Restaurant Eve $$$
American
110 South Pitt St, Alexandria, VA 22314
Tel *(703) 706-0450*   **Closed** *Sun*
A culinary showcase for chef Cathal Armstrong. The fixed-price menus in the tasting room are expensive, but the bistro and lounge are more reasonably priced alternatives.

The sunny patio with bay views at The Crab Claw

For more information on types of restaurants *see p181*

SHOPPING IN WASHINGTON, DC

Washington's vast selection of stores makes shopping in the capital a pleasurable experience. Souvenirs can be found anywhere from fashion boutiques and specialist food stores to museum and gallery gift shops. The many museums on the Mall and around the city sell a wide variety of unusual gifts, reproduction prints, and replica artifacts selected from all over the world. Although the many smart shopping malls and department stores in the DC area can provide hours of shopping, Georgetown offers visitors a far more lively and authentic environment in which to browse. It is a neighborhood packed with fashionable clothing boutiques and endless interesting shops that sell everything from antiques to hair dye, from one-dollar bargains to priceless works of art.

The shopping area at Union Station

Opening Hours

Most department stores, shopping malls, and other centers are open from 10am until 8 or 9pm, Monday through Saturday, and from noon until 6pm on Sunday. Smaller shops and boutiques are generally open from noon until 6pm on Sundays, and from 10 until 6 or 7pm on all other days. Convenience stores such as local grocery stores may open for longer hours. Increasingly, drugstores (pharmacies) and supermarkets are open 24 hours.

How to Pay

Goods may be paid for in cash, in traveler's checks (in US dollars), or by credit card. VISA and MasterCard are the most popular credit cards in the United States, while American Express is often, but not always, accepted. A tax of 5.75 percent is added to all purchases at the cash register.

Sales

Department stores, such as **Macy's** in the Penn Quarter area and **Nordstrom** farther out in Arlington, often hold sales during holiday weekends, including Memorial Day, the 4th of July, Labor Day, and Columbus Day. Check the newspapers for advertisements to find good prices on electronics, jewelry, kitchenwares, shoes, and clothing. White sales (towels and bedlinen) occur in January.

Museum Shops

All the museums on the Mall have a wide selection of products on sale in their shops. The **National Gallery of Art** sells artwork reproductions, books, art-related games and children's toys, and the **National Museum of African Art** offers a range of African textiles, ceramics, basketry, musical instruments, and books. In Penn Quarter, the **Smithsonian American Art Museum** shop has decorative items, books, and original handmade craft pieces.

The **National Museum of American History** shop carries a range of souvenirs such as American crafts, reproductions, and T-shirts, including merchandise inspired by the Star-Spangled Banner, as well as a range of books on American history. They also sell recordings from the 1940s to the 1970s, including Doo Wop, Motown, and Disco, from the Smithsonian Recordings and Smithsonian Folkways labels. Products can be purchased online too.

Also well worth a visit, near the White House, is the shop at the **Decatur House Museum**, home of Stephen Decatur, a naval hero from the War of 1812. It has a collection of items for sale related to Washington's history, art, and architecture.

For a selection of interesting books on architecture, contemporary design, and historic preservation, as well as a range of toys, ties, frames, and gifts, pay a visit to the **National Building Museum** shop at Judiciary Square.

Stalls selling an eclectic range of goods at Eastern Market

Window-shoppers looking at wares in an Urban Outfitters store, Georgetown

Malls and Department Stores

There are a few small-scale shopping malls in central Washington. **Union Station**, the beautifully renovated train station in the Capitol Hill area *(see p57),* houses 130 shops and restaurants on three levels, in a very pleasant environment. There are name-brand stores as well as an extensive collection of specialty shops that sell clothing, gifts, jewelry, crafts, souvenirs, and more. Many of the shops have been closed for a renovation of the station.

Two small shopping malls – **Mazza Gallerie** and **Chevy Chase Pavilion** – are located on upper Wisconsin Avenue in the Friendship Heights neighborhood. The metro is convenient, but there is also plenty of parking for cars. Visitors can shop at Bloomingdale's, Neiman Marcus, Saks Fifth Avenue, or Lord and Taylor department stores, or the specialty boutiques and name-brand stores.

The larger malls are located in the Maryland and Virginia suburbs. The **Fashion Center at Pentagon City** is easily reached by metro. Discount-hunters should head for the 230 outlets at **Potomac Mills**, situated 30 miles (48 km) south of the city on I-95. Several discount stores have also opened on the periphery of Georgetown Park including **T.J. Maxx** and **Homegoods**.

Galleries, Arts, and Crafts

Visitors will discover a cornucopia of art galleries and crafts shops in three of Washington's neighborhoods – Georgetown, Dupont Circle, and Adams-Morgan. Here visitors can spend a few hours feasting their eyes on the delightful objects on display.

Work by local artists is on sale in the **Addison/ Ripley Fine Arts**, located in Georgetown. Some of the best pottery can be found in the **Appalachian Spring** shops in Georgetown and at Union Station. **Eastern Market** in Capitol Hill offers a vibrant mix of stalls from antiques to ethnic artifacts, and is best at weekends. Art lovers should browse along 7th Street, NW, between D Street and the Verizon Center. Out of town, in Alexandria, the **Torpedo Factory Art Center** is excellent for lovers of all kinds of arts and crafts.

Torpedo Factory
Art Center logo

Souvenirs

Collectors' items and DC memorabilia are abundant at Political Americana and Made in America, two shops in **Union Station**. The **Old Post Office Pavilion** (closed for renovation) near Metro Center, is also worth a visit for DC souvenirs. The gift shops in the **Kennedy Center** sell gifts and books about the performing arts and Washington in general. People looking for religious items or unusual souvenirs should try the **Washington National Cathedral** museum and book shop in the basement of the cathedral. Other souvenir items are sold on the second level of the parking garage.

Clothes

Wisconsin Avenue and M Street in Georgetown are home to a wide range of clothing stores. National highstreet chains include **The Gap**, while those seeking something a little more out of the ordinary should visit **Urban Outfitters**, Intermix, and Cusp. **H & M**, the international discount store, sells clothing for men, women, and children at reasonable prices.

The space formerly known as Georgetown Park, situated on the intersection of Wisconsin Avenue and M Street, maintains street-facing modern shops while its Victorian-style interior is being redeveloped. There are high-end boutiques here as well as branded clothing stores. There is also a variety of clothes shops to browse in the Friendship Heights neighborhood.

Food and Wine

On Capitol Hill, you can shop for snacks and fresh produce or sit down for lunch in the bustling food hall of the Eastern Market, which also hosts an open-air farmers' market on Tuesdays.

For something more unusual, tasty, or exotic in the culinary field, there are several delicatessens worth visiting in Washington. In particular, try **Dean & Deluca** in Georgetown, which stocks an excellent selection of gourmet foods and also offers a fine range of American and European wines. While you are there, take the opportunity to sample the food and drinks available in the pleasant on-site café.

The magnificent National Cathedral

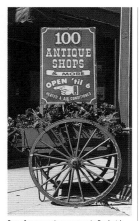
One of many antique centers in Frederick

Antiques

There are some wonderful hidden treasures to be discovered in the many antique stores scattered throughout Washington. Along Wisconsin Avenue, between P and S streets and also along M and O streets, there are around 20 antique shops. Some specialize in expensive antiques, others in prints, lamps, silverware, perfume bottles, or just interesting knick-knacks. **Random Harvest** on Wisconsin Avenue carries both upholstered and wooden furniture from the late 1800s through to the mid-20th century. It also stocks a carefully chosen selection of home accessories, including pillows, mirrors, and lamps.

Adams-Morgan and Dupont Circle are also good neighborhoods for antique hunting. **Brass Knob Architectural Antiques**, on 18th Street, is worth visiting for their range of salvaged curiosities, including clawfoot bathtubs and unusual antique light fixtures. Customers are bound to leave with just the perfect relic for their home, which could be anything from a chandelier to an iron gate.

There is also a number of centers for antiques outside central Washington. Kensington in Maryland and Old Town Alexandria in Virginia are areas rich in antiques. **Studio Antiques** in Alexandria sells all kinds of antiques, such as dolls, china, and silver, but specializes in books. In Frederick, Maryland, there is the enormous **Emporium Antiques**. This paradise for antiques lovers houses over 100 shops that sell everything from huge pieces of furniture through household wares to jewelry.

Books and Music

Book lovers are spoiled for choice in Washington and will enjoy spending time browsing in the myriad bookstores that can be found in the city.

There are several excellent independent and second-hand bookstores, especially in the Dupont Circle area. In **Kramerbooks & Afterwords Café**, customers can sit with their new purchase while drinking a coffee. There is also a full-service restaurant. **Second Story Books** is DC's biggest second-hand store, which also offers CDs and vinyl, vintage prints and photographs, and other framed ephemera.

Farther north, on Connecticut Avenue, is the **Politics & Prose Bookstore**, a favorite among Washingtonians for its combination of books and coffee. Customers can chat with the knowledgeable staff, browse, or attend a reading. (The Sunday book review section of the *Washington Post* lists readings.) **Busboys and Poets** on 5th Street is a community hub for writers, activists, and thinkers. It combines a bookstore with a restaurant, bar, and performance space where author readings and open-mic poetry nights are held.

Miscellaneous

The many department stores in and around Washington, such as **Macy's**, **Nordstrom**, and **Neiman-Marcus**, are well-stocked with good quality household wares from linens to cutlery and crockery. They are also prepared to order any out-of-stock items for their customers.

Wake Up Little Suzie sells unusual and unique gifts, such as handmade books, jewelry, and hanging mobiles. Similarly, **Chocolate Moose**, on L Street, is a treasure trove of the unusual and unconventional, including ceramics, chocolates, jewelry, and children's toys, among other things. **Tabletop DC** on 20th Street sells everything from utensils, toys, and jewelry, to placemats, picture frames, and calendars.

Everything in contemporary products for the home, from kitchenware to furniture, can be found at **Crate & Barrel** in Spring Valley. In Georgetown is **Restoration Hardware**, which offers everything from decorative door knobs through gardening supplies and lamps, to old-fashioned toys and the popular, heavy oak Mission furniture that originated in the Arts and Crafts Movement.

A bookstore and café are combined at Kramerbooks & Afterwords Café

DIRECTORY

Malls and Department Stores

Bloomingdale's
5300 Western Ave,
Chevy Chase DC.
Tel (202) 774-3700.

Chevy Chase Pavilion
5335 Wisconsin Ave, NW.
Tel (202) 686-5335.

Fashion Center at Pentagon City
1100 South Hayes St,
Arlington, Virginia.
Tel (703) 415-2400.

Homegoods
3222 M St, NW. **Map** 1 C2.
Tel (202) 333-1040.

Lord & Taylor
5255 Western Ave,
Chevy Chase, MD.
Tel (202) 362-9600.

Macy's Department Store
1201 G St, NW. **Map** 3 C3.
Tel (202) 628-6661.

Mazza Gallerie Mall
5300 Wisconsin Ave, NW.
Tel (202) 966-6114.

Neiman-Marcus
Mazza Gallerie. **Map** 1 B1.
Tel (202) 966-9700.

Nordstrom
Fashion Center at
Pentagon City.
Tel (703) 415-1121.

Potomac Mills
Woodbridge, VA.
Tel (703) 496-9330.

Saks Fifth Avenue
Chevy Chase Pavilion.
Tel (301) 657-9000.

T.J. Maxx
3222 M St, NW. **Map** 1 C2.
Tel (202) 333-1040.

Union Station Shops
40 Massachusetts Ave,
NE. **Map** 4 E3.
Tel (202) 289-1908.

Galleries, Arts, and Craft

Addison/Ripley Fine Arts
1670 Wisconsin Ave, NW.
Map 1 C2.
Tel (202) 338-5180.

Appalachian Spring
1415 Wisconsin Ave, NW.
Map 1 C2.
Tel (202) 337-5780.

Eastern Market
225 7th St, SE.
Map 4 F4.
Tel (202) 698-5253.

Torpedo Factory Art Center
105 N. Union St,
Alexandria, VA.
Tel (703) 838-4565.

Antiques

Brass Knob Architectural Antiques
2311 18th St, NW.
Map 3 A1.
Tel (202) 332-3370.

Emporium Antiques
112 E. Patrick St,
Frederick, MD.
Tel (301) 662-7099.

Georgetown Flea Market
Wisconsin Ave, between
S & T Sts, NW.
Map 1 C3.

Random Harvest
1313 Wisconsin Ave, NW.
Map 1 C2.
Tel (202) 333-5569.

Studio Antiques
524 N. Washington St,
Alexandria, VA.
Tel (703) 548-5188.

Souvenirs

Kennedy Center
New Hampshire Ave &
Rock Creek Parkway, NW.
Map 2 D4.
Tel (202) 467-4600.

Old Post Office Pavilion
Pennsylvania Ave
& 12th St, NW.
Map 3 C3.
Tel (202) 289-4224.

Washington National Cathedral
Massachusetts &
Wisconsin Ave, NW.
Tel (202) 537-6600.

Books and Music

Busboys and Poets
1025 5th St, NW.
Map 4 D3.
Tel (202) 789-2227.
2021 14th St, NW.
Tel (202) 387-7638.
235 Carroll St, NW.
Tel (202) 726-0856.
625 Monroe St, NE.
Tel (202) 636-7230.

Kramerbooks & Afterwords Café
1517 Connecticut Ave,
NW. **Map** 2 E2.
Tel (202) 387-1400.

Politics & Prose Bookstore
5015 Connecticut Ave,
NW. **Map** 2 E2.
Tel (202) 364-1919.

Second Story Books
2000 P St, NW.
Map 1 B2.
Tel (202) 659-8884.

Museum Shops

Decatur House Museum
1610 H St, NW. **Map** 3 A3.
Tel (202) 842-0917.

National Building Museum
401 F St, NW. **Map** 4 D3.
Tel (202) 272-2448.

National Gallery of Art
Constitution Ave at
6th St, NW.
Map 4 D4.
Tel (202) 842-4215.

National Museum of African Art
950 Independence Ave,
SW. **Map** 3 C4.
Tel (202) 633-4600.

National Museum of American History
The Mall between
12th and 14th Sts, NW.
Map 3 B4.
Tel (202) 633-1000.

Smithsonian American Art Museum
8th and F NW.
Map 3 C3.
Tel (202) 633-1000.

Clothes

The Gap
1120 Connecticut Ave,
NW. **Map** 3 A2.
Tel (202) 429-0691.

H & M
Georgetown Park
(Wisconsin Ave and
M St, NW). **Map** 1 C2.
Tel (202) 298-6792.
1025 F St, NW. **Map** 3 C3.
Tel (202) 347-3306.
1133 Connecticut Ave,
NW. **Map** 2 F3.
Tel (855) 466-7467.
50 Massachusetts Ave, NE.
Map 4 E3.

Urban Outfitters
3111 M St, NW.
Map 1 C2.
Tel (202) 342-1012.

Food and Wine

Dean & Deluca
3276 M St, NW.
Map 1 C2.
Tel (202) 342-2500.

Miscellaneous

Chocolate Moose
1743 L St, NW.
Map 2 F3.
Tel (202) 463-0992.

Crate & Barrel
4820 Massachusetts Ave,
NW. **Tel** (202) 364-6100.

Restoration Hardware
1222 Wisconsin Ave, NW.
Map 1 C2.
Tel (202) 625-2771.

Tabletop DC
1608 20th St, NW.
Map 2 E2.
Tel (202) 387-7117.

Wake Up Little Suzie
3409 Connecticut
Ave, NW.
Tel (202) 244-0700.

ENTERTAINMENT IN WASHINGTON, DC

Visitors to Washington will never be at a loss for entertainment, from flying a kite in the grounds of the Washington Monument to attending a concert at the Kennedy Center. The city's diverse, international community offers a rich array of choices. If you are looking for swing dancing you will find it; you will also hear different beats around town, including salsa, jazz, and rhythm and blues. Outdoor enthusiasts can choose from cycling on the Rock Creek bike path to canoeing on the Potomac River. If you are looking for something less active, take in a film at the Smithsonian. Theater-goers have a wide range of choices, from Shakespeare through highly respected repertory companies to Broadway musicals. No matter what your budget is, you will find something to do – there are more free activities in DC than in any other American city.

Information Sources

The best places to find inform-ation on plays, movies, and concerts are the **Washington City Paper** and the Weekend section of Friday's edition of the **Washington Post**. Internet users can check out *Style Live*, the entertainment guide on the *Washington Post* website.

The "Where & When" section in the monthly **Washingtonian** magazine also lists events.

Auditorium of the Shakespeare Theatre on 7th Street

Booking Tickets

Tickets may be bought in advance at box offices, or by phone and through the Internet. Tickets for all events at the **Kennedy Center** can be obtained through **Instant Charge**. Tickets for the Verizon Center, the Jiffy Lube Live, and the Warner Theater can be bought by phone through **Ticketmaster**. For Arena, Lisner Auditorium, Ford's Theatre, Merriweather Post Pavilion, and Woolly Mammoth tickets, contact **Tickets.com**.

Façade of the John F. Kennedy Center for the Performing Arts

Discount Tickets

Most theaters give group discounts, and several offer student and senior discounts for same-day performances. Half-price tickets for seats on the day of the performance may be obtained in person at **Ticketplace**, at 407 7th St, NW, or on their website.

In addition, theaters offer their own special discounts: The Arena sells a limited number of "Hottix," half-price seats, 30 to 90 minutes before the show. The Shakespeare Theatre offers 20 percent off for senior citizens Sunday through Thursday, 50 percent one hour before curtain rise for students, and discounts for all previews. The Kennedy Center has a limited number of half-price tickets available to students, senior citizens, and anyone with permanent disabilities. These go on sale at noon on the day of the performance (some are available before the first performance). Standing-room tickets may be available if a show is sold out.

Free Events

The daily newspapers provide up-to-date listings of free lectures, concerts, gallery talks, films, book signings, poetry readings, and shows.

Local and international artists offer free performances on the Millennium Stage at the Kennedy Center every evening at 6pm.

The **National Symphony Orchestra** gives a free outdoor concert on the West Lawn of the Capitol on Labor Day and Memorial Day weekends, and on the Fourth of July. In summer, various military bands such as the **United States Marine Band**, the Navy, Air Force or the **US Army Band** give free concerts (contact them direct for details).

From October to June, the **National Gallery of Art** sponsors free Sunday evening concerts at

Tourists outside the National Gallery of Art

7pm in the West Garden Court, and also free summer jazz concerts on Friday evenings in the Sculpture Garden. Free lectures and gallery talks are held at the **Library of Congress** and at the National Gallery of Art.

Open-Air Entertainment

During the summer months at **Wolf Trap Farm Park for the Performing Arts** world-famous performers can be seen on any night. Check their calendar of events and find your favorite form of entertainment – opera, jazz, Broadway musical, ballet, folk, or country music. You can bring a picnic to enjoy on the lawn.

On Thursday evenings in summer, the **National Zoo** hosts concerts on Lion Tiger Hill. They start at 6:30pm.

If you are in Washington in June try to catch the **Shakespeare Theatre Free for All** held at the Sidney Harman Hall in Penn Quarter.

The *Washington Post* lists the local fairs and festivals, held every weekend in warm weather. On the first weekend in May, the **Washington National Cathedral** sponsors the Flowermart, a festival featuring an old-fashioned carousel, children's games, crafts, and good food. The **Smithsonian Folklife Festival**, a two-week extravaganza held on the Mall at the end of June and early July, brings together folk artists from around the world. For details of other annual events in the city, see Washington, DC Through The Year (*pp38–41*).

Facilities for the Disabled

All the major theaters in Washington are wheelchair accessible. The Kennedy Center publishes a list of its upcoming sign-interpreted, audio-described, and captioned performances. For details of these and information on the venue's other accessibility services, check its website.

Many theaters, including the Kennedy Center, Ford's Theatre, the Shakespeare Theatre, and Arena Stage, have audio enhancement devices, as well as a limited number of signed performances. For the hearing impaired, TTY phone numbers are listed in the Weekend section of the *Washington Post*.

The National Gallery of Art provides assisted listening devices for lectures. Sign-language interpretation is available with three weeks' notice, and a telecommunications device for the deaf (TDD) can be found near the Concourse Sales Shop. For those with limited sight, the theater Arena Stage offers audio description, touch tours of the set, and program books in large print and Braille.

DIRECTORY

Information Sources

Washington City Paper
washingtoncitypaper.com

Washington Post
washingtonpost.com

Washingtonian
washingtonian.com

Booking Tickets

John F. Kennedy Center for the Performing Arts
New Hampshire Ave at Rock Creek Parkway, NW. **Map** 2 D4.
Tickets booked via Instant Charge **Tel** (202) 467-4600 or (800) 444-1324.
kennedy-center.org

Ticketmaster
Tel (202) 397-7328.
ticketmaster.com

Tickets.com
Tel (800) 955-5566.
tickets.com

Discount Tickets

Ticketplace
407 7th St, NW.
Map 3 C3.
ticketplace.org

Free Events

Library of Congress
1st St & Independence Ave, SE. **Map** 4 E4.
Tel (202) 707-5502.
loc.gov/concerts

National Gallery of Art
Constitution Ave at 6th St, NW. **Map** 4 D4.
Tel (202) 737-4215.
nga.gov

National Symphony Orchestra
Tel (202) 467-4600.

US Army Band
Tel (703) 696-3399.
usarmyband.com

US Marine Band
Tel (202) 433-4011.
marineband.usmc.mil

Open-Air Entertainment

National Zoo
3001 Connecticut Ave, NW. **Tel** (202) 633-4800.
nationalzoo.si.edu

Shakespeare Theatre Free for All
Sidney Harman Hall, 610 F St, NW. **Map** 4 D3.
shakespearetheatre.org

Smithsonian Folklife Festival
Tel (202) 633-1000.
festival.si.edu

Washington National Cathedral
Massachusetts and Wisconsin Aves, NW.
Tel (202) 537-6200.
nationalcathedral.org

Wolf Trap Farm Park for the Performing Arts
1645 Trap Rd, Vienna, VA.
Tel (703) 255-1900 (info).
Tel (877) 965-3872 (tickets).
wolftrap.org

Cultural Events

For an evening out, Washington has much to offer. A seafood dinner on the waterfront followed by a play at Arena Stage, Washington's oldest repertory company; dancing at one of the clubs on U Street; jazz in Georgetown; a late-night coffee bar in Dupont Circle; or opening night at the opera at the Kennedy Center and a nightcap in the West End. Or if you are staying downtown and do not want to venture far from your hotel, see a show at the Warner or the National Theater, where the best of Broadway finds a home.

Dancing to live music at the Kennedy Center

The façade of the Warner Theatre on 13th Street

Film and Theater

Independent and foreign-language films, as well as classic revivals, are screened at the state-of-the-art **Landmark's E Street Cinema**. Film festivals are held at the **Kennedy Center**. Museums such as **The National Gallery of Art** show films relating to current exhibitions. **The Library of Congress** offers a free film series of documentaries and films related to the exhibits in the museum, shown in the Mary Pickford Theater. The DC Film Festival is based at the Lincoln Theatre.

National touring theater companies bring shows to the **John F. Kennedy Center for the Performing Arts**, the **Warner**

Theatre, and the **National Theatre**. For a more intimate setting, try **Ford's Theatre**. **Arena Stage** has a well-established repertory company. **The Studio** and the **Woolly Mammoth Theatre** produce contemporary works.

The **Shakespeare Theatre** produces works in a modern, elegant setting. For plays performed in Spanish, seek out the **Gala Hispanic Theater**.

Opera and Classical Music

Based at the Kennedy Center, the **Washington National Opera Company** is often considered one of the capital's crown jewels. Although many performances do sell out, standing room tickets are sometimes available. The **National Symphony Orchestra** performs classical and contemporary works.

A rich variety of chamber ensembles and choral groups perform regularly around the city. The **Washington Performing Arts Society** brings internationally renowned performers to DC.

Dance

The Kennedy Center offers a magnificent ballet and dance season every year, with sell-out productions from the world's finest companies including the Bolshoi, the American Ballet Theater, the Royal Swedish Ballet, and the Dance Theater of Harlem.

Dance Place showcases its own professional modern dance companies, as well as international contemporary dance companies.

If you would prefer to take to the floor yourself, make your way to **Glen Echo Park** where people from ages 7 to 70 enjoy evenings of swing dancing, contra dancing (line dancing), Louisiana Cajun zydeco dancing, and waltzes. The Kennedy Center also occasionally offers dancing to live bands.

Rock, Jazz, and Blues

To see the "biggest names and the hottest newcomers" in jazz, head for the KC Jazz Club at the Kennedy Center. Oscar Brown, Jr., Phil Woods, Ernie Watts, and many more are featured here. You can hear international jazz stars at **Blues Alley** in Georgetown, or visit **Madam's Organ** in Adams-Morgan, home to some of the best R&B in Washington.

If you want to hear big-name rock stars or jazz artists, head to the **Verizon Center** (see p104), the **Merriweather Post Pavilion** in Columbia, Maryland, or the **Jiffy Lube Live** in Manassas, Virginia.

Performers at the highly respected Shakespeare Theatre

Clubs, Bars, and Cafés

For late-night dancing and clubbing, try the U Street neighborhood. One of the most highly recommended is the **9:30 Club**.

For salsa try the **Rumba Café** in Adams-Morgan. If you fancy a cigar and a martini, then check out **Ozio Martini and Cigar Lounge** downtown. **Black Cat**, with its schedule of both local and international bands, is the place for live independent and alternative music. Billiard parlors are also popular, as are the city's many coffee bars. **Cosi Dupont North** in Dupont Circle serves coffees and cocktails.

Gay Clubs

Many of the gay bars in DC can be found in the Dupont Circle area. **JR's Bar and Grill** attracts young professionals. **The Fireplace** is popular and stays open late. If you're looking for a good meal, visit **Annie's Paramount Steak House** on 17th Street.

Interior of Rumba Café

DIRECTORY

Film and Theatre

Arena Stage
1101 6th St, SW.
Map 4 D5.
Tel (202) 554-9066.
W arenastage.org

Ford's Theatre
511 10th St, NW.
Map 3 C3.
Tel (202) 347-4833.
W fordstheatre.org

Gala Hispanic Theater
3333 14th St, NW.
Tel (202) 234-7174.

Kennedy Center
New Hampshire Ave &
Rock Creek Parkway, NW.
Map 2 D4.
Tel (202) 467-4600 or
(202) 467-4600.
W kennedy-center.org

**Landmark's
E Street Cinema**
Lincoln Square Building
at 555 11th St, NW.
Map 3 C3.
Tel (202) 783-9494.
W landmarktheatres.
com

Library of Congress
Mary Pickford Theater,
Madison Building,
101 Independence Ave, SE.
Map 4 E4.
Tel (202) 707-5677.
W loc.gov

**National
Gallery of Art**
Constitution Ave at
6th St, NW.
Map 4 D3.
Tel (202) 737-4215.
W nga.org

National Theatre
1321 Pennsylvania Ave,
NW. **Map** 3 B3.
Tel (202) 628-6161.
W nationaltheatre.org

Shakespeare Theatre
450 7th St, NW.
Map 3 C3.
Tel (202) 547-1122.
W shakespeare
theatre.org

The Studio Theatre
1501 14th St, NW.
Map 3 B1.
Tel (202) 332-3300.
W studiotheatre.org

Warner Theatre
13th St (between E and F
Sts), NW. **Map** 3 C3.
Tel (202) 783-4000.
W warnertheatre.com

**Woolly
Mammoth Theatre**
641 D St, NW.
Map 3 C3.
Tel (202) 393-3939.
W woollymammoth.net

Opera and Classical Music

**National Symphony
Orchestra**
Tel (202) 467-4600.

**Washington
Performing
Arts Society**
Tel (202) 785-9727.
W wpas.org

Dance

Dance Place
3225 8th St, NE.
Tel (202) 269-1600.

Glen Echo Park
Spanish Ballroom,
7300 MacArthur Blvd,
Glen Echo, MD.
Tel (301) 634-2222.

Rock, Jazz, and Blues

Blues Alley
1069 Wisconsin Ave, NW.
Map 1 C3.
Tel (202) 337-4141.

Jiffy Lube Live
7800 Cellar Door Drive,
Bristow, VA.
Tel (703) 754-6400.
W nissanpavilion
online.com

**Madam's
Organ**
2461 18th St, NW.
Map 2 F1.
Tel (202) 667-5370.

**Merriweather
Post Pavilion**
Columbia, MD.
Tel (410) 715-5550.
W merriweather
music.com

Clubs, Bars, and Cafés

9:30 Club
815 V St, NW.
Tel (202) 265-0930.
W 930.com

Black Cat
1811 14th St, NW.
Map 3 B3.
Tel (202) 667-4527.
W blackcatdc.com

**Cosi Dupont
North**
1647 20th St, NW.
Map 3 A1.
Tel (202) 332-6364.

**Ozio Martini and
Cigar Lounge**
1813 M St, NW.
Map 3 A2.
Tel (202) 822-6000.

Rumba Café
2443 18th St, NW.
Tel (202) 588-5501.
W rumbacafe.com

Gay Clubs

**Annie's
Paramount
Steak House**
1609 17th St, NW.
Map 2 F2.
Tel (202) 232-0395.

The Fireplace
2161 P St, NW.
Map 2 E2.
Tel (202) 293-1293.

**JR's Bar
and Grill**
1519 17th St, NW.
Map 2 F2.
Tel (202) 328-0090.

Sports and Outdoor Activities

Washingtonians are known for putting in long hours – whether on the floor of the Senate, the office of a federal agency, or in a newsroom. They compensate, however, by taking their leisure hours very seriously by rooting for their favorite teams or spending as much time as possible outdoors. You can join in the fun at the Nationals Park Stadium or the Verizon Center, both of which attract hordes of fans. You can meet joggers, cyclists, and in-line skaters on the Mall and around the monuments.

Cyclists enjoying the fine weather outdoors in DC

Spectator Sports

Fans of the NHL Capitals (National Hockey League), the NBA Wizards (National Basketball Association), and the WNBA Mystics (Women's National Basketball Association) should purchase tickets at the **Verizon Center**, an impressive sports arena that opened in 1997 and has helped revitalize the downtown area.

Depending on the season, you might also see Disney on Ice, the Harlem Globetrotters, or the Ringling Brothers Circus. Visit the Verizon's National Sports Gallery, which houses sports memorabilia and interactive sports games. There is plenty to eat at the Verizon Center, but you may prefer to slip out to one of the restaurants in Chinatown, which surrounds the center.

If you are not a season-pass holder, it is very difficult to get a ticket to a Washington Redskins game at the **FedEx Field** stadium, but you can always watch the game from one of Washington's popular sports

Redskins team member

bars. The DC United soccer team plays at the **RFK Stadium**. College sports are also very popular in DC – you will find Washingtonians cheering either for the **Georgetown Hoyas** or the **Maryland Terrapins**. Baseball fans lend their support to the Washington Nationals at **Nationals Park Stadium** in the southeast of the city.

Fishing and Boating

From April to October, to fish or boat on the Potomac River, head to **Fletcher's Boat House** at Canal and Reservoir Roads. You will need to obtain a permit if you are between 16 and 64, which lasts for a year but does not cost much. You can fish from the riverbank or rent a row-boat, canoe, or kayak, which are available by the hour or the day.

In Georgetown there are boats for rent at **Thompson's Boat Center** and **Key Bridge Boat House**. Fletcher's sells snacks; if you go to Thompson's or Jack's there are cafés and restaurants along the waterfront.

Cycling

Rock Creek Park is one of Washington's greatest treasures and offers amazing respite from busy city life. Closed to traffic on weekends, it is a great place for cycling. Another popular trail is the Capital Crescent, which starts on the C&O Canal towpath in Georgetown and runs to Maryland.

One of the more beautiful bike trails in the area will take you 16 miles (26 km) to Mount Vernon. Bikes can be rented at Fletcher's Boat House, Thompson's Boat Center, **Bike and Roll**, **Capital Bikeshare**, or **Big Wheel Bikes** in Georgetown. For maps or trail information call or write to the **Washington Area Bicyclist Association**, or consult one of the bike rental shops in the city.

Tennis, Golf, and Horseback Riding

Many neighborhood parks have outdoor tennis courts, available on a first-come, first-served basis. Two public clubs in the city accept reservations: **East Potomac Tennis Center** at Hains Point, and the **Rock Creek Tennis Center**. Each has outdoor and indoor courts.

If you want to take in views of the monuments while walking the golf fairways, go to the **East Potomac Golf Course & Driving Range**. (There is an 18-hole miniature golf course here as well.) Two other courses are open to the public: **Langston Golf Course** on the Anacostia

Fans enjoy a game at Nationals Park Stadium

River and **Rock Creek Golf Course**, tucked into Rock Creek Park. You will also find **Rock Creek Park Horse Center**, where you can make reservations for a guided trail ride.

Exploring Nature

For an amazing array of trees and plants, visit the **National Arboretum** (see p146), which covers 444 acres (180 ha) in northeast Washington. There is something interesting to see all year round in the arboretum. Special displays, such as the National Bonsai Collection of miniature plants, can be enjoyed at any time of year. To catch the best of the flowering shrubs, the beautiful camellias and magnolias flower in late March through early April, and the stunning, rich colors of the azaleas, rhododendron, and dogwood appear from late April through early May. There is a 1,600-ft (490-m) long "touch and see trail" at the garden for visually impaired visitors. An

The beautiful and tranquil grounds of the National Arboretum

alternative to the arboretum is **Kenilworth Park and Aquatic Gardens** (see p146), which has ponds with more than 100,000 water lilies, lotuses, and other plants. It is a good idea to plan a trip early in the day when the blooms are open and before the sun gets too hot. Frogs and turtles can be seen regularly along the footpaths around the ponds. Park naturalists conduct

nature walks around the gardens on summer weekends.

One of the most enjoyable ways to spend time outdoors is with a picnic in the park. Visit **Dumbarton Oaks Park** in Georgetown when the wildflowers are in bloom, or visit **Montrose Park**, right next door to Dumbarton Oaks, where you can enjoy the variety of birds and the boxwood maze.

DIRECTORY

Spectator Sports

FedEx Field
Arena Drive,
Landover, MD.
Tel (301) 276-6800.
W redskins.com

Georgetown Hoyas
Tel (202) 687-4692.
W guhoyas.com

Maryland Terrapins
Tel (800) 462-8377.
W umterps.com

Nationals Park Stadium
1500 South Capitol St, SE.
Tel (202) 675-6287.

RFK Stadium
2400 East Capitol St, SE.
Tel (202) 587-5000.

Verizon Center
601 F St, NW.
Map 4 D3.
Tel (202) 628-3200.

Fishing and Boating

Fletcher's Boat House
4940 Canal Rd, NW. **Map** 1
A2. **Tel** (202) 244-0461.

Key Bridge Boat House
3500 K St, NW. **Map** 2 D3.
Tel (202) 337-9642.

Thompson Boat Center
Rock Creek Parkway &
Virginia Ave, NW. **Map** 2
D3. **Tel** (202) 333-9543.
W thompsonboat
center.com

Cycling

Big Wheel Bikes
1034 33rd St, NW. **Map** 1
C2. **Tel** (202) 337-0254.
W bigwheelbikes.com

Bike and Roll
1100 Pennsylvania Ave,
NW. **Map** 3 C3.
W bikeandroll.com

Capital Bikeshare
Tel 877-430-BIKE.
W capitalbikeshare.com

Washington Area Bicyclist Association

2599 Ontario Rd, NW.
Tel (202) 518-0524.
W waba.org

Tennis, Golf, and Riding

East Potomac Golf Course
972 Ohio Drive, SW at
Hains Point. **Map** 3 A5.
Tel (202) 479-2596.

East Potomac Tennis Center
1090 Ohio Drive, SW
at Hains Point. **Map** 3 A5.
Tel (202) 554-5962.
W eastpotomac
tennis.com

Langston Golf Course
26th St & Benning Rd, NE.
Tel (202) 397-8638.

Rock Creek Golf Course
1600 Rittenhouse St, NW.
Tel (202) 882-7332.

Rock Creek Park Horse Center

Military & Glover Rds, NW.
Tel (202) 362-0117 (ext 0).
W rockcreekhorse
center.com

Rock Creek Tennis Center

16th & Kennedy Sts, NW.
Tel (202) 722-5949.
W rockcreektennis.com

Exploring Nature

Dumbarton Oaks Park
Entrance on Lovers Lane,
off R & 31st Sts, NW.
Map 1 C1.
Tel (202) 339-6400.

Kenilworth Park and Aquatic Gardens
1550 Anacostia Ave, NE.
Tel (202) 426-6905.

Montrose Park
R & 32nd Sts, NW.
Map 1 C1 & 2 D1.

National Arboretum
24th & R Sts, NE.
Tel (202) 245-2726.

Children's Washington, DC

Visiting the city's monuments can be one of the most memorable activities for children in DC. Book online in advance to arrange a tour with a park ranger, during which you take a trip in the elevator to the top of the Washington Monument *(see p80)*, then walk down the steps. Young children will like feeding the ducks at the Reflecting Pool or Constitution Gardens. You can view the Jefferson Memorial from a paddleboat on the Tidal Basin *(see p81)*, and before you leave Washington be sure to see the monuments lit up against the night-time sky.

Children in front of the National Museum of Natural History

Practical Advice

A good source of information on specific events for children can be found in the "Going Out Guide" of *The Washington Post*. It also lists family-friendly museums and dining options. As you would expect in a major city, food is widely available in DC, whether it is hot dogs from a seller along the Mall or even strange space food (such as freeze-dried ice cream) from the **National Air and Space Museum** gift shop *(see pp64–7)*.

Outdoor Fun

For a trip into the past, take a ride on a mule-drawn barge on the C&O Canal from April to mid-October at Great Falls (contact the **C&O Canal Visitor Center** for details). Park Service rangers are dressed up in 19th-century costumes to add to the experience.

Sea lion at the National Zoo

The beautiful wooded park of the **National Zoo** *(see pp140–41)* is a good place for a walk, and you can also enjoy watching elephant training, panda feeding, and sea lion demonstrations.

For a break from the Mall museums, take a ride on the **Carousel on the Mall** (open all through the year), in front of the Arts and Industries Building. Also worth a visit is the carousel in **Glen Echo Park** (open in summer only), built in 1921. From December to March, ice skaters can head for the **National Gallery of Art Sculpture Garden Ice Rink**. Skate rental equipment is available and visitors can also take part in group skating lessons.

Museums

The Discovery Center, a vast educational complex with an IMAX® theater, is housed in the **National Museum of Natural History** *(see pp72–3)*.

If you want to experience outer space, then see "To Fly!" and the Albert Einstein Planetarium at the **National Air and Space Museum**. A series of children's films and family programs are run by the **National Gallery of Art** *(see pp60–62)*. Children can discuss paintings and take part in a whole range of hands-on activities.

The **National Museum of the American Indian** *(see pp70–71)* has many events, workshops, films and demonstrations designed for the family. Similarly, the **National Museum of African Art** *(see p69)* hosts educative music and storytelling events.

Children are always fascinated by the **National Postal Museum** *(see p55)*, with its many intriguing hands-on activities.

Children's Theater

The Ripley Center of the Smithsonian houses the **Discovery Theater**, which stages puppet shows and plays. See a puppet show or fairytale production at the **Adventure Theatre** in Glen Echo Park. The theater company **Imagination Stage**, located north of Washington in Bethesda, Maryland, presents lively theater productions for children.

The **Kennedy Center** *(see pp120–21)* and **Wolf Trap Farm Park for the Performing Arts** also provide information on all sorts of children's events in the city.

Children's tour in Cedar Hill, the historic home of Frederick Douglass

A Little Bit of History

Children studying American history will be fascinated by a visit to Cedar Hill, once the home of **Frederick Douglass**, in Anacostia. The video in the visitors' center helps to tell the amazing story of this American hero.

You can take a tour of **Ford's Theatre** (see p98) where President Lincoln was shot and the house across the street where he died.

The **Washington National Cathedral** (see pp144–5) provides a free brochure to take children on a self-guided scavenger hunt seeking carvings, specific images in stained-glass windows, and gargoyles. The National Building Museum (see p105) runs special programs for children on Saturdays.

Shopping

The **National Museum of Natural History** (see pp72–3) shops stock a wide variety of goods that will keep children enthralled. Favorites include books, natural history toys, games related to sea life, dinosaurs, and nature, as well as science kits that allow children to reproduce at home some of the wonders of the natural world on display in the museum.

The spacious seating arena at Ford's Theatre

DIRECTORY

Outdoor Fun

C&O Canal Visitor Center
1057 Thomas Jefferson St, NW.
Map 2 D3.
Tel (202) 653-5190.

Carousel on the Mall
Arts and Industries Blg, 900 Jefferson Drive, SW.
Map 3 B4.
Tel (202) 633-1000.

Glen Echo Park Carousel
7300 MacArthur Blvd, Glen Echo, MD.
Tel (301) 320-1400 or (301) 634-2222.
w glenechopark.org

National Gallery of Art Sculpture Garden Ice Rink
7th St & Constitution Ave, NW.
Map 4 D4.
Tel (202) 737-4215.

National Zoo
3001 Connecticut Ave.
Tel (202) 633-4888.

Museums

National Air and Space Museum
6th St & Independence Ave, SW.
Map 4 D4.
Tel (202) 633-4629 (IMAX® film schedule).

National Gallery of Art
Constitution Ave between 3rd & 7th Sts, NW.
Map 4 D3.
Tel (202) 737-4215, (202) 789-3030 (children's film program).

National Museum of African Art
950 Independence Ave, SW.
Map 3 C4.
Tel (202) 633-4600.
w nmafa.si.edu

National Museum of American History
Constitution Ave between 12th & 14th Sts, NW.
Map 3 B4.
Tel (202) 633-1000.

National Museum of the American Indian
4th St & Independence Ave, SW.
Map 4 D4.
Tel (202) 633-1000.
w americanindian.si.edu

National Museum of Natural History
10th St & Constitution Ave, NW.
Map 3 C4.
Tel (202) 633-1000 (general information).
Tel (202) 633-4629 (IMAX® film schedule).

National Postal Museum
2 Massachusetts Ave, NE.
Map 4 E3.
Tel (202) 633-1000.

Children's Theatre

Adventure Theatre
7300 MacArthur Blvd, Glen Echo Park, Md.
Tel (301) 634-2270.

Discovery Theater
1100 Jefferson Drive, SW.
Map 3 C4.
Tel (202) 633-8700.
w discoverytheater.org

Imagination Stage
4908 Auburn Ave, Bethesda, MD.
Tel (301) 280-1660.
w imaginationstage.org

Wolf Trap Farm Park for the Performing Arts
1551 Trap Rd, Vienna, VA.
Tel (703) 255-1900.
w wolftrap.org

A Little Bit of History

Ford's Theatre
511 10th St, NW. **Map** 3 C3.
Tel (202) 347-4833.
w fordstheatre.org

Frederick Douglass National Historic Site
1411 W St, SE.
Tel (202) 426-5960.

Washington National Cathedral

Massachusetts & Wisconsin Aves, NW.
Tel (202) 537-6200 (Gargoyle tour).
w cathedral.org

Shopping

National Museum of Natural History Shops
10th St & Constitution Ave, NW.
Map 3 C4.
Tel (202) 633-2060.
w mnh.si.edu

U St/African-Amer
Civil War Memorial/
Cardozo

← U St/ African-Amer
Civil War Memorial/
Cardozo
• Columbia Heights
• Georgia Ave-
Petworth
Fort Totten

• West Hyattsville
• Prince George's Plaza
• College Park-U of Md
Greenbelt

→ U St/ African-Amer
Civil War Memorial/
Cardozo
• Shaw-Howard Univ
• Mt Vernon Sq 7th St-
Convention Center
• Gallery Pl-Chinatown
• Archives-Navy Mem'l
• L'Enfant Plaza ⓜ ⓜ
• Pentagon ⓜ
• Pentagon City
• Crystal City
• Ronald Reagan
Washington
National Airport
• Braddock Road
• King Street ⓜ
• Eisenhower Ave
Huntington

• Waterfront-SEU
• Navy Yard
• Anacostia
• Congress Heights
• Southern Ave
• Naylor Road
• Suitland
Branch Ave

SURVIVAL GUIDE

PRACTICAL INFORMATION

Washington, DC is the heart of the American political world. It is a visitor-friendly place, especially for children and the disabled, since wheelchair accessibility is required almost everywhere, and most museums (including all under the Smithsonian umbrella *see pp100–103*) are free. The whole city shuts down on federal holidays, as well as anytime the government requires it to. With the US President and other world leaders coming and going, unexpected delays and closures can occur. Spring and fall are the best times to visit as the summers can be very hot and winters very cold.

Entrance to the White House Visitor Center

Visas and Passports

Citizens of the UK, most western European countries, Japan, Australia, and New Zealand, need a valid passport and return ticket to enter the US, and must register with the online Electronic System of Travel Authorization (ESTA) before departure. Visit https://esta.cbp.dhs.gov to obtain the ESTA; there is a small charge but it is valid for two years. Citizens of all other countries require a valid passport and a tourist visa. Entry requirements may change. Be sure to check with the US embassy in your country before you travel. Be aware that anyone entering the US on a visa will be photographed and have their fingerprints checked.

Visitors should carry photo identification at all times. Your possessions will be checked before entering museums and some places have metal detectors.

Travel Safety

Visitors can get up-to-date travel safety information from the Foreign and Commonwealth Office in the UK, the State Department in the US and the Department of Foreign Affairs and Trade in Australia.

Tourist Information

The Washington area is very welcoming to tourists. Visitor information desks at the airports can provide guides and maps, and staff will be able to answer questions. Major hotels usually have a guest services desk. Before you travel it may be worth contacting the **Destination DC** tourist office. The website provides information on special offers, local events, and free things to do.

Opening Hours

Most banks and offices in DC are open from 9am to 5pm, Monday through Friday. Some banks are also open on a Saturday morning. Malls or department stores are open daily and have extended hours on a certain day of the week. Stores rarely close for holidays.

All Smithsonian Museums are open on federal holidays. Some museums are closed on Mondays. Many gas stations, convenience stores, and select pharmacies *(see p209)* stay open 24 hours.

Taxes and Tipping

Taxes will be added to hotel and restaurant charges, theater tickets, some grocery and store sales, and most other purchases. Be sure to ask whether the tax is included in the price displayed. Sales tax is 6 percent, hotel tax is 14.5 percent, with 10 percent tax on food and beverages.

Tipping is expected for most services: in restaurants tip 15–20 percent of the bill, give $2 per bag to airport and hotel porters, and $2 to valet parking attendants. Bartenders expect 50 cents to $1 per drink; if you visit a hair salon or barbershop, 15 to 20 percent of the bill should suffice.

Alcohol and Cigarettes

The legal minimum age for drinking alcohol in Washington is 21, and you will need photo identification (I.D.) as proof of your age in order to purchase alcohol and be allowed into bars. It is illegal to drink alcohol in public parks or to carry an open container of alcohol in your car, and penalties for driving under the influence of alcohol are severe. Cigarettes can be purchased by those over 18 years old; proof of age will be required.

Smoking is prohibited in all public buildings, bars, restaurants, and stores.

Electricity

Electricity flows at the standard US 110–120 volts, and a two-prong plug is required. For non-US appliances you will need a plug adapter and a voltage converter.

International Student Identity Card, accepted as I.D. in America

Student Travelers

While students from abroad should purchase an International Student Identity Card (**ISIC**) before traveling to Washington, they may not use it often as many sights have free entry. Paying museums such as the Phillips Collection give a $2 discount on their regular admission. The ISIC handbook lists places and services in the US that offer discounts to card holders, including accommodations, museums, and theaters. The **Student Advantage Card** is available to all American college undergraduates and offers a range of discounts.

Senior Travelers

Senior citizens are eligible for certain discounts with the appropriate proof of age. Amtrak gives a discount of 15 percent for persons over 62 on most trains (not valid for business or first class). Many movie theaters give reduced admission (usually $1 off the regular price) to those aged 60 or over. Most private museums offer a senior's discount similar to the student discount.

The **American Association of Retired Persons** is open to the over-50s. Members qualify for discounts of 5–30 percent on tours, hotels, and travel.

Disabled Travelers

Washington is a model of accessibility and almost all public buildings, including most hotels and restaurants, are required to be wheelchair accessible. Streets have curb cuts and there are elevators at all Metro stations. The exceptions are historic areas like Georgetown, where 18th-century buildings and cobblestone streets make using a wheelchair problematic. For general advice, contact the **Society for Accessible Travel and Hospitality**.

Gay and Lesbian Travelers

In 2009, Washington, DC passed a gay marriage act – one of the few places in the US to recognize same-sex union. The city's lively gay scene centers around Dupont Circle and the adjacent 17th, 14th, and P Streets. The **Human Rights Campaign**

Headquarters is home to the national organization for gay rights.

Responsible Tourism

Like many places in the US, Washington, DC is increasingly aware of environmental issues. Visitors can be assured that most public organizations and many restaurants recycle their trash and, in 2009, the city enacted a law charging 5 cents for every plastic and paper bag given at grocery stores.

Local and organic produce are widely available, especially at weekend markets such as the Eastern Market (7am–6pm Sat, 9am–5pm Sun) and the Dupont Circle Farmers' Market (8:30am–1pm; Jan–Mar: 10am–1pm). The mother of the organic food movement in eastern USA is Restaurant Nora (see p190).

Many hotel chains touting their green credentials have representatives in DC, including Fairmont Hotels (see p178), cited as the best hotel chain by treehugger.com.

Local produce on sale at the Eastern Market

DIRECTORY

Embassies

Australia
1601 Massachusetts Ave, NW. **Map** 2 F2.
Tel (202) 797-3000.
🅦 usa.embassy.gov.au

Canada
501 Pennsylvania Ave, NW.
Map 4 D3.
Tel (202) 682-1740.
🅦 canadainternational.gc.ca/washington

Ireland
2234 Massachusetts Ave, NW. **Map** 3 A1.
Tel (202) 462-3939.
🅦 irelandemb.org

New Zealand
37 Observatory Circle, NW. **Tel** (202) 328-4800.
🅦 nzembassy.com/usa

United Kingdom
3100 Massachusetts Ave, NW.
Tel (202) 588-6500.
🅦 britainusa.com

Tourist Information

Destination DC
901 7th Street, NW.
Map 4 C2.
Tel (202) 289-7000.
🅦 washington.org

Student Travelers

ISIC
🅦 isic.org

Student Advantage Card
🅦 studentadvantage.com

Senior Travelers

American Association for Retired Persons
601 E St, NW.
Map 4 D3.
Tel 888-687-2277.
🅦 aarp.org

Disabled Travelers

Society for Accessible Travel and Hospitality
Tel (212) 447-7284.
🅦 sath.org

Gay and Lesbian Travelers

Human Rights Campaign Headquarters
1640 Rhode Island Ave, NW.
Tel (202) 628-4160.
🅦 hrc.org

Personal Security and Health

Although as in any major city there is crime, Washington has made great efforts in reducing problems and cleaning up its streets, and with success. If you stick to the tourist areas, avoid straying into outlying districts, and take common sense precautions as in any big city, you should not run into any trouble. The main sights are located in safe areas where there are many people, and serious crime is rare. When visiting sights off the beaten track, take a taxi to and from the destination. Most importantly, pay attention to your surroundings, especially after dark.

Law Enforcement

There are several different police forces in Washington, DC, including the Secret Service, the FBI (Federal Bureau of Investigation), and the more widespread M.P.D.C. (Metropolitan Police, Washington, DC) police. Many major sights also have their own police forces, such as the National Zoological Park Police and the United States Capitol Police.

At monuments, you will see green-uniformed Park Rangers. Their role is largely crowd control and as a source of information; many are trained historians.

Because the city is home to the President, whenever he travels, members of the law enforcement agencies follow. When foreign political leaders visit, the police are even more visible than usual: you will see them on horseback, on bicycles, in cars, and even on top of buildings.

As a visitor, should you encounter any trouble, approach any of the blue-uniformed M.P.D.C. officers that regularly patrol the city streets. All M.P.D.C officers carry weapons.

The DC police are well-known for their strict interpretation of the law. In other words: don't talk back, don't argue, and never offer money in the form of a bribe; this could land you in jail.

M.P.D.C. officer

What to be Aware of

Serious crime is rarely witnessed in the main sightseeing areas of Washington. However, avoid wandering into areas that you have no reason to visit, either during the day or at night. Pickpockets do operate in the city and will target anyone who looks like a tourist. Panhandlers (beggars) are also common, gathering near Metro stations and at shopping malls. It is best to keep walking, ignore their requests for money, and avoid engaging in conversation. Police officers regularly patrol the tourist areas, but it is still advisable to prepare the day's itinerary in advance, use common sense, and stay alert. Try not to advertise that you are a tourist; study your map before you set off, avoid wearing expensive jewelry, and carry your camera or camcorder securely. Carry small amounts of cash; credit cards are a more secure option. Keep these close to your body in a money belt or inside pocket. Before you leave home, make a photocopy of important documents, including your passport and visa, and keep them with you, though separate from the originals. Also make a note of your credit card numbers, in case of theft or loss. Keep an eye on your belongings at all

Hospital sign

times. It is a good idea to put any valuables in the hotel safe – do not carry them around with you. Most hotels will not guarantee the security of any belongings that you leave in your room.

In an Emergency

Call 911 for police or fire assistance, or if you need an ambulance. If you are involved in a medical emergency, go to a hospital emergency room.

Lost and Stolen Property

Although the chances of retrieving lost or stolen property are slim, you should report all stolen items to the police. Call the **Police Non-Emergency Line** for guidance. Make sure you keep a copy of the police report, which you will need when making your insurance claim.

In case of loss, it is useful to have a list of serial numbers or a photocopy of all documents; keep these separate as proof of ownership.

If you can remember to do so, it is useful to make a mental note of the taxi company or bus route you use; it might make it easier to retrieve lost items.

If your passport is lost or stolen, get in touch with your country's embassy or consulate (see p207). If you lose your credit card, most card companies have toll-free numbers for reporting a loss or theft (see p210).

Hospitals and Pharmacies

It is possible to visit a doctor or dentist without being registered with them, but you will be asked to pay in advance. Keep all receipts for medical costs to make a claim on your insurance later. Depending on the limitations of your insurance, it is better to avoid the overcrowded city-owned hospitals and opt instead for one of the private hospitals. If

Police car

Ambulance

Fire engine

taken by ambulance, however, drivers are required to take you to the nearest hospital. If you require a dentist you can call the **District of Columbia Dental Society**, which provides a free referral service.

Pharmacists are usually able to offer basic medical advice, and there are some pharmacies with clinics attached to treat common illnesses and small injuries. Patients are seen by nurse practitioners or physician assistants. One such clinic is the **CVS Minute Clinic**, which has six locations in DC, and several in the Virginia and Maryland suburbs.

If you need a prescription, there are plenty of pharmacies in and around the city, some staying open 24 hours. CVS is the most common chain.

Travel and Health Insurance

It is strongly recommended to obtain travel insurance before traveling to the United States. It is particularly important for visitors to have sufficient insurance for emergency medical and dental care, which can be very expensive in the States. Even with medical cover, you may have to pay for the services, then make a claim for reimbursement with your insurance company when you return home. Hospitals accept most credit cards, as do most doctors and dentists. Should you go to a hospital or seek medical assistance, be sure to take proof of your insurance with you. If you usually take medication, it is a good idea to bring a back-up supply with you and to ask your doctor to provide a copy of the prescription in case of loss or the need for more.

It is advisable to make sure your personal property is insured and to obtain cover for lost or stolen baggage and travel documents, as well as trip cancellation fees, legal advice, and accidental death or injury. Your insurance company or travel agent should be able to recommend a suitable policy.

Legal Assistance

Non-US citizens requiring legal assistance should call their embassy (see p207). Embassies will not lend you money but can help with advice on legal matters in emergencies. Should you be arrested for any reason, it is advisable to be cooperative, but you have the right to remain silent.

Restrooms

Washington, DC does not have public restrooms. There are free bathrooms available in all visitor's centers, museums, and galleries, and all hotels and restaurants also have restrooms, but they may only be available to paying customers.

DIRECTORY

In an Emergency

Police, Fire, Medical (all emergencies)
Tel Call 911,
or dial 0 for the operator.

Lost and Stolen Property

Police Non-Emergency Line
Tel 311.

Hospitals and Pharmacies

Area Hospitals
Tel Call 411 for directory assistance.

CVS 24-Hour Pharmacy
1199 Vermont Ave, NW.
Map 3 B2.
Tel (202) 628-0720.
6 Dupont Circle, NW.
Map 2 F2.
Tel (202) 785-1466.
1350 Connecticut Ave, NW.
Map 3 F3.
Tel (202) 223-7252.
W cvs.com

CVS Minute Clinic
Several locations.
W minuteclinic.com

DC Dental Society
Tel (202) 367-1163.
W dcdental.org

George Washington University Hospital
(Private.) 900 23rd Street, NW.
Map 2 E3.
Tel (202) 715-4000.

Georgetown University Hospital
(Private.) 3800 Reservoir Road, NW.
Map 1 B1.
Tel (202) 444-2000.

Medical Referral Services
Tel (202) 342-2400.

Washington Hospital Center
(Private.) 110 Irving Street, NW.
Tel (202) 877-7000.

Logo for CVS pharmacies, a common pharmacy chain in Washington, DC

Banking and Currency

Throughout Washington there are various places to access and exchange your money, from banks to cash machines to bureaux de change. The most important thing to remember is not to carry all your money and credit cards with you at once, and to be prepared to use ATM machines on Sunday when most banks and currency exchange offices are closed.

DIRECTORY

Main Banks

Bank of America
700 13th St, NW.
Map 3 C3. **Tel** (202) 624-4413.
ⓦ bankofamerica.com

Capital One Bank
701 Pennsylvania Ave, NW.
Map 3 C3. **Tel** (202) 737-4950.
ⓦ capitalone.com

Sun Trust Bank
1445 New York Ave, NW.
Map 3 B3. **Tel** (202) 879-6308.
Tel (888) 786 8787.
ⓦ suntrust.com

TD Bank
1753 Connecticut Ave, NW.
Tel 202-232-4837.
ⓦ tdbank.com

Foreign Exchange

American Express Travel Service
1501 K St, NW. **Map** 2 F3.
Tel (202) 457-1300.

Thomas Cook/Travelex
Tel 516-300-1622
(general information.)
ⓦ travelex.com
Branch at:
1800 K St, NW.
Map 3 A2.
Tel (202) 872-1428.

Lost or Stolen Cards

American Express
Tel 1-800-992-3404.

MasterCard
Tel 1-800-627-8372.

Visa
Tel 800-847-2911.

Wiring Money

MoneyGram
ⓦ moneygram.com

Western Union
Tel 1-800-225-5227.
ⓦ westernunion.com

Banks and Foreign Exchange

Generally, most banks are open Monday through Friday from 9am to 5pm (although some may close later,) and Saturday mornings from 9am to noon or 1pm. Most banks are closed on Sundays and federal holidays *(see p41)*. The exception is **TD Bank**, which has many branches with Sunday hours and is open on federal holidays.

Always ask if there are any special fees before you make your transaction. At most banks, traveler's checks in US dollars can be cashed with any photo identification, but passports are usually required to exchange foreign currency.

Foreign currency exchange is available at the main branches of large banks or at independent exchange offices. Among the best known are **American Express Travel Service** and **Thomas Cook/Travelex**, both of which have branches in and around DC. Exchange offices are generally open weekdays from 9am to 5pm. Most exchange offices charge a fee or commission, so it is worth looking around to get the best value rates. Many major hotels can also change currency, but they often charge a higher rate of exchange or commission. The most cost-effective way to acquire American currency is via debit card at a participating bank machine. Some banks waive foreign transaction fees.

ATMs

Automated teller machines (ATMs) are found all over Washington, usually near the entrance to banks, or inside convenience stores and supermarkets. Widely accepted bank cards include Cirrus, Plus, Maestro, NYCE, and credit cards such as VISA or MasterCard. A fee may be levied on your withdrawal (a pop-up screen should tell you the fee and ask if you want the transaction to continue). To minimize the risk of robbery, use ATMs in well-lit, populated areas only. Avoid withdrawing money at night, and be aware of the people around you.

American Express credit cards

Credit and Debit Cards

VISA, MasterCard/Maestro, and most international debit cards are widely accepted almost everywhere in Washington, from theaters and hotels to

ATMs are found throughout the city

restaurants and shops. Note that American Express is increasingly not accepted. It is advisable to carry a credit card as it may be required to reserve a hotel or rental car and to pay for gasoline (petrol), especially at self-service stations.

If your credit card is lost or stolen, contact your card company immediately.

Card Security

Because of the increasing problem of identity theft and card cloning, merchants may ask for photo identification when making a purchase.

If you are traveling overseas, alert your bank of your plans, or they may put a hold or an alert for fraud on your account if they see untoward charges.

Emergency Funds (Wiring Money)

MoneyGram and **Western Union** both offer immediate money transfer for a fee. Both sender and recipient will need to locate an agent to set up the transfer and collect the funds (Western Union also has an online facility for sending funds.)

Coins

American coins come in 1-dollar, 50-, 25-, 10-, 5-, and 1-cent pieces. There are also goldtone $1 coins in circulation and State quarters, which feature an historical scene on one side. Each coin has a popular name: 25-cent pieces are called quarters, 10-cent pieces are called dimes, 5-cent pieces are called nickels, and 1-cent pieces called pennies.

1-cent coin
(a penny)

5-cent coin
(a nickel)

10-cent coin
(a dime)

25-cent coin
(a quarter)

An American Eagle
on a $1 gold coin

Bills (Bank Notes)

The units of currency in the United States are dollars and cents. There are 100 cents to a dollar. Bank notes come in the following denominations: $1, $5, $10, $20, $50, and $100. Security features include subtle color hues and improved color-shifting ink in the lower right hand corner of the face of each note.

1-dollar bill ($1)

5-dollar bill ($5)

10-dollar bill ($10)

20-dollar bill ($20)

50-dollar bill ($50)

100-dollar bill ($100)

Communications and Media

The almost universal use of cell phones has caused the demise of coin-operated pay phones. It is now difficult to find a public pay phone in the street, although they are still available at main stations. Like most major cities, Washington, DC is thoroughly wired for Internet access. Free Wi-Fi is provided in many public places and there are several other ways to get online. Since Washington, DC is the political capital of the United States, news is readily available from newspapers, magazines, television, and radio.

Cell Phones

Cell phone service in Washington is generally excellent. If you are coming from overseas and want to guarantee that your cell phone will work, make sure you have a quad-band phone. Tri-band phones from outside the US are also usually compatible but, because the US uses two frequency bands itself, it is recommended to contact your service provider for clarification before you travel; you may also need to activate the "roaming" facility.

Other options include buying a prepaid cell phone in the US or a SIM chip for a US carrier. Many car rental companies also rent cell phones for customers (*see p219*).

Public Telephones

In the last decade, the number of public pay phones in the United States has decreased by half and Washington is no exception. However, public pay phones are still available at Union Station, the Smithsonian Museums, and some Metro stations, and occasionally on the street. The area code for Washington is 202. When dialing within the district, omit the code. When dialing outside the district from within DC, you will need to use the appropriate area code. The area code for the Maryland suburbs is 301 and for the Virginia suburbs, 703.

Credit card calls can be made by calling 1-800-CALL-ATT. Directory Assistance is 411 and calls are charged at the local rate. Phone cards of various values can be purchased from most supermarkets, 24-hour stores, newspaper stands, and some branches of Western Union.

Telephone Charges

Local calls cost around 50 cents for 3 minutes from pay phones. Calls made from hotel rooms will cost much more, so it is a good idea to use a public pay phone or your cell. Operator assistance can also be used to help you connect your call, but again, this will cost more.

Internet Access

In Washington, many public places – such as bookstores, cafés, airports, and the Mall – have a free wireless service. Most hotels in the city have wireless Internet in their rooms, and many also have a dedicated business center (with computers) within the hotel. For those without their own laptops, computers (with Internet) are available for use in public libraries and in stores such as FedEx, DHL, and UPS.

Using the Internet in the reading room of a Washington public library

Post Service

Post offices are open from 9am to 5pm, Mondays through Fridays, and have limited Saturday service, usually 9am to noon. Post offices are closed on all federal holidays. Stamps can also be bought from most major supermarkets, such as Giant and Safeway.

If the correct postage is affixed, you can send a letter by putting it in one of the blue mailboxes found on street corners all over Washington. Times of mail pickup are written inside the mailbox's lid; there are usually several collections a day. It is mandatory to use a five-digit zip code when sending mail. Be aware that small packages may not be posted in mailboxes for security reasons; they must be taken to a post office.

Depending on how far the mail needs to travel in the US, it can take from one to five days to

Useful Dialing Codes

- To make a direct-dial call outside the local area code, but within the US and Canada, dial 1 before the area code. Useful area codes for DC and the surrounding area include: Washington, DC 202; Baltimore 410; MD 301, 240; Delaware 302; Northern Virginia 703; West Virginia 304.
- For international calls, dial 011 followed by the appropriate country code. Then dial the area code, omitting the first 0, and the local number.
- To make an international call via the operator, dial 00; note that the call is charged at a higher rate.
- For international operator assistance, dial 01.
- For local operator assistance, dial 0.
- For international directory inquiries, dial 00.
- For local directory inquiries, dial 411.
- For emergency police, fire, or ambulance services, dial 911.
- 1-800 and 888 indicate a toll-free number.

arrive at its destination. The most economical way to send inter-national mail is First Class International at less than $1 per ounce, depending on the destination. Express and Priority mail are also available at the post office for a faster, though more expensive, service. If you are a visitor to the city and you wish to receive mail, poste restante, you can have it sent to you by addressing it care of "General Delivery" at the **Main Post Office**, or any other main post office, quoting the city name. They will hold the mail for 30 days for you to collect.

It is worth noting that USPS refers to the United States Postal Service, while UPS is a private courier company.

Courier Services

Courier services are a popular, if more expensive, alternative to the postal service. Many hotels will arrange for your packages and letters to be shipped either by Federal Express (**FedEx**), **DHL**, a division of Deutsche Poste, or **UPS**. DHL only operates internationally while FedEx and UPS handle both national and international letters and packages. FedEx services are available at Fedex

US mailbox

Office Centers (easily recognizable by the FedEx arrow logo); DHL is offered at independent office storefront locations like Parcel Plus. FedEx and UPS also have self-service kiosks throughout the city for letters and flat packages. Registration for self-service packages is completed online, and a label down-loaded to attach to the package.

Television and Radio

Televisions are everywhere in the United States, from bars and restaurants to hotels and stores. Most have cable hook-up, allowing access to more than 60 different channels. Some of the best to view are CBS, NBC, CNN, ABC, and Fox. For those interested in the political goings-on in the city, tune in to channels C-Span 1 and C-Span 2 to watch the proceedings in Congress as they are broadcast live. Radios can be found in most hotel rooms, as well as in rental cars, and offer a wide range of music, from country through classical and jazz to rock. Popular radio stations include National Public Radio (WAMU at 88.5), modern rock on WHFS (99.1), and soft rock on Easy 101 (101).

Street dispensers with newspapers

Newspapers

The most widely read newspaper in the DC area is *The Washington Post*, which is also one of the best newspapers published in the country. The local *Washington Express* is widely available as are *USA Today*, *The Wall Street Journal*, and *The New York Times*. Newspapers can be bought from street dispensers (boxes on the sidewalk that dispense newspapers), newsstands, gas stations, convenience stores, hotel lobbies, and bookstores. They are also all available online. Newsstands and some book-stores carry newspapers from most large US cities and many foreign countries.

DIRECTORY

Postal Services

Georgetown Station
3050 K St, NW. **Map** 2 D2.

Main Post Office
Brentwood Station, 900 Brentwood Road, NE, Washington, DC 20066.
Tel (202) 636-1581.

Martin Luther King Jr. Station
1400 L St, NW. **Map** 2 F3.
National Capitol Station
2 Massachusetts Ave, NE.
Map 4 E3.

Temple Heights Station
1921 Florida Ave, NW. **Map** 2 E1.

Courier Services

DHL
Branches all over the DC area.
For customer services call:
Tel (800) 225-5345.
w dhl.com

FedEx
Branches all over the DC area.
For customer services call:
Tel (800) 463-3339.
w fedex.com

UPS
Branches all over the DC area.
For the nearest branch call:
Tel (800) 275-8777.
w ups.com

Washington Time

Washington is on Eastern Standard Time. Daylight Saving Time begins on the second Sunday in March, when clocks are set ahead 1 hour, and ends on the first Sunday in November, when clocks go back 1 hour.

City and Country	Hours + or – EST	City and Country	Hours + or – EST
Chicago (US)	−1	Moscow (Russia)	+8
Dublin (Ireland)	+5	Paris (France)	+6
London (UK)	+5	Sydney (Australia)	+15
Los Angeles (US)	−3	Tokyo (Japan)	+14
Madrid (Spain)	+6	Vancouver (Canada)	−3

TRAVEL INFORMATION

Washington is easy to get to via any mode of transportation. Three airports serve the DC area; they are used by most major airlines for domestic and international flights. Intercity bus lines also operate to the city, as do Amtrak trains, which arrive at and depart from Union Station, right in the center of Washington. Visitors often tend to travel first to DC, base themselves in the city, and then arrange day or weekend trips into Maryland and Virginia.

Glass-walled interior of Reagan National Airport

Arriving by Air

There are three main airports in the Washington, DC area: **Dulles International Airport**, **Reagan National Airport**, and Baltimore-Washington International Thurgood Marshall Airport (known as **BWI**). Most of the major carriers, including American Airlines, British Airways, Air France, and United Airlines, fly to at least one of these airports. The majority of international and overseas flights land at Dulles International, 26 miles (42 km) west of Washington in Virginia. Dulles is not directly served by a Metro but there is a connecting shuttle service, the **Washington Flyer Silver Line Express Bus**, to take new arrivals to Wiehle-Reston East Metro. Between the coach service and the Metro, expect to spend up to an hour-and-a-half to reach the city center. Alternatively, the **SuperShuttle** share-ride bus service runs every hour and will drop passengers at their door. It is a cheaper option than a taxi but journey times depend on detours made to drop off the other passengers. Taxis are plentiful and are the quickest but most expensive option. **Uber** and its rival, **Lyft**, are web-based taxi services that can be booked through your cell phone if you have pre-registered a credit card with them.

Located about 5 miles (8 km) outside the city in Arlington County, Virginia, the Reagan National Airport is the most convenient airport for central Washington. The city is easily accessible using the Metro, or by taking the SuperShuttle (every 30 minutes), or a taxi.

BWI Airport, 30 miles (48 km) northeast of DC, tends to be used by low-cost airlines. The Maryland Rail Commuter Service (**MARC**) is the cheapest way to get from the airport to the city, but it runs only on weekdays. Amtrak *(see p215)* offers the next-best train service for just a few dollars more. The SuperShuttle is also available from BWI, but it is more costly and takes longer than a train ride. The taxi fare from BWI into central DC is rather expensive.

For security reasons, anyone arriving in the US on a visa is now photographed, and will have their fingerprints taken, before being allowed into the country *(see p206)*.

Air Fares

The busiest season for travel to the US is March through June and September through early November. Christmas and Thanksgiving are also busy. Flights will be at their most expensive during these periods. Flights in June and July are usually the most expensive but there are many discounted accommodations at this time. Weekend flights are usually less expensive than weekdays, while Apex tickets are often the best deal. Apex tickets must be booked at least one week in advance, and your visit must include a Saturday night. Cheap air fares can be obtained by shopping around, so it is worth checking with the airlines and websites such as **Expedia**, **Kayak**, and **Priceline**.

The Washington Flyer Silver Line Express Bus

Airport	Information	Distance/Time to Washington, DC	Taxi Fare	SuperShuttle
Dulles	(703) 572-2700	26 miles (42 km) 40 minutes	$60–65	$26–35
Reagan National	(703) 417-8000	5 miles (8 km) 15 minutes	$20	$13–23
BWI	(410) 859-7111	30 miles (48 km) 50 minutes	$100	$32–42

Main concourse at Union Station

Arriving by Train

Amtrak is one of the best ways to travel to the DC area. Trains from other cities arrive in Washington at Union Station. Trains are also available from Union Station to Baltimore, Philadelphia, Richmond, and Williamsburg. Amtrak offers a deluxe train service to New York City, called the Acela, which travels slightly faster and more comfortably than the regular train, but is more expensive. Trains (either the Acela or the slower Northeast Regional) to New York leave every hour. **MARC,**

Maryland's commuter train, departs on weekdays to Baltimore.

Arriving by Car

The center of Washington, DC is surrounded by Interstates I-95 and I-495, which together form the congested Capital Beltway. Driving on the Beltway, especially during rush hour, can be intimidating for the inexperienced driver. Interstate I-66 connects Washington to West Virginia, and Interstate I-50 heads east from DC to Annapolis, Maryland, and the surrounding areas. Beyond the

Beltway, Interstate I-95 goes north toward Baltimore, Philadelphia, and New York. Interstate I-270 heads north to Frederick, Maryland.

Arriving by Bus

Intercity buses are a great, economical way to get to Washington. As well as the traditional **Greyhound** buses, there are half a dozen bus companies serving DC, including **Megabus, Bolt Bus, Vamoose,** and the **Washington Deluxe.** Many are equipped with restrooms, free Wi-Fi, power outlets, and even DVD players. Tickets are sold on a scale – one-way to New York is generally about $25, but may be as little as $1 with advance purchase.

Greyhound buses depart from the bus terminal near Union Station, but many of the other bus companies leave from more central locations.

Greyhound bus, an inexpensive way to see the whole country

DIRECTORY

Arriving by Air

BWI Airport
Linthicam, MD.
Tel (410) 859-7111 or (800) I-FLY-BWI. Lost & Found
Tel (410) 859-7387.
ⓦ bwiairport.com

Dulles International Airport
Chantilly, VA.
Tel (703) 572-2700. Lost & Found **Tel** (703) 572-8479.
ⓦ metwashairports.com

Lyft
ⓦ lyft.com

Reagan National Airport
Arlington, VA.
Tel (703) 417-8000. Lost & Found **Tel** (703) 417-8560.
ⓦ metwashairports.com

SuperShuttle
Tel (800) 258-3826 or (800) BLUE-VAN.
ⓦ supershuttle.com

Uber
ⓦ uber.com

Washington Flyer Silver Line Express Bus
Tel (888) 927-4359 or (888) WASH-FLY.
ⓦ washfly.com

Air Fares

Expedia
Tel 1-800-EXPEDIA.
ⓦ Expedia.com

Kayak
ⓦ kayak.com

Priceline
Tel (800) 774-2354.
ⓦ priceline.com

Arriving by Train

Amtrak
Union Station, 50 Massachusetts Ave, NE.
Tel 1-800-872-7245.
ⓦ amtrak.com

MARC
Tel (410) 539-5000 or 1-866-743-3682.
ⓦ mtamaryland.com

Arriving by Bus

Bolt Bus
Tel 1-877-265-8287.
ⓦ boltbus.com

DC2NY
Tel (202) 332-2691.
ⓦ dc2ny.com

Greyhound Busline
Tel 1-800-752-4841.
ⓦ greyhound.com

Megabus
Tel 1-877-462-6342.
ⓦ megabus.com

Vamoose
Tel (212) 695-6766 or (301) 718-0036.
ⓦ vamoosebus.com

Washington Deluxe
Tel 1-866-287-6932 or 1-718-387-7523.
ⓦ washny.com

Getting Around Washington, DC

Washington has a very comprehensive public transportation system. Visitors and locals alike find that it is easier to get around by public transportation than by car, especially as they do not then have the aggravation of finding a much-coveted parking space. All the major tourist attractions in the capital are accessible on foot, by Metrorail, by Metrobus, or by taxi.

Busy night-time traffic in central Washington, DC

Green Travel

With such an excellent public transportation system, it is easy to get around Washington, DC without causing undue harm to the environment. Almost every tourist sight is accessible via public transportation. Furthermore, Metrobus runs a fleet of buses powered by Compressed Natural Gas (CNG), a cleaner alternative to gasoline (petrol).

Cycling has become an increasingly popular way to travel in Washington, and there is an excellent network of cycle lanes throughout the center. Cycling has been further encouraged with the Capital Bikeshare self-hire scheme (see p217).

If it is necessary to use a taxi, visitors can encourage green practices by requesting a "hybrid" taxi, powered by a combination of battery and gasoline, although these cabs are not always available. If using a taxi in the Virginia suburbs, **Envirocab** runs an all-hybrid fleet. They are not licensed to operate in the District, however.

All car rental companies offer hybrid cars, but with limited availability. Book ahead to make sure your request is considered.

Getting your Bearings

It is important to know that the city is made up of four quadrants: northeast (NE), northwest (NW), southeast (SE), and southwest (SW), with the US Capitol at the central point. Every address in DC includes the quadrant code (NE, and so on) and, with building numbers running into the thousands on the same street in each quadrant, its use is necessary to distinguish the location.

A useful tip for when you are first trying to find your way around the city is to remember that most numbered streets run North and South, and most lettered streets run East and West. However, be aware that there is no "J," "X," "Y," or "Z" Street, and that "I" Street is often written as "Eye" Street.

Walking

Washington is a terrific city for walking, as long as you wear comfortable shoes and keep your wits about you. Many of the main sights are clustered around the Mall. In Georgetown, walking is the best way to soak up the atmosphere.

Metrorail

A map of the Metrorail (see back endpaper and City Map) is one of the most important pieces of information visitors will need when trying to get around DC. The system takes some getting used to, and the instructions are in English only, so allow plenty of time when first using the Metrorail (or "Metro," as it is also called).

The cost of the fare depends on the time and distance you wish to travel, and ranges from $1.70 to $5.75. There is an additional fee for traveling during rush hour. Tickets, or "farecards," for single or multiple trips can be bought from vending machines. Coins and bills (but no bills over $20) can be used to pay the exact fare; or add more money if you wish to use the card again. Passengers need to swipe their farecards through the turnstile at the beginning and end of the trip. If there is any unused fare left at the final destination the ticket will be returned to you; if not, the ticket will be retained. You can top up tickets for further trips. Metrorail passes are on offer for one day ($15) and seven days' ($40.50) travel. These can be used to transfer from Metro to bus. SmarTrip cards are also available. These are plastic rechargeable farecards that cost $2 and can be used on other modes of public transportation in DC. Five Metrorail lines operate in downtown DC, with frequent services: the Orange Line; Blue Line; Red Line; Yellow Line; and Green Line. Trains run from 5:30am to midnight Monday through Thursday, from 5:30am to 3am on Friday and 7am to 3am on Saturday, and from 7am to midnight on Sunday. Trains run frequently (less than 10 minutes' wait) and, on board, stops are announced at every station. The entire system is accessible for wheelchairs. One warning: Eating, drinking, smoking or littering on the Metro is grounds for arrest.

Metro sign

Washington, DC Metrobus

Metrobus

Metrobus is a fast, inexpensive way to get around. Fares can be paid either with exact change on boarding, with a SmarTrip card, or a Metrorail farecard pass (see Metrorail). The standard, off-peak fare is $1.75 (or $1.35 with SmarTrip). If paying with cash, there is a 25 cent charge for bus-to-bus transfers; if using SmarTrip, transfers are free within a 3-hour period. Up to two children under five can travel for free with a fare-paying passenger and there are discounts for disabled travelers and senior citizens. The **Circulator** bus links the main sights in the center and runs every 10 minutes. Fares are $1 for adults and 50 cents for kids.

Maps of all the bus routes are available in Metrorail stations, and maps of specific lines are posted at each bus stop.

Many Metrobuses are wheelchair accessible with a "kneeling" feature that lowers the bus for the disabled rider.

Taxis

Taxis can usually be hailed from the street corner of major arteries, but if you need to be somewhere at a specific time it is best to book. The **DC Taxi Cab Commission** can provide names of cab companies. Uber (uber.com) also provide a booking service via your cell phone. Taxi fares in DC are operated using time and distance meters. Passengers should expect to pay a starting "drop" rate of $3, and then $2.16 for every mile after this. Luggage, rush hour travel, and gas prices can all incur surcharges from 50 cents to $2, and each extra passenger costs $1.50. Be aware that drivers do not always know the way to addresses beyond the tourist center.

Driving and Parking in the City

Driving in DC need not be stressful as long as you avoid the rush hour (between 6:30 and 9:30am, and 4 and 7pm on weekdays). During these times the direction of traffic flow can change, some roads become one way, and left turns may be forbidden to ease congestion. These changes are usually marked, but always pay close attention to the road. Curbside parking is hard to find at the more popular locations, and is illegal at rush hour in many

Road sign

areas. If using metered parking, it is important to keep within the time limit; you could otherwise be fined, risk being clamped, or towed away. Parking restrictions on Sundays and public holidays are different from other days, so read the parking signs carefully.

Cycling

There is a great network of cycle paths in DC. Bike shops rent out bikes, and will be able to suggest routes. They can usually provide route maps. **Capital Bikeshare** is a 24-hour, self-service hire scheme where bikes can be rented from more than 110 stations around the city. **Bike and Roll** offers bike rentals, as well as organized tours of the city.

Guided Tours

There are many city bus tours available in DC. **DC Tours** offers a hop-on-hop-off sightseeing service with numerous pick-up points. For something a bit different, **Old Town Trolley Tours** offers a ride around the main sites in an old-fashioned trolley bus. **DC Metro Food Tours** run culinary walking tours of several DC neighborhoods. **Bike and Roll** offers bike tours in and around the city, including a 1-hour Early Bird Fun Ride and a 10 mile (16 km) Capital Sites Ride. **DC Ducks** provides a tour of the city and a tour down the Potomac River.

DIRECTORY

Green Travel

Envirocab
Tel (703) 920-3333.
W envirotaxicab.com

Metrorail and Metrobus

Circulator
Tel (202) 962-1423.
W dccirculator.com

Metrorail and Metrobus
600 5th St, NW,
Washington, DC 20001.
Tel (202) 637-7000.
Tel (202) 638-3780 TTY.
W wmata.com

Taxis

DC Taxi Cab Commission
Tel (202) 645-6018.
W dctaxi.dc.gov

Diamond Cab
Tel (202) 387-6200.

Yellow Cab
Tel (202) 546-7900.

Cycling

Bike and Roll
Tel (202)-842-2453.
W bikeandrollldc.com

Capital Bikeshare
W capitalbikeshare.com

Guided Tours

DC Ducks
Tel 855-323-8257.
W dcducks.com

DC Metro Food Tours

Tel (202)-683-8847.
W dcmetrofoodtours.com

DC Tours

Tel 888-878-9870.
W dctours.us

Old Town Trolley Tours

Tel (202) 832-9800.
W trolleytours.com

Exploring Beyond Washington, DC

There is much to see beyond Washington's city limits, and traveling by car is easy with a good map. Many of the sights are reachable by public transportation, but it is generally easier and quicker to drive. Car rental is widely available but often expensive. Buses and trains are a cheaper alternative, but your choice of destinations may be more limited.

Driving along the scenic Skyline Drive (see p167), Virginia

Car Rental

To rent a car in the US you must usually be at least 25 years old with a valid driving license and a clean driving record. All agencies require a major credit card. Damage and liability insurance is recom-mended just in case something unexpected should happen. It is advisable always to return the car with a full tank of gas; otherwise you will be required to pay the inflated fuel prices charged by the rental agencies. Check for any pre-existing damage to the car and note this on your contract.

It is often less expensive to rent a vehicle at an airport rather than in the city. Agencies with offices at the Washington airports include **Alamo**, **Avis**, **Budget**, and **Hertz**. You could also become a member of **Zip Car**, a car sharing scheme. These cars can be picked up from hundreds of locations across the city. Your car will come with fuel, insurance, and 180 miles (290 km) per day. **Car2Go** is another car sharing service with small Smart cars, but they cannot be taken outside the city.

Road sign

Rules of the Road

The highway speed limit in the DC area is 55 mph (88 km/h) – much lower than in many European countries. In residential areas the speed limit ranges from 20 to 35 mph (32–48 km/h), and near schools it can be as low as 15 mph (24 km/h).

Roads are generally well-signed but it is still wise to plan your route ahead. It is important to obey the signs, especially "No U-turn" signs, or you risk getting a ticket. If you are pulled over by the police, be courteous or you risk facing an even greater fine.

In addition, all drivers are required to carry a valid drivers' license and be able to produce registration documents and insurance for their vehicle. Most foreign licenses are valid, but if your license is not in English, or does not have a photo ID, you must get an international driver's license. Many roads are surveyed by cameras that will issue a ticket even if you are going just a few miles per hour over the speed limit. This is not limited to major arteries.

Interstate highways are abbreviated on signs with a capital "I" followed by a number. Avoid the Capital Beltway (I-495) at rush hour.

Gasoline (Petrol)

Gas comes in three grades – regular, super, and premium. There is an extra charge if an attendant serves you, but patrons can fill their own tanks at self-service pumps without incurring an extra fee. Most stations are exclusively self-service and only accept credit cards. Gas is generally cheap in the US.

Breakdowns

In the unlucky event of a breakdown, the best course of action is to pull completely off the road and put on the hazard lights to alert other drivers that you are stationary. There are emergency phones along some of the major interstate highways, but in other situations break-down services or even the police can be contacted from mobile phones. In case of break-down, drivers of rental cars should contact their car rental company first.

Members of the **American Automobile Association (AAA)** can have their vehicle towed to the nearest service station to be fixed. For simple problems like a flat tire or a dead battery, the AAA will fix it or sell and install a new battery on site.

Parking sign

Parking

Most of the major sights that lie beyond Washington have adequate parking for visitors, but there may be a charge to use the facility. In general it is good practice to read all parking notices carefully to avoid fines, being clamped, or being towed away. Do not park beside a fire hydrant, or you risk the car being towed.

Tips and Safety Advice for Drivers

• Traffic drives on the right-hand side of the road.
• Seat belts are compulsory in front seats and suggested in the back; children under three must ride in a child seat in back; belts are also compulsory in cabs.
• You can turn right at a red light as long as you first come to a complete stop, and if there are no signs that prohibit it. Be aware, however, that turning right on a red light is illegal in Virginia and will incur a fine.
• A flashing yellow light at an intersection means slow down, look for oncoming traffic, and proceed with caution.
• Passing (overtaking) is allowed on any multi-lane road, and you must pass on the left. On smaller roads safe passing places are indicated with a broken yellow line on your side of the double yellow line.
• Crossing a double-yellow line, either by U-turn or by passing the car in front, is illegal, and will incur a fine if caught.
• If a school bus stops, all traffic from both sides must stop completely and wait for the bus to drive off.

• Driving while intoxicated (DWI) is a punishable offense that incurs heavy fines or even a jail sentence. Do not drink if you plan to drive.
• Avoid driving at night if unfamiliar with the area. Washington's streets change from safe to dangerous in a single block, so it is better to take a taxi than your own car if you do not know where you are going.
• Single women should be especially careful driving in unfamiliar territory, day or night.
• Keep all doors locked when driving around.
• Do not stop in a rural area, or on an unlit block, if someone tries to get your attention. If a fellow driver points at your car, suggesting something is wrong, drive to the nearest gas station and get help. Do not get out of your car.
• Avoid sleeping in your car.
• Avoid short cuts and stay on well-traveled roads.
• Avoid looking at a map in a dark, unpopulated place. Drive to the nearest open store or gas station before pulling over.

Bus Tours

Although Greyhound buses (see p215) do serve some towns beyond DC (such as Charlottesville and Richmond, with serveral departures daily), the easiest and most enjoyable way to see the sights by bus is on a private tour. Several companies offer bus tours of DC's historic surroundings. **Gray Line** takes you on the Black Heritage tour, to Gettysburg, Colonial Williamsburg, or Monticello; DC Tours (see p217) organizes combination day trips covering Gettysburg, Mount Vernon, Arlington Cemetery, Alexandria Old Town, and Charlottesville; **All Washington DC Tours** is a national chain that represents several tour companies in the city. Most bus tours depart from Union Station. Some tours offer a hotel pickup and dropoff, at a fee.

Trains

Amtrak trains (see p215) travel from DC's central Union Station to New York City and most of the surrounding area, including Williamsburg, Richmond, and Baltimore. The MARC (see p215), Maryland's commuter rail, also runs from DC to Baltimore on weekdays for a few dollars less.

DIRECTORY

Car Rental

Alamo
Tel 1-855-533-1196.
W alamo.com

Avis
Tel 1-800-230-4898.
W avis.com

Budget
Tel 1-800-218-7992.
W budget.com

Car2Go
Tel 877-488-4224.
W car2go.com

Hertz
Tel (800) 654-3131.
W hertz.com

Zip Car
Tel (202) 737-4900.
W zipcar.com

Breakdowns

American Automobile Association (AAA)
701–15th St, NW, Washington, DC 20005. Tel (202) 481-6811.
Breakdown assistance for members:
Tel (800) 222-4357. W aaa.com

Bus Tours

All Washington DC Tours
Tel 702-749-5720.
W allwashingtondctours.com

Gray Line
Union Station, 50 Massachusetts Ave, NW. Tel 1-800-862-1400.
W graylinedc.com

A Gray Line tour bus at the US Capitol

Street Finder Index

Key to the Street Finder

Major sight	Tourist information office	Synagogue
Place of interest	Hospital with emergency room	Pedestrian street
Other building	Police station	Ferry terminal
Railroad station	Church	State boundary
Metrorail station	Mosque	DC quadrant boundary
Bus station		

Key to Abbreviations used in the Street Finder

Ave	Avenue	NE	Northeast	SE	Southeast
DC	District of Columbia	NW	Northwest	St	Street/Saint
		Pkwy	Parkway	SW	Southwest
Dr	Drive	Pl	Place	VA	Virginia

0 meters 300
0 yards 300
1:19,100

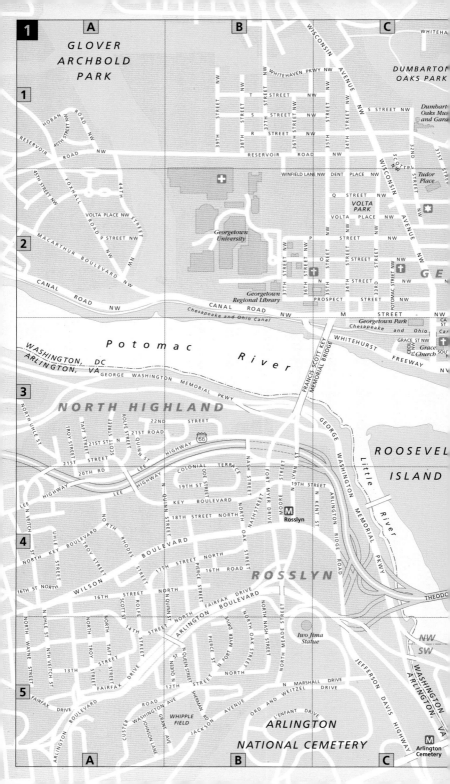

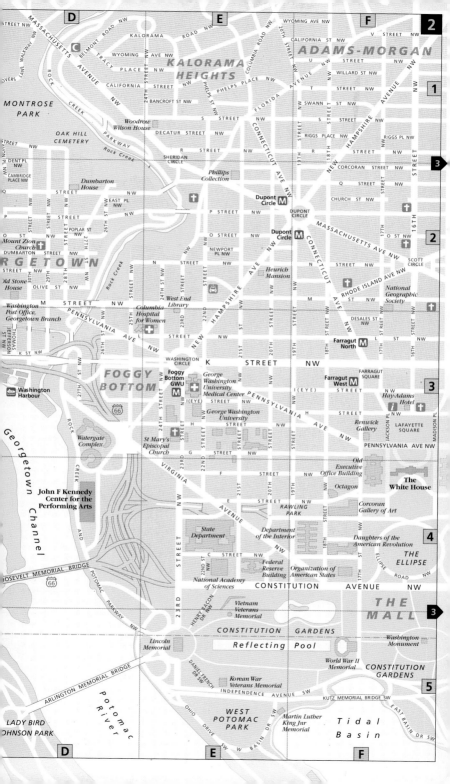

General Index

Acknowledgments

Dorling Kindersley would like to thank the following people whose contributions and assistance have made the preparation of this book possible.

Main Contributors

Susan Burke lives in Virginia and works as an editor for the Air Line Pilots Association. She has taught creative writing for many years and has been a freelance editor of many books and journals primarily in the fields of sociology, economics, and politics.

Alice Powers is a freelance writer living in Washington, DC. She has written many articles for the *Washington Post* and other newspapers. She has also written several literary anthologies and teaches writing at the Corcoran College of Art and Design.

Jennifer Quasha lives in New York City but has a long association with Washington. She has written many articles on subjects ranging from travel to health, and has worked on other Dorling Kindersley books, including *Walking With Dinosaurs*.

Kem Sawyer has lived in Washington for over 20 years and has written children's books, feature articles, and book reviews. She particularly enjoys writing about local history.

Design and Editorial

Managing Editor Louise Lang
Factchecker Litta W. Sanderson
Art Director Gillian Allan
Design and Editorial Assistance Sue Megginson, Johnny Pau, Hugh Thompson.
Proofreader Stewart Wild
Indexer Hilary Bird
Researcher Sarah Miers

Special Assistance

Particular thanks go to Kathleen Brooks at the National Air and Space Museum, Jessie Cohen and Leah Overstreet at the National Zoological Park, Julie Heizer at the Washington, DC Convention and Visitors' Association, Sarah Petty and Brennan Rash at the National Museum of American Art, Shannon Roberts at the National Gallery of Art, and Morgan Zinsmeister at the National Museum of American Art. Thanks also to Dumbarton House, National Headquarters of The National Society of The Colonial Dames of America.

Additional Photography

Max Alexander, Frank Greenaway, Paul Franklin, Dave King courtesy of Natural History Museum, Tim Mann, Ian O'Leary, Rough Guides/Angus Osborn, Rough Guides / Paul Whitfield, Jon Sawyer, Kim Sayer, Giles Stokoe, Clive Streeter, Scott Suchman, Matthew Ward, Stephen Whitehorn.

Additional Illustration

Arun K. Pottirayil.

Additional Cartography

Uma Bhattacharya

Revisions Team

Louise Abbot, Namrata Adhwaryu, Ashwin Adimari, Emma Anacootee, Shruti Bahl, Tessa Bindloss, Vandana Bhagra, Subhashree Bharati, Divya Chowfin, Sherry Collins, Anne Coombes, Karen D'Souza, Anna Freiberger, Camilla Gersh, Lydia Halliday, Claudia Himmelreich, Sarah Holland, Rose Hudson, Cincy Jose, Bharti Karakoti, Zafar ul-Islam Khan, Sumita Khatwani, Rahul Kumar, Esther Labi, Jude Ledger, Hayley Maher, Sam Merrell, Susan Millership, Scarlett O'Hara, Rakesh Kumar Pal, Catherine Palmi, Sangita Patel, Marianne Petrou, Pollyanna Poulter, Alice Powers, Khushboo Priya, Rada Radojicic, Pamposh Raina, Melanie Renzulli, Litta W. Sanderson, Ankita Sharma, Sands Publishing Solutions, Kem Sawyer, Azeem Siddiqui, Neil Simpson, Rituraj Singh, Susana Smith, Avantika Sukhia, Alka Thakur, Lauren Thomas, Conrad Van Dyk, Ajay Verma, Deepika Verma, Ros Walford, Dora Whitaker, Hugo Wilkinson.

Additional Picture Research

Marta Bescos, Sumita Khatwani.

Photography Permissions

Dorling Kindersley would like to thank the following for their assistance and kind permission to photograph at their establishments, as well as all the cathedrals, churches, museums, restaurants, hotels, shops, galleries, and other sights too numerous to thank individually.

Danita Delimont (Agent): David R. Frazier Photolibrary/ NASM 67c; Carol Pratt 198tr; Scott Suchman 139clb, 214cla; **Destination DC:** 206, 207crb, 215tl; **Philippe Limet Dewez:** 199tr; **Dreamstime.com:** Orhan Cam 44, 94tl; Etstock 192cl; Jiawangkun 56; Kropic 106; Jason Machado 193br; James Mattil 213tc; Mesutdogan 88; Mfschramm 200bl; Sean Pavone 203tr; Pigprox 84t; Rabbit75 32, 42-3; Raodahead 154-5; Rosepeterson 156; Alexey Yuryevich Rotanov 197tl; Vacclav 213cb; Vanessagifford 130.

Firefly Restaurant/Kimpton Hotels and Restaurants: Scott Suchman 186br; **Founding Farmers:** Greg Powers 186t; Renee Comet 182cl; **Four Seasons Hotel Washington, DC:** Tom McCavera 178tl; **Michael Freeman:** 52bc, 53cb, 64clb/br, 65tl, 67br; **Freer Gallery of Art, Smithsonian Institution, Washington DC:** 75tl.

Getty Images: AFP/Stephen Jaffe 209cla; Pablo Martinez Monsivais-Pool 29crb; **Hotel George:** 5c, 174br: **Graffiato/Know Public Realtions:** Greg Powers 180cla; **Granger Collection, New York:** 8-9, 19b, 20tr/cb, 21tr/clb/br, 22t/bc, 23tr/bc, 24bl, 25br, 28ca/clb/ bl/ bc/br, 29cla/bl, 49cra, 93ca, 93cl, 147tr.

Image Bank: Archive Photos 99br; Andrea Pistolesi 52cla, 80bl.

The Jefferson Hotel: 175tr, 179br.

Kaseman Beckman Advanced Strategies: 135tl; **Kiplinger Washington Collection:** 80cla; **Kramerbooks & Afterwords Cafe & Grill:** 194br; **Library of Congress:** Carol M. Highsmith 48bc.

Matisse Restaurant: 180cl; **Metropolitan Washington Airports Authority:** 214crb; **Michie Tavern:** 191tl; **Courtesy Mount Vernon Ladies' Association:** 162cla.

National Air and Space Museum © Smithsonian Institution: National Air and Space Museum Archives/Eric Long 65cr, 67tl; SI Neg. No. 99-15240-7–33cla; **National Gallery of Art, Washington, DC:** Samuel H. Kress Collection, Photo: Philip A. Charles *Bust of Lorenzo de' Medici* 59tl; Ailsa Mellon Bruce Fund, Photo: Bob Grove *Ginevra de' Benci* c. 1474 by Leonardo da Vinci 60tr; Samuel H. Kress Collection *A Young Man With His Tutor* by Nicolas de Largilliere, 1685–61tc; Samuel H. Kress Collection *Christ Cleansing the Temple* (d), pre-1570, by El Greco 62tr, Samuel H. Kress Collection *Madonna and Child*, 1320–1330 by Giotto 62cl; Collection of Mr. and Mrs. Paul Mellon *Woman with a Parasol*, 1875, by Claude Monet 6oclb; Harris Whittemore Collection *Mother of Pearl and Silver: The Andalusian* 1888-1900, by James McNeill Whistler 61br; Timken Collection *Diana and Endymion*, c. 1753, by Jean-Honore Fragonard 62br; Chester Dale Collection *Miss Mary Ellison*, 1880, by Mary Cassatt 63c; **National Museum of American Art/© Smithsonian Institution:** 58cl; 100tr, Gift of Mr. and Mrs. Joseph Harrison *Old Bear, a Medicine Man*, 1832, by George Catlin 101bl; *Achelous and Hercules*, 1947, © T. H. Benton and R. P. Benton Testamentary Trusts/VAGA, New York/DACS, London 2011 – 100–1c; Bequest of Helen Huntington Hull, grand-daughter of William Brown Dinsmore who acquired the painting in 1873 for "The Locusts," the family estate in Dutchess County, New York Among the Sierra Nevada, California 1868 by Albert Bierstadt 100bl; Gift of John Gellatly *In the Garden (Celia Thaxter in Her Garden)*, 1892, by Childe Hassam 101bc; © Untitled Press, Inc/VAGA, New York and DACS, London 2011 *Reservoir*, 1961, by Robert Raus-Chenberg 102cr; Gift of Anonymous Donors *The Throne of the Third Heaven of the Nations Millenium General Assembly*, c. 1950–1954, by James Hampton 102bl; Gift of the Georgia O'Keeffe Foundation Manhattan 1932 by Georgia O'Keeffe 101br; **National Museum of American history/© Smithsonian Institution:** 76cl/clb/bc, 77tl/cra, 78br, 79 all; **National Museum of the American Indian:** 70–1 all; **National Museum of Natural History/© Smithsonian Institution:** 72bl, Chip Clark 73br; Dane Penland

73tl; **National Park Service:** J. Fenney 113t, 206cla; Richard Freer 167clb; Rick Latoff, courtesy www.Parkphotos.com 69br; Mary McLeod Bethune Council House NHS, Washington D.C. 142c; **National Portrait Gallery/© Smithsonian Institution:** Gift of The Morris and Gwendolyn Cafritz Foundation and Smithsonian Institution Trust Fund *Selfportrait*, 1780– 1784, by John Singleton Copley 101ca; Gift of Friends of President and Mrs. Reagan, *Ronald Wilson Reagan*, 1989, © Henry C. Casselli 103tr; *Diana Ross and the Supremes*, 1965, © Bruce Davidson/Magnum 103br; Transfer from the National Gallery of Art, Gift of Andrew W. Mellon, 1942, *Pocahontas*, Unidentified artist, English school, after the 1616 engraving by Simon van de Passe, after 1616 – 103c; Gift of the Morris and Gwendolyn Cafritz Foundation and the Regents' Major Acquisitions Fund, Smithsonian Institution *Mary Cassatt*, 1880–1884, by Edgar Degas 101tl; Courtesy National Portrait Gallery *"Casey" Stengel*, 1981 cast after 1965 plaster by © Rhoda Sherbell 101tr; **National Postal Museum/© Smithsonian Institution:** Jim O'Donnell 55c; **National Zoological Park/© Smithsonian Institution:** Jessie Cohen 140–1; **Newseum:** 95tl; Richard T. Nowitz: 64cla, 83crb; Abe Nowitz 39c.

Octagon Museum/American Architectural Foundation, Washington DC: 117bl.

Paolo's Ristorante/Capital Restaurant Concepts: 187tr; **Phillips Collection:** 137br/c; **Popperfoto:** Reuters 30cla/cr.

Restaurant Nora: 190bl; **Rex Features:** 29tc; SIPA Press/Trippett 29cb; **Robert Harding Picture Library:** Jim West 219bl.

Mae Scanlan: 33ca, 34tr, 38bl, 79t, 202tr; **Shakespeare Theatre Company:** 196cr, 198bl; **Smithsonian National Air and Space Museum:** 66br; **Len Spoden Photography:** 149tl/tr, 150br, 151tl, 153br/tr; **Frank Spooner Pictures:** Markel-Liaison 93br; **Courtesy of The Spy Museum:** 104tl/c; STA Travel Group: 207tl; **SuperStock:** age fotostock 12cr; **Swann House Historic Dupont Inn:** 176bl.

Topham Picturepoint: 127clb; **TRH Pictures:** National Air and Space Museum 66cla.

University of Virginia: Library Special Collections Department, Manuscript Print Collection 129tl; **United States Holocaust Memorial Museum:** 83cr; Alan Gilbert 82bl.

Courtesy of the Washington, DC Martin Luther King, Jr. National Memorial Project Foundation, Inc.: Gediyon Kifle 37tl; **White House Collection, Courtesy White House Historical Association:** 110cl/b, 111t/c/bl/br, 112bl, Peter Vitale 113bl; Bruce White 113cr.

Zaytinya/Heather Freeman PR: Greg Powers and Audrey Crewe 185bc.

Front Endpaper: Corbis: Kelly-Mooney Photography Lclb; **Dreamstime.com:** Jiawangkun Rbc; Kropic Ltr; Mesutdogan Rtl; Orhancam Rtr; Rosepeterson Lbr; Vanessagifford Lbc.

Back Endpaper: © 2012 Washington Metropolitan Area Transit Authority.

Map Cover: Alamy Images: incamerastock.

Cover: Front - **Alamy Images:** incamerastock main.

All other images © Dorling Kindersley. See www.dkimages.com for more information.

Special Editions of DK Travel Guides

DK Travel Guides can be purchased in bulk quantities at discounted prices for use in promotions or as premiums. We are also able to offer special editions and personalized jackets, corporate imprints, and excerpts from all of our books, tailored specifically to meet your own needs.

To find out more, please contact:
in the US **specialsales@dk.com**
in the UK **travelguides@uk.dk.com**
in Canada **specialmarkets@dk.com**
in Australia **penguincorporatesales@ penguinrandomhouse.com.au**

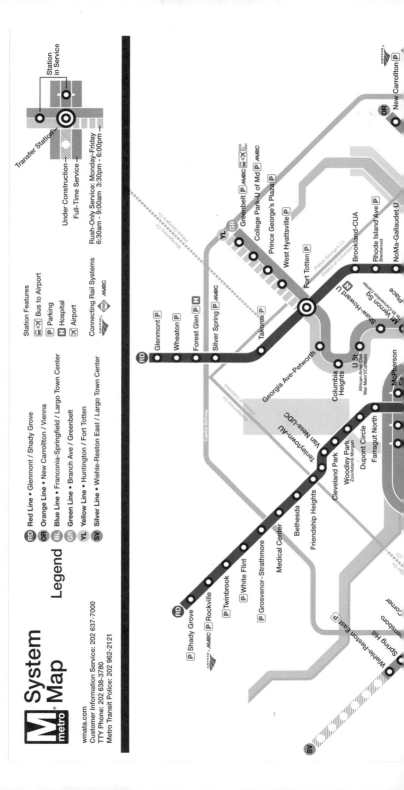